RETHINKING BECKETT

RETHINKING BECKETT

A Collection of Critical Essays

Edited by

Lance St John Butler
Lecturer in English Studies
University of Stirling

and

Robin J. Davis
Associate Librarian
University of Stirling

MACMILLAN

© The Macmillan Press Ltd 1990

All rights reserved. No reproduction, copy or transmission
of this publication may be made without written permission.

No paragraph of this publication may be reproduced, copied
or transmitted save with written permission or in accordance
with the provisions of the Copyright Act 1956 (as amended),
or under the terms of any licence permitting limited copying
issued by the Copyright Licensing Agency, 33–4 Alfred Place,
London WC1E 7DP.

Any person who does any unauthorised act in relation to
this publication may be liable to criminal prosecution and
civil claims for damages.

First published 1990

Published by
THE MACMILLAN PRESS LTD
Houndmills, Basingstoke, Hampshire RG21 2XS
and London
Companies and representatives
throughout the world

Typeset by Wessex Typesetters
(Division of The Eastern Press Ltd)
Frome, Somerset

Printed in Hong Kong

British Library Cataloguing in Publication Data

Rethinking Beckett: a collection of critical essays
1. English Literature, Beckett, Samuel, *1906–*
Critical studies
I. Butler, Lance St John   II. Davis, Robin J.
828'.91209
ISBN 0-333-49283-8

Contents

v

Notes on the Editors and Contributors

LANCE ST JOHN BUTLER is Lecturer in English Studies at the University of Stirling, Scotland. Author of *Samuel Beckett and the Meaning of Being: A Study in Ontological Parable* (1984), he has also published on other aspects of English literature, notably Hardy: *Thomas Hardy After 50 Years* (1977), *Thomas Hardy* (1978) and *Alternative Hardy* (1988).

ROBIN DAVIS is Associate Librarian at the University of Stirling and on the committee of *French XX Bibliography*. He has published a wide range of articles on librarianship and bibliography and in particular *Essai de Bibliographie des Oeuvres de Samuel Beckett* (1971) and *Checklist of Samuel Beckett's Works 1967–76* (1979). A cousin of Samuel Beckett.

THE CONTRIBUTORS

Stephen Barker has a BA in Dramatic Arts from Amherst College and an MFA (Fiction) and PhD (English–Literary Theory) from the University of Arizona. He is an Assistant Professor in the School of Fine Arts–Drama at the University of California at Irvine. He has been a professional actor, director and dancer, and has written, in addition to his work on Beckett, on Faulkner, Joyce and Nietzsche. A book on Nietzsche is near completion: *Articulation, Etrangeté and Power: Aspects of Nietzsche in Theory and Practice.*

Gottfried Büttner was born in 1926 in Dresden, Germany, studied medicine at Göttingen and Tübingen, MD 1953, general practitioner since 1956. He has published several books (two on Beckett) and numerous articles focusing on the change of consciousness he notices in contemporary works of art. Part-time lecturer for several years at the University of Hessen in Kassel, he received a PhD in English literature in 1981. Acquainted with Beckett since 1965.

Steven Connor is a Lecturer in English at Birkbeck College, University of London. He is the author of *Charles Dickens* (1985) and *Samuel Beckett: Repetition, Theory and Text* (1988), as well as articles on nineteenth- and twentieth-century literature and cultural theory. He is at present working on a study of the discourses of postmodernism.

Kevin J. H. Dettmar is a doctoral candidate in the department of English, University of California, Los Angeles. He has published essays on Yeats and Irish Romantic poetry and is currently completing a study of the carnivalesque strain in Joyce.

Ed Jewinski teaches contemporary literature and critical theory at Wilfrid Laurier University, Ontario, Canada. He is the co-editor of *Magic Realism in Canadian Literature* and he has published and delivered papers on a variety of modern writers including Beckett, Joyce, Lawrence, Pirandello, Foucault, Derrida and Lacan. With Phyllis Carey of Marquette University he is co-editing a selection of essays on the interrelationships of Joyce and Beckett.

Charles Krance teaches twentieth-century French literature at the University of Chicago. His other special interest, in addition to Samuel Beckett, lies in the writings of Céline on whom he is currently finishing a book to be entitled *The Eye/I of the Storm*.

Michael E. Mooney is Associate Professor of English at the University of New Orleans. He has published essays on Beckett, Shakespeare and Renaissance Drama in *ELH, The Journal of Beckett Studies, Shakespeare Survey, English Literary Renaissance, Comparative Drama* and *Studies in English Literature*. He is currently working on a study of Beckett's sceptical fictions.

Angela Moorjani is Associate Professor of French and chair of the Department of Modern Languages and Linguistics at the University of Maryland, Baltimore County campus. Her publications include *Abysmal Games in the Novels of Samuel Beckett* (University of North Carolina Press) and articles on psychoaesthetics and semiotic approaches to textual analysis.

Rubin Rabinovitz is Professor of English at the University of Colorado, Boulder. He is author of *The Reaction Against Experiment in the English Novel, Iris Murdoch* and *The Development of Samuel Beckett's Fiction*. His essays and reviews have appeared in the *Journal of Beckett Studies, Modern Fiction Studies, Twentieth Century Literature*, the *New York Times Book Review, New York Magazine, Byte, PC Magazine* and other publications.

Barbara Trieloff received her doctorate from McMaster University, Canada, and is currently Lecturer in the English Department there. She is currently working on a bilingual study of the language of Beckett's post-trilogy prose as it compares with the language of the dramaticules.

Paola Zaccaria is Associate Professor of English and American Literature at the University of Bari, Italy. She has published a book on Virginia Woolf (*Trama e ordito di una scrittura*, Dedalo, 1980), and articles on Joyce, Christina Rossetti, Katherine Mansfield, Tillie Olsen, Karen Blixen, Samuel Beckett, Virginia Woolf and Audre Lorde. Her research interests include contemporary narrative theory, feminist theory of literature and linguistics. She is currently working on a book about Beckett's later shorter fiction.

Introduction

Beckett is different. The very proclamation of poverty and impotence that is the keynote of his work seems to release immense critical richness and power. Unexhausted by explication, he appears to be inexhaustible.

In celebration of his eightieth year, in 1986, the present editors organised a conference at Stirling University in Scotland and asked for contributions that would, among other things, rethink, yet again and for the present moment, the meaning of his non-meanings and the success of his failure. We were not disappointed. What is offered in this volume is a selection of the best of these rethinkings: here is the Beckett that reflects and is reflected by the late 1980s.

What is different about Beckett is not that he provokes a critical response (all writers can do that), but the protean, open-ended, 'undecidable' and inexhaustible quality of the challenge he offers. In this, it seems to us, he is the poet of the poststructuralist age. Not that he was *not* the poet of other ages too, for he was: Beckett as the quintessential *nouveau romancier*, Beckett the Cartesian, Beckett the Existentialist, these have rubbed shoulders with Beckett the nihilist, Beckett the mystic and, of course, Beckett the dramatist of the Absurd and Beckett the explorer of the limitations of language. But, recuperating all of these and moving without apparent strain into new realms, deconstructionist *avant la lettre*, there is a new Beckett, thinkable only in the most recent critical terms, rethinkable now as, doubtless, also in the future.

This collection of essays tries to present some of the approaches to Beckett (or Beckett's approaches to us) made possible by this new language of criticism, but it is not insistently Derridean (for instance) and our intention has been to provide a showcase for different rethinkings of Beckett made possible by the general revisions of thought of recent years.

The first essay, by Steven Connor, challenges Robbe-Grillet's view of Beckett's theatre as an arena of *présence*, offering instead the view that the characters in the plays are in fact engaged in a process of self-erasure. The last essay, by Stephen Barker, insists that Beckett is working at that interface that is marked by the *trace* that is all human intellection, the moment of differentiation, the moment, *par excellence*, of absence. In my end is my beginning. In between these inseparable poles the race is on to deploy most forcefully and usefully linguistic and philosophical notions that reveal Beckett to us. And in every case, it seems, Beckett is different. Thus Angela Moorjani demonstrates that deixis in this writer simply does not work as it does in other writers; the terms are changed. Rubin Rabinovitz confirms, in a virtuoso display of exhaustive enumeration, the extraordinary crafting of the trilogy through repetition, a device that produces results in Beckett that are not found elsewhere. Kevin Dettmar explores *Molloy* as the novel in which a unique attempt is made to defeat metaphor.

The next four essays concern those unrivalled paradigms of the postmodern – the short texts produced since *How It Is*. Barbara Trieloff demonstrates how these texts employ incredible syntactic devices to subvert our whole notion of the *written*. Paola Zaccaria seeks for the deepest structure in *Fizzles* and finds it to reside in an opposition between the vertical and the horizontal, construed both linguistically and mimetically. Charles Krance tries, in an exploration in detail, to achieve a reading of *Worstward Ho* that will somehow be adequate to the complex play of that enigmatic text, while Ed Jewinski uses deconstructionist methods to reorientate our view of *Company*.

Thereafter, before we return to the 'absence' of the last essay, Michael Mooney and Gottfried Büttner approach *Watt* from positions, respectively, of scepticism and spiritual quest. The two essays together demonstrate, perhaps, a contradiction in which both terms manage to remain tenable – once again Beckett's uniqueness is revealed.

Our last word, which in all probability will not be our last word, is that with Beckett no last word seems possible and that rethinking is therefore an endless process.

Lance St John Butler
Robin J. Davis

University of Stirling

1

'What? Where?' Presence and Repetition in Beckett's Theatre

Steven Connor

Beckett's turn to the theatre has often been represented as the expression of a longing for an art of visibility and tangibility as a relief from the epistemological disintegrations which Beckett described in his interview with Israel Schenker in 1956 – 'no "I", no "have", no "being". No nominative, no accusative, no verb. There's no way to go on.'[1] Michael Robinson, for example, sees the theatre as 'the only direction in which a development was possible', since the theatre 'promises a firmer reality than a subjective monologue written and read in isolation; perhaps on the stage the reality behind the words may be revealed by the action which often contradicts that literal meaning'.[2] Beckett himself has testified to the sense of relief that he gets from working in drama:

> Theater ist für mich zunächst eine Erholung von der Arbeit am Roman. Man hat es mit einem bestimmten Raum zu tun und mit Menschen in diesem Raum.[3]

Perhaps the most emphatic statement of this view of Beckett's turn to the theatre is that offered by Alain Robbe-Grillet. Writing early in Beckett's dramatic career, he stressed the sense of sheer *presence* which is given by Vladimir and Estragon in *Waiting for Godot*, deprived as they apparently are of all the conventional dramatic supports of script, plot or properties. Because they have nothing to rely on, they are also free, for they have nothing to repeat; everything is happening for the first and last time. For Robbe-Grillet, Beckett's theatre embodies the Heideggerian appre-

1

hension of *Dasein*, of primordial being-there; Vladimir and Estragon are 'irremediably present'.[4]

Other writers have elaborated or modified this theme by stressing the self-reflexiveness of the plays. William Worthen argues that Beckett 'literalizes' the plight of his characters in the visibly straitened conditions in which his actors are required to work, so that a piece like *Play* 'dramatizes the essential dynamics of stage performance'.[5] Sidney Homan argues in a similar way for self-reflection as a guarantee of presence. The plays turn in on themselves, he argues, to join playwright, play and audience in a mutually-mirroring autonomy. The plays therefore no longer require reference to a pre-existing world, or the addition of any commentary to elucidate meanings which are hidden or allegorically elsewhere; the plays are simply what they are, in an elementary performing present, without before or after, the action 'complete, pure, itself – and immediately experienced by the audience'.[6] Beckett's occasional remarks about his plays have encouraged this view of their fundamental simplicity. Writing to Alan Schneider about *Endgame*, Beckett explained his insistence on 'the extreme simplicity of dramatic situation . . . Hamm as stated, and Clov as stated, together as stated, nec tecum nec sine te, in such a place, and in such a world, that's all I can manage, more than I could.'[7]

In many ways, this view of Beckett's turn to the theatre reproduces conventional views about theatre itself and its relation to the other arts, and, most notably, the opposition between the 'living' art of the theatre and the dead or abstract experience of private reading. If we merely imagine characters and events in written texts, it is often said, then in the theatre, and in other visual media, we 'actually see' those characters and events, 'actually hear' their voices. If the dramatic performance must always be secondary to the authorial text which it repeats, then there has been a desire among many modern commentators to assert, against this, the primacy of the performance over the text. One of the most representative and influential of these is Antonin Artaud. Throughout his essays of the 1930s, Artaud argues for a non-repetitive theatre, one which is not slavishly obedient to the written texts which precede and control it but instead speaks its own, intrinsically theatrical language of mime, gesture, dance, music, light, space and scene. This escape from the script is an escape from the compulsion to repeat. The spectator of the drama will no longer be forced to try to read the performance back into its original script, since what he or she beholds will be both text and performance; and closing the gap between text and performance will also close the gap between meaning and interpretation for the spectator. In such a theatre, there is no need, or even possibility of a confirming 'elsewhere': the theatre begins and ends with itself:

> We might say the subjects presented begin on stage. They have reached such a point of objective materialisation we could not imagine them, however much one [sic] might try, outside this compact panorama, the enclosed, confined world of the stage.[8]

Artaud's formulation resembles the kind of thing that is often said of Beckett's plays, especially his late plays. The claim for self-reflexive unity is found, for example, in Ruby Cohn's arguments for the increasing 'theatereality' of Beckett's plays, by which she means the increasing convergence of the space that the plays represent with the actual theatre space in which they are performed, and in Enoch Brater's claims for the identity established between word and image in *Rockaby*, in which, he says 'a verbal metaphor becomes concrete and palpable. In a word it has become real.'[9]

If, in some ways, Beckett's theatre is aptly described as a theatre of presence, or, in Artaud's terms, a theatre freed from repetition, then there are also important ways in which his work seems to undermine not only the particular claims of individual critics, but the more general cultural claims upon which they often rest and from which they derive their authority. I think it is no accident that Beckett's international fame came first of all as a playwright and not as a novelist, for it has been the prevailing critical and cultural consensus about the theatre and its strengths and capacities which has allowed his work to be absorbed and rewritten as a humanist theatre of presence, a theatre which directly and powerfully embodies real, and universal human predicaments. In various ways, and particularly in the intricate play of its different repetitions, Beckett's theatre makes this critical representation seem inadequate, and asks questions of common conceptions about the theatre as a whole.

VOICE AND WRITING

The drama's claim to embody a 'metaphysics of presence' rests largely upon two other claims: that it represents human beings with the actual bodies of other human beings, and that it represents spoken words with words spoken by those actual human beings. The relationship between these claims is an intimate and necessary one. In the case of Beckett's theatre, there is a particular potency in the promise of the audible voice, given the point which seems to have been reached in *The Unnamable*: though the speaker is surrounded and penetrated by voices, murmuring and babbling, he cannot be sure if any of those voices are his own, cannot even be sure of the existence of the voices. For Beckett, the opportunity that theatre offers for full and unambiguous speech was clearly not to be resisted. But this opportunity is also a drawback. For if one of the drives behind Beckett's work is to speak the self, to 'say I', then his work is also driven by the desire to retract, efface, or otherwise cancel out speech, to speak in order to fall silent. This must provoke the question of how an art of effacement can work with the dominating palpability of 'living' speech in the drama.

One of the important ways in which this is attempted is by a return to the repetitive and auto-citational devices of the fiction. The refrains which echo through *Waiting for Godot* and *Endgame* work against the sense of immediate utterance. As we hear the formulaic interchanges being repeated, we become aware that, faced with the giddy nothingness of being on stage and having nothing to say, Vladimir and Estragon have to fall back on what they have said before. They quote themselves, or, it might perhaps be felt, their language begins to quote them, in what comes to seem like a self-erasure.

But Beckett's later theatre goes further than this in interrogating the opposition of speech and writing. This happens most strikingly as a result of the introduction on to the stage, the place of 'living' speech, of the 'dead' language of mechanical reproduction. By doing this, Beckett transgresses the opposition between the repeatable and the non-repeatable which conventionally underlies the opposition between writing and speech. Writing is 'dead' because it is language that has been separated from its originating body and receiving context, to allow it to be reused in different contexts. Only in writing is it possible to say 'I am dead'.

But in the use of the tape-recorder in *Krapp's Last Tape*, Beckett shows us a language which is not exactly speech or writing. Though the recording retains everything that seems living about the voice, its tone, rhythms, pitch and emphasis, the mere fact that it is possible to retain this much is what makes certain the loss of continuity between the voice and its context. Where the younger Krapp can talk expertly about his mother's 'viduity', the older Krapp no longer remembers what the word means, just as he cannot remember the details set down in the ledger about the 'black ball' or the 'memorable equinox'. In fact the ledger that Krapp consults forms an interesting counterpart to the spoken voice that he hears on the tape. The effect for the viewer of seeing Krapp as puzzled by the voice as by the written redaction of what the voice has to say, though able in both cases to stop and go over the material again, is to run together the two forms of language and to highlight the ways in which recorded speech resembles writing.

The same conflation is suggested by other parallels. Beckett, as usual in his fiction and drama, insists on the material facts involved in the process of reading, stressing the weight and inaccessibility of the ledger, the difficulty Krapp has in reading the entries with his failing eyesight and, especially, the necessity of breaking off reading to turn the page – 'Farewell to – [*he turns page*] – love.'[10] The effect of bathos is intensified by the splitting of the word in the French version – 'Adieu à l'a . . . (*il tourne la page*) . . . mour' – with the obvious hint that it gives of love turning to death.[11] But Beckett exploits the simple physical fact of the turning of the page as well. Written language allows – one might almost say necessitates – gaps and interruptions, for its unchanging material form means that it can be broken off and resumed at the same point. The immediacy of speech, on the other hand, is directly related to its volatility, and speech cannot be suspended in this way, without being lost for ever. In *Krapp's Last Tape*, the possibility of introducing gaps is evident both in the written ledger and the spoken tape, this possibility in both cases being a function of iterability. The awareness of the function of gaps is likely to induce a sense of other parallels between speech and writing. The hesitations in the younger Krapp's voice, for instance, which punctuate his confidently continuous dialogue with moments of indecisive silence, open up possibilities of alteration or difference. So Krapp's 'farewell to – [*he turns page*] – love' is matched by the voice on the tape saying 'I love to get up and move about in it, then back here to . . . [*hesitates*] . . . me' (*CDW*, 217). Such a hesitation functions as an indicator of authentic speech at the same time as it reminds us of the gaps typical of writing; the younger Krapp's hesitations are like the moments when the older Krapp winds back and pauses before resuming. On a couple of occasions, the listener's interpolations of silence or commentary are run together, or counterpointed with those of the speaker on the tape:

> Ah well . . . [*Pause.*] These old P.M.s are gruesome, but I often find them – [*KRAPP switches off, broods, switches on.*] – a help before embarking on a new . . . [*hesitates*] . . . retrospect.
>
> (*CDW*, 218)

And sometimes the older and younger Krapp collude more closely in listening and responding to the words as they are being spoken:

> The voice! Jesus! And the aspirations! [*Brief laugh in which KRAPP joins.*] And the resolutions! [*Brief laugh in which KRAPP joins.*] To drink less in particular. [*Brief laugh of KRAPP alone.*]
>
> (*CDW*, 218)

Here older and younger Krapp both break up the continuity of the utterance with derisive commentary upon it. The fact that the older Krapp adds a layer of disillusion only emphasises the citational nature of the original utterance, in which the middle-aged Krapp is in turn appropriating the recorded words of *his* younger self in order to deride them.

Though Krapp's spoken journal into the tape-recorder may sound spontaneous, it is not. The voice and style of the younger Krapp suggest speech under the particular stress that the awareness of a recording brings with it, speech darkened by the threatening shadow of repeatability. This may account for the nervous hesitations in his speech; it is as though the threat of repetition redoubles itself by inducing moments of self-critical review at the moment of vocal delivery. As a performance, the younger Krapp's report shows the influence of another more obvious kind of writing, as well: the notes jotted down on an envelope from which he may be reading or improvising. The older Krapp seems to have retained this habit – in fact, when we first hear about the envelope from the younger Krapp and connect it with the envelope that the older Krapp has produced at the beginning of the play, we might even wonder for a moment whether it isn't the *same* envelope. Certainly the older Krapp gets little assistance from his notes, for he soon crumples up the envelope and resorts to improvised speech. The sense of vulnerability which this engenders may remind us of Vladimir and Estragon, who seem similarly scriptless. Like Vladimir and Estragon, the older Krapp cannot keep up the flow of speech, without resorting to repetition, the repetition of the delicious word 'spool', the repetition of his song, the allusive repetitions in the memories of Christmas and Sunday mornings on Croghan, and, finally, the repetition of the tape in place of his own words. But if Krapp resembles Vladimir, Estragon, Hamm and Clov, in having to produce unscripted language for an audience, then his predicament differs from theirs, too. His words are being recorded and so are marked in advance with the sign of writing and destined to enter into the condition of iterability.

The envelope is indeed a fit emblem for this kind of writing. Krapp's recordings are intended to provide a firm and unambiguous record of a moment of time, but instead show how every utterance can be taken up or enveloped by some other occasion, some other context of understanding. Krapp's recorded life then comes to seem less like a logically continuous series of discrete utterances, each fixed firmly in its intentional context, than a web of mutually-enveloping self-quotations, each endlessly displaced from its originating moment.

In all these ways, *Krapp's Last Tape* moves to dissolve or undermine the dramatic qualities most commonly associated with speech – immediacy, originality and continuity. In doing this, it transforms the theatre from a place of living speech to a place of writing, a place where it becomes possible – and maybe even unavoidable – to say 'I am dead'. This represents more than a simple inversion of the priority of speech over writing. As with Derrida's work, the interrogation of the speech/writing opposition in Beckett's theatre compels the sense that the stable difference *between* speech and writing is in fact repeated as an unstable difference *within* speech and writing. Derrida argues that speech itself is both living and dead, unique and repeatable. Intrinsic to the structure of every sign, spoken or otherwise, is the possibility that it allows of being quoted or repeated in some other context. This 'possibility of extraction and of citational grafting' means that any sign 'can break with every given context, and engender infinitely new contexts in an absolutely nonsaturable fashion'.[12]

Beckett's later plays carry the conflict and merging between speech and writing even further. In more and more complex ways, plays like *That Time*, *Rockaby* and *Ohio Impromptu* suggest the drama's capacity to quote non-dramatic language, such as tape-recordings, and written narrative. In each case, the effect of the repetition is to set up discrepancies between the drama and the narratives that it encloses. The voices in *That Time* belong to the listening face only in the limited sense in which Krapp's earlier voice still belongs to him; the voice in *Rockaby* seems to speak of and to the woman, but its repetitions establish an irreducible and continually-renewed split between voice and image; and the narrative in *Ohio Impromptu* quotes, and is quoted by the dramatic situation in a structure of repetition which can never 'grow to be as one'. In all these cases, the desperate desire to 'be again', to reappropriate being in living speech, depends upon repetition, even as it is repetition which endlessly estranges being from speech.

WHAT? WHERE?

To replace speech by writing, and thereby to challenge the prestige of dramatic speech, as Beckett's theatre does, is also to challenge one of the most powerful and recurrent oppositions between drama and writing – that opposition between the living, the embodied, the concrete on the one hand, and the abstract, the symbolic and the immaterial on the other. The two alleged characteristics of drama, its phonic immediacy and its physicality, are closely connected, of course, for the critical ascendancy of voice in the theatre derives from and is reinforced by the sense of the origin of the voice in the body. If the language of the written book is distant and immaterial, then the language of the performed drama is conceived to be intimately alive because it is physical.

As many have observed, Beckett's theatre displays a deep and continuous concentration on the physical in all its senses.[13] In its rigorous attention to spacing, movement and position, Beckett's theatre seems to emphasise the irreducible physicality of human bodies in the spaces they actually inhabit. For Beckett's characters, the stage has its own tangible presence, usually in the sense of a limit or boundary, as, most especially, in *Act Without Words I*, where the function of the offstage area is to stress that there is no other place permitted for the actor than the stage. What is more, the limits of this available area in Beckett's theatre have tended to shrink remorselessly. Whereas, in *Waiting for Godot* the two tramps range vigorously over the whole stage and even leave it from time to time, in *Endgame*, only one character can move around freely, thus turning the large empty space around the characters from a functional, habitable space into a space of ironic unavailability. Though Krapp has the run of the stage and of a small offstage area, the action is effectively concentrated in the pool of light in the centre; in an important way, Krapp is only a character for the audience when he is in this restricted area of light. From this play onwards, characters are restricted to smaller and smaller spaces, either by lighting, as with the reduced area provided in *Footfalls*, or the spotlight on the face in *That Time* and on the mouth in *Not I*, or by physical restraint, as with Winnie in *Happy Days*, or the speakers in *Play*. It is as though Beckett were seeking to narrow the stage around the bodies of his actors and to abolish the difference between them, in a version of that process described in *All Strange Away*, in which the narrator progressively collapses the cube to eliminate the empty space opened up by a change in position.[14] The claustrophobic narrowing of the stage space is also to be found enacted in an unpublished fragment called 'Mongrel Mime', which, apparently, requires the passage of an actor from right to left over the stage through three progressively smaller chambers.[15] One of the advantages of writing for television for Beckett is that it provides a mobile frame, allowing, in *Eh Joe*, *Ghost Trio*, . . . *but the clouds* . . . and the television version of *Not I*, the exploitation of the constricting effects of close-up.

All this might seem to evidence an attention to stage space which is self-reflexive, in an affirmation of the limited autonomy of the theatre similar to that by Artaud. But to make this kind of affirmation is to ignore the resistant difference within self-reflection. Even if it represents itself alone, the stage is still an imaginary place, which is different from the 'actual' stage known during the day by cleaners, scene-shifters and rehearsing actors. The stage affirms itself as elementary and irreducible space, by representing itself as such. Beckett's theatre, for all its simplicity and directness with regard to stage space, time and again shows us actual space repeating itself in this way, or moving from the simplicity of the concrete into the complex condition of the represented. Pozzo, enquiring of Vladimir and Estragon whether they are in 'the place known as the Board' learns that the place is not quite 'like nothing,' because it has a tree in it, so concludes, 'Then it's not the Board' (*CDW*, 80).

Perhaps the play which gives the strongest sense of self-sufficient location in Beckett's work is *Endgame*. Hugh Kenner, answering his own 'where is this place?' declares, 'it is here, that is all we can say, here before us, on stage. The set does not *represent*, the set is itself.'[16] Beryl and John Fletcher similarly affirm the play's freedom from repetition, saying that the stage has 'a particular reality. It is not a facsimile of a middle-class living room . . . but a place in its own right.'[17] But this is to underestimate the complexity of what happens to conventional expectations of theatrical space during the course of this play. Normally, in a play that insists on the unity of place, we are given a sense of accessory or contingent spaces, extending outside and adjacent to what we see before us on stage. In fact, we gain our sense of the solidity of the stage space by reference to this imagined context. *Endgame* makes it difficult for the audience to place its stage space within these imaginary coordinates. Sometimes, as when Hamm declares, 'Outside of here it's death', or when Clov announces that all he can see out of the window is 'Zero', it may seem that this contracted space is the whole world. But at other times, we are given the opposite impression, that this space is a sort of non-locality, a provisional or hypothetical space where time is absent, or never gets going; to borrow the paradoxical notion of *Worstward Ho*, it might be a 'grot in the void', a fold of imaginary space within vacancy itself.[18] If this is so, then the stage space might seem less 'real' even than the reduced exterior that Clov sees, or imagines he sees. Nor should we forget Clov's kitchen. Is this part of the stage space, part of the surrounding 'zero', or some intermediate zone, perhaps even some other stage somewhere? *Endgame* asks us to conceive of a place which is both absolute and relative. The stage space both is and isn't its own space.

On top of this, our experience of the limiting space of the play is made ambiguous by Hamm's blind experience of it. Hamm's blindness seems to induce in him the vertigo of placelessness, for he feels surrounded by 'infinite emptiness . . . like a little bit of grit in the middle of the steppe' (*CDW*, 109–10). He tries to counteract this sensation by having Clov move him round the walls and back to the centre of the stage, but in neither place does he seem to achieve the sense of full occupancy. Sitting at the centre, he feels the need to confirm the limiting circumference of the room at the wall. Once at the wall, the feeling of eccentricity to himself overtakes him and he makes Clov hurry him back to the centre of his world – but, once there, is unable to content himself that he really is at the centre. He seems to be suffering from a version of the anxiety suffered by Watt at the sight of the disjoined centre and circumference. Hamm presumably wishes to be at the centre because that is the place of least movement, and the defining place of stability. But his blindness means that the centre is likely to become detached in his mind from its circumference – for, obviously, a centre can only function as such when the circle of which it is the centre is also perceived, or structurally present in it. This means that, far from abolishing or negating the circumference, the centre continually requires or internally repeats the circumference. Considered as a structural necessity as well as a perceptual function, this is as true for a sighted person as for a blind one.

Hamm's centripetal movement inwards is therefore likely to be converted at any moment to a centrifugal movement outwards to his own periphery and vice versa. What makes this more complex is that where a circumference only has one centre, a given centre has an infinite number of possible circumferences. Hamm seems to enact this on his return to the centre:

> I feel a little too far to the left. [*Clov moves chair slightly.*] Now I feel a little too far to the right. [*Clov moves chair slightly.*] I feel a little too far forward. [*Clov moves chair slightly.*] I feel a little too far back. [*Clov moves chair slightly.*]

> (*CDW*, 105)

His obsessive attempts to stabilise himself actually mark out the beginnings of another circle, as any attempt to find a centre must.[19] Hamm can never *be* in the place where movement is cancelled out, for the movement between centre and circle is continual and repeated.

In a recent play which is devoted entirely to movement, *Quad I* and *II*, a similar compulsion to oscillate between centre and periphery is found. Each of the four hooded players tramps in a series of triangles down two sides of a square and diagonally across the centre – though without actually touching the centre. As with Hamm in *Endgame*, the movement round the edge of the square seems to require or bring about a deviation into the middle, and the approach to the middle seems to project the players back out again to the edge. This seems to be a refiguring in miniature of the larger oscillation of the players between movement into and movement away from the square. Like comets, they are drawn repeatedly into the gravitational pull of the square, only to be flung off into outer darkness at the end of their courses. As with Hamm, again, the exact centre is never reached, but skirted round in a movement which, when all four players are moving at once, creates an anticlockwise circle inside the square.

Though the square seems to be a simple given – we see it ready for the players to occupy before they enter – it is not long before their movement seems to take over and internalise its shape. But, once absorbed like this, the shape of the square loses its permanence and seems to have to be inscribed and anxiously reinscribed by their movement. It may be that, in this, Beckett is insisting on the specificity of the TV medium, which relies not upon the presence of images before us, but on the retinal persistence of interrupted lines of light which shuttle back and forth across the screen. Just as a still image can only be produced by the rapid, exactly repeated motion of these lines, so the sense of poise and completeness of design in *Quad* is made up from the repeated movements of the four players. *Quad* therefore collapses and complicates the relationship of outside and inside. The players arrive in the square, and, moving round it, may seem, like Dante's damned, to be the prisoners of their movement. But, since the movement they describe creates a space, they may be said to be outside it. They are therefore, in different senses, prisoner and jailor, inside and outside and the simple, apparent space of the mime has become a complex space of metaphor, repetition and representation.

A feature of Beckett's theatre which is just as surprising is the giving over of the stage space not to action, but to the preparation preliminary to action, which makes the audience unsure where the 'real' action is to take place. This is apparent in *What Where*, in which the stage space is made into a kind of animated doodle-pad, into which the absent author can project his first thoughts and rewrites. This process is carried even further in *A Piece of Monologue*, in which the actual stage is given over to the delivery of what sounds like a script for some other play. It is as though the actor were standing on stage describing himself performing a mime: 'Gropes to window and stares out. . . . Gropes back in the end to where the lamp is standing. Was standing. When last went out' (*CDW*, 425). He also describes the stage on which he stands, in terms which repeat with only small modifications the words that we read in the stage-directions at the beginning of the play: 'White hair catching light. White gown. White socks. White foot of pallet edge of frame stage left' (*CDW*, 428–9). To repeat stage-directions in performance is to enact again the supplanting of voice by text and, at the same time, to dissolve the solidity of the perceived space of the play; this now becomes merely a potential space, which the audience must fill with imaginary action – indeed, we may succeed so well in this that it is hard to believe at the end of the performance that we have not witnessed the actions that we have heard described so often. The stage has been converted from a place where action takes place visibly before us, to a space of text, initiating action which is staged elsewhere, in imagination or memory.

Artaud objected to the status of the stage space as repetition, as a sort of subsidiary emptiness, called into being by, and subordinate to the absent text which projects and controls it; he wanted the space of the stage to be 'full' and immediate, not the shadow of some other text or controlling intention. We have seen that Beckett's late theatre pushes in exactly the opposite direction. Instead of closing the gap between text and enacting space, a play like *A Piece of Monologue* incorporates, even 'stages' that gap, so that what is usually thought of as a division *between* the script and the perform-ance becomes a division displayed *within* the performance (and therefore within the text, too).[20]

Of course, this repetitive structure extends beyond simple dual-ity, for every script may be staged in an infinite number of ways, none of them exactly coincidental with the original. This can involve repetitions within repetitions, as when a particular production of a play is adapted for another medium, such as television. Indeed, such a double repetition is made possible in the passages of *A Piece of Monologue* which allude to terms used in TV and film scripts, such as the description of the grave 'seen from above', an image which is 'held for thirty seconds' before the instruction 'fade' (*CDW*, 428).

Footfalls similarly accompanies its multiplication of ghostly loca-tions, the room, the church, the supper-table, with a multiplication of implied media. M. suspends her pacing in order to speak to us, of some other 'tangle of tatters', in some other place, and then tells the story of old Mrs Winter and her daughter. The language of her narrative mimics written forms 'Amy – the daughter's given name, as the reader will remember' – and, more disconcertingly, the printed form of the playscript:

> Amy: Just what exactly, Mother, did you perhaps fancy it was? . . . Mrs W: You yourself observed nothing . . . strange? Amy: No, Mother, I myself did not to put it mildly. Mrs W: What do you mean, Amy, to put it mildly, what can you possibly mean, Amy, to put it mildly?
>
> (*CDW*, 403)

This capacity for 'quotation' of other representational media further erodes the specificity of the stage-performance, so that we cannot be absolutely sure of the appropriate form or medium of the play. It may sit oddly with Beckett's often-quoted strictures about the specificity of medium of his plays, and his attempts to restrain adaptations, but nearly every one of his plays makes important internal gestures towards other media.[21] In *Waiting for Godot*, there are hints of other kinds of theatrical context, like the circus and the music hall, in which the play might be staged – though, as we might expect, Beckett resisted Roger Blin's initial idea of making this explicit by turning the theatre into a circus ring.[22] *All That Fall*, which, as we have seen, Beckett thought of as intrinsically a radio play 'for voices rather than bodies', is actually the most spatially concrete of radio plays, requiring of the listener or reader a staging in some interior mental space, even as it parodies the conventions which allow the construction of this space. If one had to imagine what a mixture between a radio play and a stage play would be like, however, it would probably be something like *Krapp's Last Tape*, written shortly after *All That Fall*, which is a kind of 'staging' (as opposed to an adaptation) of a radio play, since it mingles, without attempting to unify, the visibility of bodies on the stage and the placeless voices 'coming out of the dark' of the radio play. This may have been anticipated in the use of blind characters in *Waiting for Godot* and *Endgame* to unsettle the audience's sense of visible location.

Beckett's later writing for the theatre demands of it technicalities of lighting and staging which suggest video and film – the separation and dismemberment of the body, with isolation of faces and lips, or the effect of hovering and bird's-eye view, and consequent concentration of focus, as well as the separation of voices from bodies, to give the effect of voice-over, as in *Footfalls* and *Rockaby*. His writing for TV, on the other hand (though it is difficult to imagine it being staged in quite the same way in any other medium), retains and even highlights many of the features of the stage play – the single unchanging set, for instance, and the restriction of viewpoint.

Not I is a particularly good example of this variability of medium. Even though he had nothing to do with the making of it, Beckett actually at one time preferred the TV version, which dispensed with the figure of the auditor, in favour of a claustrophobically close focus on the mouth. The mouth in the theatre seems magically remote, as though produced in some space of illusion, and may make audiences think of something other than a physical mouth (a member of one audience described the mouth as being like a flickering candle-flame), while the mouth in the TV version is inescapably physical, enforcing a fascinated attention to the violent, erotic struggle of lips, teeth, tongue and spittle. The point is not really which version of the play is better, or more faithful, for the play includes both versions, and in a sense consists in the self-distancing movement across different media which these two versions bring about. The case is analogous to what happens with Beckett's self-translations. The two versions of a text each require the other to complete them, even though the 'other' version never does complete the text, but instead introduces complexity or discrepancy.

Beckett has also extended this principle of transferability to his prose work. The close attention to details of space and position in the related texts *The Lost Ones*, *Ping*, *Imagination Dead Imagine* and *All Strange Away*, as well as the theatrical language often used in these works, suggests a doubling of medium, as though the texts included within themselves the possibility of their staging in some other theatrical form. Indeed, such stagings have taken place, and have sometimes been endorsed by Beckett.[23] One of the most recent prose works, *Company*, seems to have a particularly dense overlayering of references to and possibilities for staging in other media; the voice which 'comes to one in the dark' throughout this text has many of the qualities of the voices 'coming out of the dark' of radio drama, while the details of the listener's position remind us remarkably of the listening face of *That Time*, a stage play that itself uses some of the properties of radio drama. The careful attention in *Company* to the physical space in which the listener lies, and the division of this space from the imaginary spaces of quotation/remembering suggest the insistent physicality of some of Beckett's late drama, while the use of intercutting and flashback, as well as the close visual attention paid to certain items within the narrative, such as the watch-face, suggest continuities with visual media.

These internal allusions to a plurality of different places for staging make *Company* typical of Beckett's late writing (and especially his dramatic writing), rather than an exception to it. If it remains true that Beckett's dramatic works assert the specificity of their media, it is because they are placed at the representative edges of those media, rather than at their centres. It is these boundaries which constitute the specificity of the medium, even as they mark the dubious place where they touch and perhaps cross into different media. Beckett's plays mark this tenuous place of difference as the most representative. The simple 'thereness' of the plays depends upon their repeatability in other spaces of staging.

In suggesting that presence is never simple but always subject to the possibility or necessity of various kinds of repetition, Beckett's theatre points outside itself, to implicate in this redoubling readers' and audiences' attempts to make sense, to 'stage' the plays in the spaces of interpretation. To say this is not to imply an infinite or open range of possibilities for reading. Rather it is to induce a self-reflexive sense of the often invisible limits of reading and interpretation, a sense of the conventions which regulate and are occasionally resisted by criticism. In other words, the staging of Beckett's work in interpretation involves issues of power, and this staging has a particular significance because of the uniquely prestigious place that he occupies in literary culture; no other living author can claim Beckett's near-mythological status. For this reason, Beckett's texts, theatrical and otherwise, and the criticism which constitutes and reproduces them, legitimate power at many levels; the power of beliefs about the integrity and authority of the artist, beliefs in the place and function of theatre and, indeed, of high culture itself. These connect with institutional structures of power, maintaining the special place of the discipline of English within universities and within society as a whole. At a more general level still, Beckett studies reproduce and confirm a whole range of more general beliefs about the nature and purpose of interpretation, the continuity and singleness of the subject and the nature of the unchangeably human. It is in the affirmation of *presence*, the belief that Beckett's plays give us something positive and self-identical, in a positive and identifiable place, which underpins these affirmations. Ruby Cohn's open declaration of the universal value of Beckett's work makes it plain how, for criticism, to 'say where' is closely bound up with being able to 'say what': 'Beckett's play lies in the precision of its wide human embrace. In Vladimir's sentence: "But at this place, at this moment, all mankind is us, whether we like it or not." '[24]

This is not to argue that Beckett studies are monolithic and without contradiction. In fact, the contradictions within Beckett criticism, as within most kinds of cultural criticism, are often massive and fundamental. The most obvious of these contradictions is in the way that Beckett criticism attempts to control and to make knowable and readable texts that acknowledgedly undo the bases on which such knowability and readability rests. It is not so much that criticism is here being simply unfaithful to the texts it constitutes – although criticism based on the need to affirm origin and presence is usually blind to most of the features of Beckett's texts which resist these metaphysical absolutes – as that criticism remains unaware of its own deep implication in the production and staging of those texts as knowledge. If questions of cultural politics may seem to some to be particularly inappropriate for Beckett's texts, then this is a measure of the power of the protocol which excludes or invalidates them. The point of such contradictions is usually that they should remain structurally invisible. They are unlikely to become visible, unless criticism is prepared to stage itself with the same degree of analytic self-reflexiveness as do Beckett's texts and plays.

Acknowledgement

Steven Connor's contribution to this volume appears by kind permission of Blackwell. It was first published in *Samuel Beckett: Repetition, Theory and Text*, 1988.

Notes

1. 'Moody Man of Letters', *New York Times*, Sunday, 6 May 1956, sect. 2, p. 3.
2. *The Long Sonata of the Dead: A Study of Samuel Beckett* (New York: Grove Press, 1969), p. 230.

3. Quoted in Michael Haerdter, *Materialen zu Becketts Endspiel* (Frankfurt: Suhrkamp, 1967), p. 88.

4. Alain Robbe-Grillet, 'Samuel Beckett, or Presence on the Stage,' in *Snapshots and Towards a New Novel* (London: Calder and Boyars, 1965) pp. 119–26.

5. 'Beckett's Actor', *Modern Drama*, 26:4 (December 1983), p. 420.

6. Sidney Homan, *Beckett's Theaters: Interpretations for Performance* (London and Toronto: Associated University Presses, 1984), p. 49.

7. Samuel Beckett, *Disjecta: Miscellaneous Writings and a Dramatic Fragment*, ed. Ruby Cohn (London: John Calder, 1983), p. 109.

8. Antonin Artaud, 'On the Balinese Theatre,' *The Theatre and Its Double*, trans. Victor Corti (London: Calder and Boyars, 1970), p. 43. My account of Artaud's writings on the theatre and of critical attitudes towards Beckett's theatre depends heavily on Jacques Derrida's discussions of Artaud in 'The Theater of Cruelty and the Closure of Representation' and 'La Parole Soufflée', in *Writing and Difference*, trans. Alan Bass (London: Routledge & Kegan Paul, 1978). The relationship between Beckett's and Artaud's work has been discussed in Maurice Blackman, 'Acting Without Words: Artaud and Beckett's Theatrical Language,' in *Journal of Australian Universities' Modern Language Association*, 55 (1981), pp. 68–76.

9. Ruby Cohn, *Just Play: Beckett's Theater* (Princeton, NJ: Princeton UP, 1980), pp. 27–33; Enoch Brater, 'Light, Sound, Movement, and Action in *Rockaby*,' *Modern Drama*, 25:3 (September 1982), p. 345.

10. Samuel Beckett, *Complete Dramatic Works* (London: Faber & Faber, 1986), p. 217. All references hereafter in text to *CDW*.

11. *La Dernière Bande* (Paris: Editions de Minuit, 1959), p. 13. One can compare the page-turning in *Krapp's Last Tape* with the similar suspension of the action to turn the page in *Ohio Impromptu* (*CDW*, 446).

12. Jacques Derrida, 'Signature, Event, Context', in *Margins of Philosophy*, trans. Alan Bass (Sussex: Harvester Press, 1982), p. 320.

13. See, for example, Pierre Chabert's 'The Body in Beckett's Theatre', in *Journal of Beckett Studies*, no. 8 (Autumn, 1982), pp. 23–28 and the discussion of theatrical location in the chapter 'At This Place' in Cohn, *Just Play*, pp. 17–33.

14. Samuel Beckett, *Collected Shorter Prose 1945–1980* (London: John Calder, 1984) pp. 123–4.

15. 'Mongrel Mime for One Old Small' is the heading for this sketch of a play, abandoned in 1983 and held in the Humanities Research Center in Austin, Texas.

16. Hugh Kenner, *A Reader's Guide to Samuel Beckett* (London: Thames & Hudson, 1973), p. 121.

17. Beryl S. and John Fletcher, *A Student's Guide to the Plays of Samuel Beckett* (London: Faber & Faber, 1985), p. 93.

18. Samuel Beckett, *Worstward Ho* (London: John Calder, 1983), p. 16.

19. The shape described is also that of a cross, a shape which recurs in Beckett's theatre and staging; see the discussions of cruciform movements in Cohn, *Just Play*, p. 32 and Martha Fehsenfeld, 'Beckett's Late Works: An Appraisal,' in *Modern Drama*, 25:3 (September 1982),

p. 358. The cross shares with the circle a structural interdependence between centre and periphery.

20. Pierre Chabert draws explicitly on Artaud's work when he argues for the absolute identity between text and production which comes about when Beckett directs his own plays: 'Beckett as author and director is one and the same person. . . . The mise-en-scène, depending as it does on a change in status between speech and space no longer constitutes an activity secondary to that of writing. It is the act of translation, illustration, derivation of which Artaud spoke', 'Beckett as Director', trans. M. A. Bonney and J. Knowlson, in *Krapp's Last Tape: Theatre Workbook*, ed. J. Knowlson (London: Brutus, 1980), p. 86.

21. Writing to Barney Rosset about a proposed stage-adaptation of *All That Fall*, for example, Beckett protested that the play was 'a specifically radio play' whose quality 'depends upon the whole thing's *coming out of the dark'*. Later in the letter, Beckett's general adherence to the principle of the specificity of medium is made clear: 'If we can't keep our genres distinct, or extricate them from the confusion that has them where they are, we might as well go home and lie down' (quoted by Claus Zilliacus, *Beckett and Broadcasting: A Study of the Works of Samuel Beckett for and in Radio and Television*, Acta Academiae Aboensis, Ser. A. Humaniora, Vol. 51 [Abo, Finland, 1976], p. 3).

22. Deirdre Bair, *Samuel Beckett: A Biography* (London: Pan Books, 1980), p. 342.

23. See the chapter 'Jumping Beckett's Genres', in Cohn's *Just Play*, pp. 207–29 for details of transpositions of Beckett's works from one medium to another.

24. Cohn, *Just Play*, p. 14.

2

Beckett's Devious Deictics

Angela Moorjani

When Beckett began *The Unnamable* with 'Where now? Who now? When now?', he was toying with the narrative convention that demands that at the beginning of stories narrators orientate their audience in respect to time, place, and person. The beginning of *Molloy*, for example – 'I am in my mother's room. It's I who live there now' – appears to fulfil just such an orientating function by means of the indexical forms of language, the shifters or deictics that anchor person, time, and place to the perspective of the speaker. Deictic terms, which include personal pronouns, such as Molloy's *I*, temporary forms, such as *now* and verb tense (*am*), and spatial terms (*there*), can be fully understood only if the hearer or reader reconstructs the position of the speaker. Such terms differ from other linguistic signs in that they are signifiers whose reference (but not signifieds) shifts according to when, where, and by whom they are used.[1] ('Beckett's Shifty Shifters' would be a useful alternative title for this chapter.)

In my discussion of the devious categories of person, place, and time in Beckett's imaginary, I will begin with place and the situation of loss so crucial to the Beckett canon, where timelessness and selflessness, if not placelessness, abound. What is this place from which the voice speaks?

According to psychoanalytic theories of mourning, recently extended by Nicholas Abraham and Maria Torok, whose work Derrida discusses in *Fors*, a lost one is introjected into the psyche as still living. After a period of time, in the normal process of mourning, the lost one is declared dead. And the living go on with living. In abnormal mourning, on the other hand, the living dead is permanently incorporated into an inner crypt – a 'cleavage' in the ego, Freud called it – with no possibility of decrypting. The living dead, with whom the mourner identifies, is thus maintained in this cryptic space, with its status of an exteriority within an interiority or a closed-off place of exile marked out within the ego.

20

Beckettians will have recognised the similarity of this place with the preferred theatre of Beckettian drama, the tomblike womb and the womblike tomb in the darkness of the mind in which the living are unborn and the dead do not die.

The introjecting/incorporating/encrypting process of mourning, moreover, has much in common with the introjection of parental power, both life-sustaining and life-threatening, the maternal first, the paternal next, and according to Kleinian psychoaesthetic theories, with the artistic process. The mourner and the artist both rehearse or repeat the infant's earliest ties and experiences of loss, first the fantasmatic loss of self because of a destructive (m)other, then, in reverse, the loss of the (m)other because of a destructive self. Such sacrificial fantasies bring with them a depressive load of guilt – that familiar Beckettian refrain – and the desire to make reparation. It is the function of the work of art ultimately to repair what has been lost in fantasy to this orgy of destruction and fragmentation, in this sense, restoring to life what has been introjected as damaged and lifeless. Through mourning, with time, we let the lost one die in the psyche, a second death, so that we can go on living; in art, we bring to life what has been lost in fantasy (Klein 210–18, 262–89). Incorporation or encrypting, on the other hand, blocks both moves in a simultaneous deathlessness and lifelessness, suspended between libidinal and destructive forces.

Beckett's work has relentlessly explored this unchartered place, this *'fors intérieur'*, this artificial unconscious (Derrida 21) of the preverbal and artistic imaginary. If this is the place from which Beckett's cast of voices speaks, the many fragments of the Unnamable, then in what terms are they to speak of the unspeakable lifelessness, deathlessness, and timelessness of the crypt? This cryptic enclosure in the ego is surely the most non-deictic of places, paradoxically containing a speaker outside an inner self, a 'not I' outside an inner history. This then is not the unconscious structured like a language, but a *topos* outside the signifying practice of language, to which neither symbolic naming, indexical or deictic pointing, or iconic likenesses can properly refer. To refer to it the writer must unsay all that is said, fade out all that is shown.

If then, as Benveniste holds in his famous article, 'De la subjectivité dans le langage', it is through language, by referring to ourselves as *I* that we accede simultaneously to our status as subjects and to the intersubjective dimension of human discourse,

the *I* implying a *you* and the *you* an *I*, each *I* becoming a *you* for
self and other, and each *you* becoming an *I* in turn, then this
paradoxical and fragmented voice without a self cannot say *I*, only
perhaps a pseudo-*I* without a *you*, or a pseudo-*you* without a
corresponding *I*, pointing to a discourse without a subject and
without an interlocutor. As the voice puts it in *Company* to the
encrypted body: 'the first person singular and a fortiori plural
pronoun had never any place in your vocabulary' (61). But what
about *Company*'s voice itself; in saying *you* to the hearer is not its
own first person implied? And what of the speaker–listener couples
of many other texts that would seem to illustrate the interpersonal
nature of discourse? The Beckettian interlocutors, however, even
though their existence in discourse depends on the presence of
the other, turn out to be the fictional projections of a single other
who slips into a company of masks to conceal the abysmal void
lurking beneath. Thus *Company*'s narrator, voice, and hearer are
the fragments of always still another narrator who embeds his
figments in the devious discourse that fails to contain him. And
were the voice and hearer to refer to themselves, they would do
so in the third person. Similarly, the speakers and/or listeners of
Not I, *A Piece of Monologue*, and *Ohio Impromptu*, among others,
have the ghostly status of third-person simulacra of the anonymous
cryptic other.

That the many first-person narratives, including those of the
trilogy, too, are masquerades or fictionalisations for the inhabitant
of the crypt, is clearly marked in the text. First of all, in the trilogy,
the narrative *I* is even more shifty than usual, since instead of
referring steadily to one narrative speaker, as readers have come
to expect, it keeps splitting and shifting from one speaker to
another, each divided from the other myriad fragments of a nonself (Kerbrat-Orecchioni 66). The Unnamable's narrative accordingly
is punctuated with allusions to the not-I status of both the teller
and the told – 'I seem to speak, it is not I, about me, it is not
about me' (291) – and to the cryptic situation – 'the unthinkable
unspeakable, where I have not ceased to be, where they will not
let me be' (335) or 'what's all this about not being able to die, live,
be born . . .'. (370).

The reference by speakers/narrators to themselves in the not-I
form, the projection or exile of the first person into a distant other,
certainly a common literary diversion, is analysed by Greimas and
Courtés in their semiotic dictionary as a '*schizie créatrice*' or creative

splitting. What these theorists have done is to divide Jakobson's concept of the shifter into two operations, *débrayage* and *embrayage*, which may be translated as 'shifting-out' and 'shifting-in'. For them, shifting-out is the prior operation by means of which a not I/not now/not here is disconnected from the I/now/here anchored to the speaker's utterance. In a radicalisation of Benveniste, Greimas and Courtés point out that in the shifting irreality of discourse, even the pronoun *I* and the terms *here* and *now* are already projections or simulacra of the actual speaker and the attendant time and place. The not I, not here, not now, then, put an even further distance between locutionary agents and their representations in language. Shifting-in, on the other hand, is the procedure whereby the prior disconnection is reversed by an attempted fusion of speaker and spoken-about, a return in direction towards the unattainable source of the utterance.[2]

Literary examples of *embrayage* would be autobiographies for first-person shifting-in, the Flaubertian *'Madame Bovary, c'est moi'* for third-person *embrayage*, and for the second person, Butor's narrator in *La Modification* identifying with the narrative's *vous*, and finally the Barthian use of the first, second, and third persons to speak of himself in *Roland Barthes par Roland Barthes*. Except for Barthes, who qualifies his devious use of pronouns as the unravelling of an imaginary self, the other examples constitute a distancing from self to speak all the better about the self, emphasising the colossal egocentricity of discourse.[3]

How Beckett deviates from even such deictic detours can be illustrated as follows. The *débrayage–embrayage* progression moves from a source of utterance to an *I* then on to *not I* before returning to the *I*:

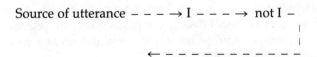

In Beckett, however, the speaking of self as divided from self, the *débrayage* or splitting is not reversed by *embrayage*, the return to the speaking subject. The source of utterance is projected first into the 'unspeakable', and then into a multitude of *I*s and *not I*s, with no return from each successive exile: the *not I* remains divided from the *I* which is uncoupled from the unspeakable as it is from the source of utterance, resulting in a radical form of *débrayage* or *schizie créatrice*:

Source of utterance – – → Unspeakable – – → I – – → not I – – →

A total *embrayage*, on the other hand, would permit the identity of the *not I* and the *I* with the source of the utterance, a process that Greimas and Courtés consider inconceivable, since it would erase all traces of discourse (1:119). In Beckettian terms it would constitute the impossible silence.

Instead of shifting back to the source of utterance, Beckett's early texts already sabotage the literary *embrayage* between the narrated *not I* and the narrator's *I*. In *More Pricks than Kicks*, the narrator says of Belacqua, 'I gave him up in the end . . .' (38); and in *Watt*, the split between Watt (third person) and Sam (first person) is extended by the schism between Watt (first person, in turn) and the ineffable within. With the trilogy and beyond, a furious progression of deictic masks, a fantastic theatre of illusions, continues to conceal the anonymous lost one.

Spatio-temporal *débrayage* in Beckett works in quite similar ways, with a time of utterance exiled into a timelessness that is masked by disconnected *now*s and *not now*s:

Time of utterance – – → Timelessness – – → now – – → not now – →

In asking about time, the Unnamable thus wonders 'why it buries you grain by grain neither dead nor alive, with no memory of anything . . . no history and no prospects . . . time is one thing, I another' (389), a situation outside of time that brings to mind not only *Happy Days* but also *Godot* and *Endgame*, among others. As in the manipulations of personal deixis, the projections into pseudo-*I*s and *not I*s, the temporal projections into a *now* and *not now* serve to disguise the ultimate timelessness.

One of the favourite temporal surrogates then is the road on which the Unnamable would like to think of 'moving, between a beginning and an end' (314). It is the road on which the pseudo-couples wander, on which Pozzo and Lucky pass, and which reappears on the set of *'but the clouds . . .'* and in the fables of *Company* and *Worstward Ho*. But just as the personal and interpersonal presence of self in discourse is displaced, so the dynamic progression along a time-line or deictic temporal reference is denied by as dazzling a series of attacks on linearity as can be found in postmodernist writing. The time-flow from a beginning to an end that would permit the return to an origin is thus contested by turning the steps in time into an infinite round, which in turn fades away, as in *Footfalls*, or by reducing the dynamic coming and going into a static moment as at the end of *That Time*, or by substituting conceptual time for linear time and embedding the moments of a pulverised storyline one inside the other in an infinite regression, as throughout the trilogy, or again by merging all tenses that are anchored to speaker's time into an omnitemporal repetition, as in *Molloy*'s 'mythological present', all of which ultimately dissolve into timelessness.

In this connection, it is important to distinguish between non-deictic forms that are nevertheless timebound, such as the cyclical, static, abysmal or labyrinthine, and omnitemporal conceptions of time mentioned above, and timelessness itself. Such devious temporal conceptions, which can be traced back to the earliest philosophers of time, recall the shifty use of pronouns, both of which, however, are just Beckettian games within the context of timelessness and personlessness.

What is of particular interest too in relation to the above notions of time is that they illustrate the progressive temporalisation of space or spatialisation of time, which the English and French languages share with many others and which pervades the conceptual horizon of the twentieth century from the visual arts to scientific theory. Such space–time expressions suggest a conceptual structure in which time-relationships are derived from spatial ones and help explain the Beckettian spatio-temporal imaginary (Lyons, *Semantics* 718–24; Traugott 207–16). In *The Unnamable* it is put as follows: 'And even should the notion of time dawn on his darkness . . . . Involving very naturally that of space, they have taken to going hand in hand, in certain quarters, it's safer' (362–3).

Besides being masked by the static, non-deictic notions of time, the ultimate timelessness is betrayed by the frequent deictic projections into the past. Of these, the narratives of *That Time* and *Company* are of particular interest to a study of Beckettian temporal *débrayage*. In both texts, since the fables to which the hearers listen, and which they refuse to admit as their own, contain recognisable moments of Beckett's own past, whether autobiographical or 'authorbiographical', the writer posits an implied self as the source of utterance to which the personal and temporal projections, including the not-now of memories and stories, cannot return. (Along with such autobiographical reminiscences, Beckett has of course alluded all along to his radical disjunction from his creations by mirroring himself in the disconnected Sams, Hacketts, and Lemuels and in the schizo-writing/narrating and recently directing and mourning activities of many of his fictional and dramatic participants.)

Finally, to return now to the spatial deixis with which I began, it is the crypt, the place of exile of the source of utterance, that the many Beckettian places, the *here*s and *not here*s, caricature and which is at the basis of the temporal and personal dislocations:

Place of utterance – – → Crypt – – → here – – → not here – –

If one considers the Unnamable's description of the crypt, 'I'm . . . a wordless thing in an empty place, a hard shut dry cold black place' (386), it would seem most appropriate to imagine it in terms of what in semantics is called an 'abstract location' (Lyons, *Semantics* 719), here the state of living death. The many metaphoric displacements of the crypt, the head and hell, asylums and dungeons, post-nuclear desolation, urns and entombment, the womb, the room, the bed, the rocker, gardens, mansions, seas, and forests, can be seen as so many attempts to project into a *here* and *not here*. The strange status of these places of containment, from which Beckettian time's abysmal structure is derived, emphasises simultaneously an afterlife and a pre-life, as do the devious forms of person analysed above. And just as the *I* is ousted by the *not I*, the deictic forms of time by the non-deictic, the *here* gives way to the *not here* before it is in turn unsaid.

A quick consideration of the locative adverb *there* will serve as an example of Beckettian spatial *débrayage*. In paying close attention to *Molloy's* opening declarations – 'I am in my mother's room. It's I who live there now' – one wonders why the narrator uses *there* instead of the expected *here*. Why not, 'It's I who live here now'? From the beginning of the novel, a devious *there*, pointing to the place where the speaker is not, usurps the place of *here*, indicating the location where the speaker is. Moreover, on comparing the English translation of the beginning passage of *Molloy* with the French original – '*Je suis dans la chambre de ma mère. C'est moi qui y vit maintenant'* – an interesting difference comes to light between French and English locative adverbs. In the French version, Beckett used the deictic *y* which refers back cotextually to *'dans la chambre de ma mère'*, but indicates neither nearness nor farness in relation to the speaker. In order to render the *y* into English, however, the translator must opt for either proximity or distance, for *here* (where the speaker is) or *there* (where the speaker is not). Even though *Molloy* was translated by Patrick Bowles in collaboration with the author, the choice of the deviant *there* in the place of *here* would appear to be Beckett's, since it corresponds to the many other examples of *débrayage* analysed.

The adverb *there*, however, can also have a non-deictic, 'existential' meaning, as in *being there* or *not being there* (Lyons, *Semantics* 723). It is of course in this sense that is to be understood Amy's 'I was not there' in *Footfalls*, which in the French *Pas* becomes the equally deictically neutral, *'Je n'étais pas là.'* Like the non-deictic expressions of time, the non-deictic *there* points to the displacement of the speaker or the source of utterance.

To what extent the readers, listeners, and viewers implied by the Beckettian texts are deprived of deictic anchors is obvious from the preceding analysis. For Beckett's devious deictics, instead of orientating the audience, ultimately function to disorientate by annulling all attempts to position a self in relation to a narrative I/here/now.

Although in the early French fiction, in particular, the role of the reader or narratee is emphasised by frequent asides, such as *Molloy*'s 'For the old pain, do you follow me, I had got used to it . . .' (77), Gianni Celati has convincingly linked this presence of a *you* to a form of hysterical posturing. The narrative *I*, he finds, is as if dispossessed by the fantasised narratee's discourse (226, 229). This then resembles a discourse limited to a *you* without an *I*, a shifting-out of the hysterical subject into a *you*. (That the hysterical personality avoids the first person in discourse is pointed out by Luce Irigaray in her 1967 article.) The hysterical dispossession of the narrative *I*, then, is another way of unsaying the subject, and along with it the *you* of the reader/narratee, given the dependence of the *you* on the *I* in discourse.

In conclusion, in focusing briefly on the encrypting process that I have hypothesised as occasioning the Beckettian *débrayage*, one could say that until roughly the 1960s – and since then, in such works as *A Piece of Monologue*, *That Time*, and *Company* – it is the encrypted lost self that is being mourned, the aborted being that the artist feels within himself that he has the obligation but not the means to release.[4] The deictic masks here are male. And the reversable tormentor/tormented couples and the recurring identification with the sacrificed divine son point to the experience behind the incorporating/encrypting process. It is the projection of this inner torment into time, the repetition of the sacrificial experience in history, that has led Beckett the man and writer to political action, despite the horizon of hopeless repetition and ultimate timelessness. Then, beginning with *Happy Days*, *Eh Joe*, *Not I*, and continuing with *Footfalls*, *Rockaby*, and *Ill Seen Ill Said*, the simulacra are female (as happened sporadically before, for example in *Molloy*). What appears encrypted here is the mother whose release needs to be effected along with the child's. (Does not the enigmatic child of *Godot*, *Endgame*, and *Ghost Trio* carry the message of the always-deferred release from the timelessness of the crypt? Nor is it surprising in this connection that *Godot*'s supposed maleness is usurped by the female voice of *Ghost Trio*.)

In *Ill Seen Ill Said*, the 'tenacious trace' of the maternal figure, more tenacious than the paternal because more archaic, reminiscent here of depictions of the mythic Great Mother, the source of all creation, the origin of love, life, and death, nevertheless shares the living-dead exile of the Unnamable: 'No shock were she already dead. As of course she is. But in the meantime more convenient not. Still living then she lies hidden' (41). Among *Ill Seen Ill Said*'s metaphors of containment, it is perhaps the coffer that most vividly suggests cryptic exile. For according to the Greek version of the Ishtar–Tammuz story, Aphrodite put Adonis into a chest which she gave to Persephone for safekeeping. When the goddess of the underworld refused to return the chest to Aphrodite, the goddess of love descended into hell to save Adonis from the dead. In a repetition of the Demeter–Persephone myth, Adonis subsequently divided his time between the upper world and the underworld, between the divine mothers of life and death (Frazer 11). In suggesting the cryptic living dead, *Ill Seen Ill Said*'s empty coffer once again mocks the attempt to create a self by a return to the centre of creation, an *embrayage* blocked whether the return be toward a source of utterance or a male or female origin of life and death.

Notes

1. In his influential work, *Sprachtheorie* (1934), Karl Bühler first distinguished between deictic terms which depend for their meaning on the speech event and symbolic linguistic signs which are less dependent on context. See also Benveniste, Jakobson, Kerbrat-Orecchioni, and Lyons for discussions of deixis.
2. See *débrayage* and *embrayage* in Volume 1 of Greimas and Courtés; and Morot-Sir's discussion of these concepts.
3. See Barthes, 'Vingt mots-clé pour Roland Barthes', p. 32 and *Roland Barthes par Roland Barthes*, p. 171; and Kerbrat-Orecchioni, pp. 63–6, 152–6.
4. Beckett has mentioned the impression he has of such a lost creature to several people, among whom recently Charles Juliet whom he told: *'J'ai toujours eu la sensation qu'il y avait en moi un être assassiné. Assassiné avant ma naissance. Il me fallait retrouver cet être assassiné. Tenter de lui redonner vie'* (16).

Works Cited

Abraham, Nicolas, and Maria Torok, *Cryptonymie: Le Verbier de l'homme aux loups* (Paris: Aubier-Flammarion, 1976).
Barthes, Roland, *Roland Barthes par Roland Barthes* (Paris: Seuil, 1975).
——, 'Vingt mots-clé pour Roland Barthes', *Magazine Littéraire* 97 (1975): 28–37.
Beckett, Samuel, *Collected Shorter Plays* (New York: Grove Press, 1984).
——, *Company* (New York: Grove Press, 1980).
——, *En attendant Godot* (Paris: Minuit, 1952).
——, *Endgame* (New York: Grove Press, 1958).
——, *Happy Days* (New York: Grove Press, 1961).
——, *Ill Seen Ill Said* (New York: Grove Press, 1981).
——, *Molloy* (Paris: Minuit, 1951).
——, *More Pricks than Kicks*, 1934 (New York: Grove Press, 1970).
——, *Pas* (Paris: Minuit, 1978).
——, *Three Novels: Molloy, Malone Dies, The Unnamable*, 1955, 1956, 1958 (New York: Black Cat–Grove Press, 1965).
——, *Watt*, 1953 (New York: Grove Press, 1959).
——, *Worstward Ho* (New York: Grove Press, 1983).
Benveniste, Emile, 'De la subjectivité dans le langage', *Journal de Psychologie* 51 (1958): 257–65. Reprinted in *Problèmes de linguistique générale*, by Benveniste, 2 vols (Paris: Gallimard, 1966–74), 1: 258–66.
——, 'Le Langage et l'expérience humaine', *Diogène* 51 (1965): 3–13.
Bühler, Karl, 'The Deictic Field of Language and Deictic Words', *Sprachtheorie: Die Darstellungsfunktion der Sprache*, 1934 (Stuttgart: Fischer, 1965). Reprinted in Jarvella and Klein, trans. Jarvella and Klein, pp. 9–30.
Celati, Gianni, 'Beckett, l'interpolation et le gag', *Poétique* 14 (1973): 225–34.

Derrida, Jacques, 'Fors: Les mots anglés de Nicolas Abraham et Maria Torok', Abraham and Torok, pp. 7–73.

Frazer, Sir James George, *The Golden Bough: A Study in Magic and Religion*, 3rd edn, 13 vols (New York: Macmillan, 1955), Vol. 7.

Freud, Sigmund, 'Mourning and Melancholia', 1917. *Standard Edition of the Complete Psychological Works*, trans. James Strachey (London: Hogarth Press, 1953–74), 14: 239–58.

Greimas, Algirdas Julien, and Joseph Courtés, *Sémiotique: Dictionnaire raisonné de la théorie du langage*, 2 vols (Paris: Hachette, 1979–86).

Irigaray, Luce, 'Approche d'une grammaire d'énonciation de l'hystérique et de l'obsessionnel', *Langages* 5 (1967): 99–109.

Jakobson, Roman, 'Shifters, Verbal Categories, and the Russian Verb' [Cambridge, Mass.]: Harvard University, Dept of Slavic Languages and Literatures, Russian Language Project, 1957. Reprinted in *Selected Writings*, 2 vols (The Hague: Mounton, 1971), 2: 130–47.

Jarvella, Robert J., and Wolfgang Klein (eds), *Speech, Place, and Action: Studies in Deixis and Related Topics* (New York: Wiley, 1982).

Juliet, Charles, 'Un Vivant', *Magazine Littéraire* 231 (1986): 16–17.

Kerbrat-Orecchioni, Catherine, *L'Enonciation de la subjectivité dans le langage* (Paris: Colin, 1980).

Klein, Melanie, *Love, Guilt and Reparation and Other Works*, 1921–45 (London: Hogarth, 1975).

Lyons, John, 'Deixis and Subjectivity: *Loquor, ergo sum?*' Jarvella and Klein, pp. 101–24.

——, 'Deixis, Space, and Time', *Semantics*, 2 vols (Cambridge: Cambridge University Press, 1977), 2: 636–724.

Morot-Sir, Edouard, 'Texte, référence et déictique', *Texte: Revue de Critique et de Théorie Littéraire* 1 (1982): 113–42.

Traugott, Elizabeth Closs, 'Spatial Expressions of Tense and Temporal Sequencing: A Contribution to the Study of Semantic Fields', *Semiotica* 15 (1975): 207–30.

3

Repetition and Underlying Meanings in Samuel Beckett's Trilogy

Rubin Rabinovitz

To many readers, the style of Samuel Beckett's trilogy of novels –
Molloy, Malone Dies, and *The Unnamable* – initially seems rambling
or chaotic. In part, this impression is enforced by the repetitiousness
of the prose, a factor that intensifies as the trilogy progresses. In
the last two pages of *The Unnamable,* for example, there are over a
dozen sets of recurring passages. Ostensibly, the repetition is part
of an approach which involves (as Beckett's narrator puts it) saying
'any old thing, to pass the time.'[1]

In fact, as in many of Beckett's other works, first impressions
can be unreliable. As one begins to keep track of the reiterated
elements it becomes obvious that their presence could hardly be
haphazard. The repetition in the trilogy, as in many of Beckett's
other works, is part of a highly structured pattern underlying the
apparent chaos of its surface meanings.[2]

Often, short recurring passages serve as clues to more elaborate
forms of repetition. Thus phrases like 'I know, I know' or 'heard
and heard distinctly' may at first seem unimportant, but they often
are linked to longer repeated elements:

MD 52.19   though clothes don't matter, I know, I know
MD 68.27   though acts don't matter, I know, I know

M 27.32   heard, and heard distinctly, not being hard of hearing
M 66.27   heard, and heard distinctly, having quite a sensitive
          ear

Noticing such recurring pairs can lead to the discovery of others
where a different phrase is repeated:

M 66.27   having quite a sensitive ear [Molloy]
M 66.19   I had quite a sensitive ear [Molloy]
M 175.12   I have an extremely sensitive ear [Moran]

Molloy is the speaker in two of these examples, and Moran is the speaker in the third: this acuteness of hearing is only one of the many traits that link different protagonists in the trilogy.

Some repeated phrases appear many pages apart; it is improbable that this would occur with any frequency if the repetition were accidental. In the following example – a set of comments about how Molloy and Malone reached the rooms they inhabit – the recurring passages are in different volumes of the trilogy:

M 7.2   I don't know how I got there. Perhaps in an ambulance, certainly a vehicle of some kind. I was helped.
MD 5.21   I do not remember how I got here. In an ambulance perhaps, in a vehicle of some kind certainly.

Molloy and Moran begin their narratives in similar circumstances: in rooms where they are cared for by anonymous strangers. The recurring passages stress these similarities.

Mahood also refers to an ambulance; he fears that his longed-for death will be prevented by a passerby summoning help with the cry, 'we must call an ambulance' (U 76.20). Molloy says he was helped; Malone never mentions help; and the Unnamable dreads being helped: an ambulance will drag him back into the world of the ambulatory. The repetition is striking because there are few references to ambulances in the trilogy; as it happens, the word 'ambulance' is mentioned only three times, in the passages just cited.[3]

Examples like this one lead to central questions in the trilogy, such as whether the different protagonists can be seen as aspects of a single personality. The recurring passages also hint at subtle connections among the three volumes of the trilogy. As has often been noted, the opening statement of Molloy's narrative ('This time, then once more . . . then perhaps a last time') can be understood as a reference to the three volumes of the trilogy as well as to the protagonists' quests. In fact, there are three versions of this three-part statement in *Molloy*:

M 8.30   This time, then once more I think, then perhaps a last time

M 9.6   I'll manage this time, then perhaps once more, then perhaps a last time

M 33.11   let me cry out this time, then another time perhaps, then perhaps a last time

The recurring elements 'this time . . . then . . . then perhaps a last time', which appear in all of these passages, call attention to the pattern of repetition as well as to the links among the three volumes of the trilogy.

The pattern of repetition is pervasive enough that recurring elements are to be found on virtually every page of the trilogy. The three novels contain over 1500 sets of recurring elements with an average of three items in each set; thus some 4500 items figure in the pattern of repetition. In the Grove three-volume edition, the text of the trilogy runs for 540 pages; this averages out to about eight items per page.[4] The amount of repetition in the French version of the trilogy is about the same: the translation is in general faithful to the French original.[5]

VARIETIES OF REPETITION

Beckett makes use of many types of recurring elements in the trilogy. Words, phrases, sentences, actions, episodes, and ideas are repeated, and occasionally, even sounds. Here, for example, he uses rhyme and alliteration for a euphonic type of repetition:

M 96.23   a little more insistent, a little more resistant

M 234.15   constant contact with my incontinences

M 235.6   a few flitters of silk fluttering from the stays

The majority of recurring elements, however, consist of short phrases. In many instances only portions of such phrases are reproduced verbatim. This kind of reiteration is often used for qualifying or redefining ideas:

MD 3.16   There I am, back at my old aporetics.

MD 4.1   There I am, back at my old quibbles.

A similar type of repetition is used to underline the parallel structure of a series of statements:

U 163.25   or another, let us be fair
U 163.26   or up into another, let us be impartial
U 163.28   or in another, let us be just

Here the iterated phrases are easy to notice because they appear within a few lines of one another. But a similar kind of repetition can occur over a series of pages:

U 7.3   And yet I am troubled.
U 18.27   And yet I am anxious.
U 20.7   And yet I am afraid

In some instances, distant parallel elements become easier to detect when they are enforced by internally repeated phrases, such as 'done with' in the following passages:

U 29.19   done with saying, done with listening.
U 36.4   done with speaking, done with listening.
U 149.32   done with speech, done with listening.

Repetition of this type sometimes signals a change in approach or attitude. As Moran progresses in his journey he becomes more disenchanted with his old bourgeois life. This idea is reflected in the following passages where he describes the lights of a distant town:

M 218.28   brave little lights of men
M 222.16   foul little flickering lights of terrified men

Beckett sometimes uses a similar technique for a humorous effect. Here the juxtaposition of two seemingly unrelated phrases suggests that Malone is slyly deriding rationality:

MD 25.9   all pigs are alike when you get to know their little ways
MD 51.23   ideas are so alike when you get to know them

Often, the restating of an idea introduces irony:

M 193.22   What a boon it is from time to time, a little real conversation.

M 194.2   What a restful change it is from time to time, a little
    dialogue.

After giving his son an enema Moran tells him, 'Let it soak well
in.' Later his son repeats this remark when Moran is applying
iodex to his knee, and Moran realises he is being mocked. 'He
would pay for that later on', says Moran (M 162.19, 163.27).

Another type of repetition alludes to the tedium of life or the
predictability of human behaviour. Here this idea emerges in a
story whose redundancy hints at its banality:

U 167.29   she weeps, with emotion, at having loved him, at
    having lost him
U 168.6   she weeps, weeps again, with emotion again, at having
    lost him again
U 168.10   she weeps, weeps louder, at having loved him, at
    having lost him

In some instances two narrated events resemble one another,
although neither words nor sounds are repeated. The following
set of passages, narrated by Molloy and Moran, is an example:

M 35.2   In the ditch the grass was thick and high, I took off my
    hat and pressed about my face the long leafy stalks.
M 174.24   I offered my face to the black mass of fragrant
    vegetation

In another series of related passages, Molloy, Moran, and Malone
react in similar ways to the cries of birds:

M 20.31   the awful cries of the corncrakes
M 125.5   I hear the eagle owl. What a terrible battle cry!
MD 56.7   the dreadful cries of the gulls

This series of passages is in turn related to others about birds:
again, noticing one reiterated element leads to the discovery of
others.[6]

LINKED SETS OF RECURRING ELEMENTS

An important type of repetition involves different types of duplicated elements that reinforce one another. Beckett often links recurring sets in order to call attention to underlying similarities in apparently unrelated episodes. This occurs, for example, in two scenes where Molloy and Moran encounter shepherds. Various types of repetition are used to suggest parallels between these two scenes: each hero finds it difficult to speak, but questions the shepherd nevertheless; and each shepherd seems reluctant to respond to these questions. In each scene there are references to the shepherd and his dog watching the protagonist; to the profound silence; and to black sheep.[7] In addition, both heroes make similar remarks about the region:

M 38.20   Good God, what a land of breeders
M 217.10   What a pastoral land, my God.

Parallel scenes like these again raise questions about how the trilogy's protagonists are related to one another.

PARALLEL SYMMETRY

Molloy's and Moran's experiences are often similar, and at times the details linking the two heroes are introduced in a parallel sequence. The two parts of *Molloy* are about equal in length; and the ordering of events is such that Moran, in a given section of Part II, undergoes experiences that resemble Molloy's at a similar place in Part I. Each half of the novel begins with a protagonist's explanation that recently concluded events are to be recounted; then moves back in time to the beginning of a journey; and then goes on to a description of the journey itself.

A sense of the similarity of the two halves of the novel is intensified by recurring details that appear at roughly the same place in each of the two parts. There are many examples of this effect in the early pages of each narrative. (In the following list, the numbers in parentheses to the left of the texts indicate on which page of Part I or II an event occurs; thus the events in the first example occur on the opening pages of Parts I and II.)

(1) Molloy is in his mother's house writing (M 7).
(1) Moran is in his house writing (M 125).

(2) A man who encourages him to write comes, 'every Sunday apparently' for Molloy's completed pages (M 8).
(1) Gaber arrives at Moran's house on a Sunday; later it will be revealed that Gaber asked Moran to write his report (M 125).

(2) Molloy's visitor is 'always thirsty' (M 8).
(4) Moran offers Gaber beer (M 128); Gaber asks for more (M 129).

(2) Molloy speculates about whether he has a son (M 8).
(2) Moran mentions his son (M 126).

(2) Molloy speaks about a chambermaid (M 8).
(3) Moran speaks about his maid (M 127).

(13) Molloy owns a bicycle, discusses transportation problems (M 19), repeats phrases related to travel ('This is how I went about it', M 19.25, M 114.1; 'my arms on the handlebars', M 20.24, M 25.31).
(9) Moran owns a bicycle, discusses transportation problems (M 134), repeats phrases related to travel: ('leave on your autocycle', M 134.14, M 135.7; 'the problem of transport', M 134.23, M 134.28).

(17) Molloy regrets being born (M 23).
(18) Moran regrets having begotten his son (M 142).

(28) Molloy's use of the present tense when speaking of the past is called the 'mythological present' (M 34).
(25) Moran's use of the present tense when framing imperative statements is called the 'prophetic present' (M 149).

(31) Molloy on first awakening sees things most clearly; then a 'mist' forms which 'veils the world' (M 37).
(27) Moran can best see through 'the outer turmoil's veil' while reclining; arising, he drowns in a 'spray of phenomena' (M 151).

(35) Molloy discusses the problems of using language, 'the icy words . . . the icy meanings . . .' (M 41).
(35) Moran says 'It seemed to me that all language was an excess of language . . .' (M 159).

Many other examples could be added to this list; and the list could be extended by including details that involve other characters in the trilogy. But these examples should be enough to illustrate the way congruent details are introduced sequentially so the parallels between the two protagonists are emphasised.

This, however, is not to say that Molloy and Moran are – or are not – versions of the same person. That they resemble one another can easily be demonstrated; that they are the same person cannot be proved. Molloy and Moran figuratively represent stages in an endless quest; the reader, looking for the evidence to link them, becomes engaged in a similar quest. Equating the two protagonists would put an end to this quest, one that leads to more interesting issues. Beckett, as will be seen, is less concerned with Molloy's identity as an older Moran than with questions about what an identity represents.

FRONT–BACK SYMMETRY

The symmetry in the two parts of *Molloy* suggests that the protagonists can be seen as figures traversing parallel paths, but this is not exactly so. If portions of their routes seem rectilinear, the paths they finally traverse are circuitous. The end of each cycle marks the beginning of a new one at a place that is at a more advanced stage than the previous one, so these routes take on a helical form.[8]

In addition to the parallel symmetry described earlier, Beckett uses a second type of symmetry that connects ends and beginnings to suggest cyclical and helical movements. One example of this front–back symmetry is the way the beginning and end of Moran's narrative are linked by the repeated sentences, 'It is midnight. The rain is beating on the windows' (M 124.1, M 241.28).

There are many other examples of front–back symmetry. When Molloy hobbles into a ditch at the beginning of his quest he predicts that he will return to it, or to a similar place (M 34.30, M 36.1). At the end of his journey Molloy pulls himself through a thicket and falls into a ditch (M 122.31). This ditch marks the end of his wanderings through a forest; Malone, soon after he begins his narrative, recalls having been in a forest (MD 6.9). Towards the end of his account the narrator of *The Unnamable* longs to be in a forest, a desire similar to one Molloy expresses at the close of his narrative (U 158.9, M 124.5).

Some recurring sets contain elements of both front–back and parallel symmetry, as when the farmer Moran meets towards the end of his journey resembles one he encountered on setting out. Moran's speculation about whether the two are the same runs parallel to questions about the identity of other minor characters, such as Molloy's visitor and Gaber, who have many traits in common. Such parallels finally serve as echoes of the question about whether Molloy and Moran can be equated (M 237.3).

Front–back symmetry can often be found in passages that recur at the beginning and end of an episode or narrative section. Thus Moran says of Gaber, 'I knew him well' when he describes their first and last meetings (M 127.7, M 225.26). In contrast, the other protagonists often repeat the phrase 'I don't know' at similar points in their accounts: it appears a number of times in the opening pages of *Molloy* and in the closing pages of *The Unnamable*.

M 7.2   I don't know [also at M 7.19, 8.1, 8.3, 8.26]
U 178.11   I don't know [also at U 178.31, U 179.4, U 179.8, U 179.23]

There are many other instances of recurring passages that mark beginnings and endings of works or their major divisions, such as the following sets that link the beginning and end of *The Unnamable*, and of the trilogy:

U 3.3   Keep going, going on, call that going, call that on.
U 179.23   you must go on, I can't go on, I'll go on.

M 8.26   it's nearly the end.
U 150.29   it's nearly the end.

The echoes in these examples do double duty by conveying ironic meanings. In the second example Molloy, at the beginning of his narrative, imagines that his quest is nearly over – a shaky hypothesis, under the circumstances. The inability to continue is expressed near the end of *The Unnamable*, but the trilogy opens and closes with the idea of going on. The Beckettian quest continues even beyond the last page of the last novel in the series.

RECURRING ACTION

In keeping with the cyclical nature of these quests, the activities related to them are often connected. Molloy and Malone cannot be equated on a literal level, but they are linked by an extended metaphor that subtly suggests that they are repeating one another's actions. This eventually leads to the idea that Beckett's protagonists are caught up in related cycles and undergoing similar experiences as they move through them.

For Beckett, living implies the redundancy of habitual actions – doing the same things, uttering the same remarks, making the same mistakes, again and again. As Molloy says,

    M 61.6   whatever I do, that is to say, whatever I say, it will always be as it were the same thing, yes, as it were.
    M 115.27   I knew how difficult it was not to do again what you have done before.

We imagine that we can break out of this repetitious cycle; but each seemingly new endeavour usually turns out to be a version of an earlier one. It finally becomes clear that for Beckett's characters the illusory hope of breaking out of this circular pattern is itself part of a habitual cycle.[9]

It is in this way – as stages in metaphorical cycles rather than as periods in a person's life – that Beckett's heroes can be seen as representing aspects of a single personality. As Molloy puts it, 'whatever I do, that is to say, whatever I say, it will always be as it were the same thing, yes, as it were' (M 61.6). With each hero one is initially aware of their differences in name, appearance and situation. But metaphorically these heroes can be linked as they begin their quests with the same belief, that after a little more effort the quest will have ended. They may reach what they consider the end of the cycle, but they do not find whatever it is they were looking for when they set out. And so each journey ends in disappointment – disappointment that gives rise to the wish to embark on a new phase of the cycle.

Progress in the quest can take place on a number of different levels, both literal (making progress in the world; moving through time) and metaphorical (achieving intellectual gains, making emotional progress, embarking on a voyage of self-discovery, and writing about these experiences). Many of the recurring passages in the trilogy refer to this metaphor, in some instances on more than two levels. Often the idea of movement or progress is suggested in such passages:

> U 163.3   that helps you on, that helps you forward, I believe in progress.
> U 167.12   that helps you forward, I believe in progress
> U 167.23   that helps you on, that helps the end to come

The need to make progress in the quest is sometimes expressed by the idea of going faster, which can refer to the protagonist's journeys in the outer and inner worlds as well as to the narrative pace used to describe them:

> M 84.24   in a moment we'll go faster, much faster.
> M 136.4   Faster, faster.
> M 240.27   I shall go faster, all will go faster

In the same way passages about interrupting or ending a journey can refer on a number of metaphorical levels to the hope that the quest will soon end:

> M 118.21   Yet a little while, at the rate things are going, and I won't be able to move, but will have to stay, where I happen to be, unless someone comes and carries me.
> M 119.28   Yet a little while, at the rate things are going, and I won't be able to move, but will have to stay, where I happen to be, unless some kind person comes and carries me.

These passages can in turn be linked to the last sentence in Molloy's narrative:

> M 124.6   Molloy could stay, where he happened to be.

Noticing that the three passages are connected leads to an understanding of why there is a comma in the concluding sentence: it reflects how the final sentence is based on a repeated segment in the other two ('will have to stay, where I happen to be, unless . . .').

The recurring action in the trilogy centres on the idea of making progress, literally or metaphorically, in a quest. Beckett often repeats passages with the verb 'to go', which suggest different aspects of the quest metaphor. Mahood says, 'To go on, I still call that on, to go on and get on has been my only care, if not always in a straight line . . .' (U 45.20). Other examples include 'you must go on', 'I can't go on', 'I'll go on', and 'I'll go there now, I'll try and go there now'; all these phrases are repeated many times.[10] Activities like riding, walking and crawling, are similarly connected to the quest metaphor: any one of them can represent an attempt to make progress in the quest.

IMAGES RELATED TO INACTIVITY

Descriptions of activities such as pausing or stopping are another important part of the quest metaphor: they often represent the period of rest at the beginning or end of a cycle, when the need to travel is dormant. Such passive phases are so predictable that some of Beckett's more experienced travellers – Molloy, Malone, and Mahood – think of them as stages in the quest:

> M 105.32   my progress reduced me to stopping more and more often, it was the only way to progress, to stop.
>
> MD 50.20   I whose every move has always been a groping, and whose motionlessness too was a kind of groping, yes, I have greatly groped stockstill.
>
> U 45.25   Never once have I stopped. My halts do not count. Their purpose was to enable me to go on.

Activities like resting, lying in a ditch, occupying a shelter, being arrested, falling to the ground, injuring one's legs, living in a room, or even losing a pencil can represent stages of the journey Mahood calls his 'halts'. Often such halts come as the result of an impasse or exhaustion:

> U 98.3   unable to go any further, because of the obstacle
> U 98.4   unable to go any further, in any case
> U 98.5   not needing to go any further for the moment
> U 98.6   he will drop
> U 98.9   He will drop

Recurring phrases link the heroes who are at rest, such as Molloy and Moran in the following example, or Molloy and Macmann in the next:

M 69.29   I lay down on the ground
M 201.28   I lay down on the ground

M 111.29   now prone, now supine
MD 70.6   now supine, now prone

The deterioration of the legs introduces the idea of forced halts:

M 104.4   having one bad leg plus another more or less good
M 104.8   I no longer had one bad leg plus another more or less good, but now both were equally bad

M 202.2   My leg was no better, but it was no worse either.
M 216.15   My leg was no better. It was no worse either.
M 240.26   My knee is no better. It is no worse either.

The process of deterioration continues with each hero, which introduces another kind of parallelism. Moran, before he sets out on his journey experiences a pain in the knee; by the end of the journey he has acquired crutches. Molloy's one good leg deteriorates; Malone's legs are useless; Mahood is finally legless. Metaphorically this progression runs parallel to Beckett's transition from descriptions of events in the outer world to mental events. His heroes focus more and more on inner activities as their ability to be active in the physical world decreases. This idea also has a self-reflexive aspect, when a crippled protagonist's slow progress hints at the difficulty of describing the complexities of the mental world.

Another kind of halt is imposed when a person prevents the hero from continuing on his quest. Thus the policeman who arrests Molloy and the farmer who questions Moran are similar figures: each one must be pacified before the journey can be resumed. The parallels between these characters are underlined in incidents where they ask the heroes what they are doing – questions they find difficult to answer properly (M 25.22, M 237.16).

These incidents end peacefully, but in some cases minor characters are dealt with in a more hostile fashion. Molloy's attack on a charcoal-burner, Moran's murder of a stranger with a moustache, and other violent episodes in the trilogy fall into this category. If the quest represents a journey into the self, the two contending figures – the traveller eager to be on his way and the antagonist who detains him – can be seen as an introspective persona and a persona that resists introspection. The policeman, the farmer, the charcoal-burner, and the moustached stranger could all represent this type of figure. Metaphorically, then, they can all be considered aspects of a single personality.

This idea is emphasised in a number of recurring incidents. Molloy encounters the charcoal-burner in a forest, where he 'dealt him a good dint on the skull' (M 113.26). Malone later recalls having been the victim of such an attack: 'But perhaps I was stunned with a blow, on the head, in a forest perhaps, yes, now that I speak of a forest I vaguely remember a forest' (MD 6.8). Still later, the personae who represent creative aspects of the self make it clear that they are ultimately the ones who have attacked these characters:

MD 63.13   How many have I killed, hitting them on the head or setting fire to them?

U 170.22   I've drowned, more than once, it wasn't I, suffocated, set fire to me, thumped my head with wood and iron, it wasn't I, there was no head, no wood, no iron, I didn't do anything to me, I didn't do anything to anyone, no one did anything to me

On a literal plane, the victims can be seen as representations of people who have been assaulted; but the narrators deliberately undermine this type of verisimilitude as they indicate that the victims are aspects of themselves or fictional characters whom they have created.

The figures who are involved in violence are usually masculine. They are counterbalanced by a series of women – often maternal figures – who interact in a less aggressive manner with the heroes. Often they provide food, shelter, and protection; at times they try to persuade the heroes to give up their quests and live with them. Many of the women who appear in the trilogy play this kind of role: Molloy's mother, Edith, Lousse, Martha, Madelaine, Moll, the woman who cares for Malone, and an unnamed chambermaid whom Molloy once loved.

Such parallels are enforced by recurring elements that link these women with one another. Molloy's mother has a 'grey wizened' head; Martha's is 'wizened, grey' (M 24.15, M 132.28). Molloy's mother and Edith give Molloy money (M 24.13, M 77.21). Moll, like Molloy's mother, is old, ugly and gives off a repulsive smell (M 24.18, MD 94.13). Ironic references to 'true love' link a chambermaid, Ruth, and Moll (M 8.10; M 76.18, 20; M 113.3; MD 94.35).

Molloy says that he sometimes associates the images of such women: 'to tell you the horrible truth, my mother's image sometimes mingles with theirs, which is literally unendurable, like being crucified' (M 79.17). The introduction of the Oedipal theme here should not overshadow another telling point: that these characters have a good deal in common. They represent figures associated with a passive phase of the quest, and this again suggests they may be aspects of a single personality. His reference to being crucified serves not only to depict Molloy's painful feelings but also to provide a connection between Moll – whose principal adornments are earrings and a tooth shaped like crucifixes – and the women Molloy describes.

SETTINGS

Often these women are associated with a house or a room that provides the hero with a place where he can rest until the next phase of the journey – an idea with epic overtones.[11] Such settings are given attributes which, like the similarities among the women who are associated with them, suggest an underlying unity. When readers note these parallels they experience a kind of *déjà vu*: a feeling of having seen the place before, that is accompanied by an uncanny feeling.

A recurring detail that links a number of haven settings is a location near a shambles: this is true of Molloy's mother's house (M 28.16), Moran's house (M 130.21), the Lamberts' house (M 37.32) and Madelaine's chop-house (MD 55.5). When Molloy leaves Lousse's house he mentions passing a wicket-gate, and Moran comments on a similar detail when he leaves home (M 70.15, M 174.19). Lousse's wicket-gate is set in a high wall topped with broken glass – a wall that resembles the one surrounding Macmann's asylum (M 70.13, MD 109.16).

Beckett's heroes often occupy shelters, a type of haven whose name suggests its role: a temporary place of refuge. A number of reiterated phrases call attention to this word:

M 201.19   I went back into the shelter
M 202.14   I went back to the shelter
M 208.11   I went back to the shelter

MD 13.25   far from help, far from shelter
MD 65.28   caught by the rain far from shelter
MD 67.21   the rain caught him far from shelter
MD 73.35   the place where the rain had caught him far from shelter

There are still other protagonists in the trilogy who occupy shelters.[12]

Another parallel that links some of these havens is their womb-like quality. The protagonists' wish to be finished with living is at times expressed as a desire to return to the womb – a metaphor as old as Job's comment, 'Naked came I out of my mother's womb, and naked shall I return thither' (Job 1:21). Molloy's journey ends in his mother's room, a phrase which sounds like 'his mother's womb'. Malone thinks he may have been born in the room he occupies; 'That', he says, 'would explain many things' (MD 77.9). Later he speaks of his impending death as a birth-like process involving a passage through 'the great cunt of existence' (MD 114.33). The narrator of *The Unnamable*, in keeping with his role as an unborn aspect of the self, seems figuratively to be occupying an amniotic sac: 'this place was made for me and I for it, at the same instant'.[13]

In general, the settings in the trilogy are important less for naturalistic than for associative qualities. Depicting a place too vividly would rob it of its ability to suggest a stage in a cycle. Hence Beckett often blurs specific details of setting so places can be linked to others associated with them. At times this idea is expressed in passages with recurring elements that emphasise the ultimate identity of different settings:

M 88.13   however far I went, and in no matter what direction, it was always the same sky, always the same earth, precisely, day after day and night after night.

U 19.23   in another place, where I shall say I have always been, of which I shall know nothing . . . but of which little by little, in spite of these handicaps, I shall begin to know something, just enough for it to turn out to be the same place as always

The trilogy's sketchy settings are sometimes attributed to the narrator's inability to focus on the landscape: 'I confuse east and west, the poles too, I invert them readily' (M 25.2). But on occasion a narrator's impatience with conventional descriptions of setting is frankly expressed: 'to hell with this fucking scenery' (MD 108.19).

OBJECTS

Like settings, the objects described in the trilogy hint at connections with metaphorical ideas related to the quest. Thus, some objects are used to establish links among the haven locales, such as a lacquer tray at Moran's house which holds 'a bowl of hot milk and a slice of bread and jam' and one at Lousse's that is large enough to hold 'a single dish and one slab of bread' (M 164.9, M 73.24). When Molloy claims that his knife is missing, Lousse gives him one; Moran takes a knife from his son and later returns it to him (M 60.10, M 179.6, M 185.20). Moran, waiting for his dinner, plays with a knife-rest; Molloy describes a knife-rest that he stole from Lousse; and Moll reports having found one among Macmann's possessions (M 158.17, M 85.4, MD 87.12). The reference to Macmann's knife-rest comes just after his clothes are taken from him for cleaning; this resembles a similar episode involving Molloy at Lousse's house.[14]

For the most part, the objects Beckett describes have to do with travel. Bicycles are often mentioned in *Molloy*, a fitting vehicle in a novel that deals with two cycles; and a number of passages about bicycles are reiterated. Here, for example, the idea of duality is emphasised by the word 'second-hand':

M 193.12   I said, buy a bicycle to fit you, second-hand for preference.

M 195.19   Second-hand for preference, I said

M 195.22   I didn't tell you second-hand, I said, I told you second-hand for preference

M 195.29   You see no difference between second-hand and second-hand for preference, I said

M 193.30   if you can't find one second-hand? I said. You told me second-hand, he said.

M 193.32   if you can't find one second-hand? I said . . . . You didn't tell me, he said.

M 196.3   if you can't find a second-hand bicycle buy a new
bicycle. I repeat. I repeated. I who had said I would not repeat.

In the last passage the word 'repeat' is reiterated: here where the
repetition calls attention to itself.

Bicycles are also used to establish connections among the
protagonists. After an accident the back wheel of Moran's bicycle
is 'slightly buckled perhaps', and Molloy speaks of 'the buckled
wheel that carried me' (M 215.15, M 88.26). Molloy describes in
detail how he manages to propel his bicycle with only one leg;
after losing the use of a leg Moran predicts that he will learn to
pedal with one leg (M 19.23, M 221.2). Both Molloy and Moran
find bicycles an enjoyable topic of conversation:

M 19.30   Dear bicycle. . . . To describe it at length would be a
pleasure.
M 212.32   it must once have been quite a good bicycle. I would
gladly describe it

A comment of Malone's is reminiscent of these:

MD 80.36   I should have liked to speak of the cap of my bicycle
bell

Molloy, however, makes it clear that his bicyle has a horn and not
a bell (M 20.2). Just as the evidence for equating these protagonists
is lacking, so their bicycles are not identical. Here, as elsewhere in
the trilogy, the similarities serve to encourage inquiries rather than
to terminate them prematurely.

Crutches are another tool for making progress, and a number of
the protagonists – Molloy, Moran, Malone, and Mahood – make
use of them.[15] In the same way, many of the characters in the
trilogy are associated with sticks, clubs or poles. In different
episodes the sticks are used in different ways: for support, for help
in walking, or for recovering lost objects, as when Malone retrieves
a notebook so he can continue writing. All these examples have
obvious connections with the quest metaphor.

References to sticks are also used to link characters in different
sections of the trilogy:

M 16.15   the man with the stick [Molloy's narrative]

M 18.2   the man with the stick did not pass by [Molloy's narrative]
M 207.14   he wanted to know if I had seen an old man with a stick pass by [Moran's narrative]
M 211.5   Would they not suspect the old man with the stick? [Moran's narrative]

Clothing is another prop that Beckett uses to suggest parallels among the characters. Like Molloy, Macmann wears a greatcoat, and Malone calls attention to this coat with a repeated phrase:

MD 54.22   Now with regard to the buttons of this coat
MD 54.22   Now with regard to the material of this coat

Macmann acquires a hat that may once have belonged to a 'sporting gentleman', and Moran encounters a man whose hat produces a 'highly sporting effect' (MD 55.16, M 206.24). The description of Macmann's hat echoes another passage about the acquisition of the hat and the greatcoat:

MD 55.14   And it would not surprise me to learn that this hat had once belonged to a sporting gentleman
MD 55.14   And it would not surprise me to learn that they had been bought, one at the hatter's, the other at the tailor's, perhaps the same day, by the same toff

For Molloy and Moran, donning a hat can be an expression of anger:

M 122.10   I banged [the hat] down on my skull
M 210.2   I jammed the straw hat down on my skull

Molloy, Moran, and Macmann use laces to retain their hats, but in each case this arrangement proves to be imperfect (M 122.9, M 208.24, MD 73.25). The hats are not all the same, nor are the methods for affixing them: again, the repetition suggests comparable but not identical situations. Thus the narrator of *The Unnamable* makes it clear that the descriptions of clothing in earlier settings are his own fictional creations: 'Am I clothed? I have often asked myself this question, then suddenly started talking about Malone's hat, or Molloy's greatcoat, or Murphy's suit' (U 23.1).

CHARACTERISATION

As the last passage suggests, the objects associated with various figures are the inventions of a persona who, when inquiring about his own condition, begins describing other characters. This is part of an attempt to learn about the deeper self by making up characters who represent aspects of the self and then telling stories about them. The clothing worn by these characters is ephemeral; even the activities of individual characters – when they are not approximating the actions of the deeper self – are unimportant. Malone suggests this when he speaks about a character he is creating, Macmann:

MD 53.19   though clothes don't matter, I know, I know
MD 68.27   though acts don't matter, I know, I know, nor thoughts

What is more important than descriptions of individual characters is the way a series of portrayals can combine and collectively approximate an indefinable self. This self cannot be portrayed in a direct or literal fashion, but each character can be seen as an attempt to represent the self metaphorically.

Such an approach makes the characterisation in the trilogy very different from that of more conventional novels. A typical goal in characterisation is to stress differences among the characters in order to obscure their common origins in the author's imagination. Beckett's method is to use the differences among his characters as a way of preventing them from being equated, and the similarities as a way of suggesting that they are aspects of a single underlying self.

Hence Beckett sometimes uses repetition to underline both the similarities and the differences among his characters. In the following example the similarities are stressed when three passages call attention to Molloy's acute hearing and a fourth indicates that Moran resembles him in this respect:

M 27.32   what I have just heard, and heard distinctly, not being hard of hearing
M 66.27   the words I heard, and heard distinctly, having quite a sensitive ear

M 66.20   I had quite a sensitive ear
M 175.11   I have an extremely sensitive ear.

Despite this parallel, two of the later heroes are hard of hearing. This idea is expressed in similar terms: Malone says he is 'more than half-deaf half of the time'; and Mahood says, 'I am half-deaf' (MD 45.18, U 80.4).

A similar effect of contrasting similarities and differences occurs when a character refers to figures who preceded him in the Beckett canon. The characters' differences are emphasised when a protagonist speaks of his predecessors as if they were independent entities; their similarities are used to suggest that the earlier characters are the protagonist's inventions.

Those figures in the trilogy who play narrative roles all have the ability to recall characters who appeared in earlier works. Molloy refers to Watt; Moran mentions Murphy, Watt, Mercier, and Camier; Malone alludes to Murphy, Mercier, Molloy, and Moran; and the narrator of *The Unnamable*, in some forty references, discusses all of these characters as well as Youdi and Malone.[16]

In addition to naming them, Beckett's narrators also refer indirectly to characters and episodes in the earlier works. Malone's memories of a hunchback and a butler are references to Hackett, in *Watt*; and to the old boy, in *Murphy* (MD 2.25, MD 63.17). Malone gives details of an incident described in the story, 'The End'; the narrator of *The Unnamable* quotes the opening line of that story.[17] The references in the trilogy to unwavering gulls' eyes, to London, and to studying astronomy all introduce themes that were important in *Murphy*.[18]

Such references encourage readers to summon up memories of these earlier works as they puzzle over where they have encountered recurring details. This retrospective activity runs parallel to that of Beckett's narrators, and helps readers blend images of the characters in a way that will lead to the formation of composites based on their underlying similarities.

In conventional fiction, characterisation originates in observations of a person as he or she appears in the outside world; in Beckett's, it originates in mental images of a person that, when superimposed, begin to approximate an identity. Beckett uses readers' memories of parallel situations in different parts of the trilogy as the basis of this process. Hence the repetition is an integral part of Beckett's new type of characterisation.

NAMES

Beckett is also very original in the way he names his characters. Readers soon notice that many of the protagonists have the two-syllable Irish names that begin with the letter M. There are links among names; for example, Molloy is uncertain whether Sophie's last name is Loy or Lousse, and Moran is unsure whether the man he is pursuing is named Molloy or Mollose (M 44.7, M 152.27).

A related factor is the way Beckett continually undermines the fixity of the characters' names. Moran – the most conventional character in the trilogy – retains his name; virtually every other important character's name is in some way called into question or altered. Though his mother calls him Dan, Molloy denies that this is his name; and when a policeman interrogates him he claims to have forgotten what his name is. Malone speaks for a long time before he gives his name, and when he finally does he adds, 'this is what I am called now' (MD 48.19).

Many of the characters in the trilogy are given names that are later changed; a few are even renamed a second time, as the following list indicates:

Original Name	*New Name or Names*
Dan (M 21.16)	Molloy (M 29.18), Mollose (M 152.27)
Ma (M 21.27)	Mag (M 21.25), Mother Molloy (M 153.23), Mother Mollose (M 153.23)
Ruth (M 76.1)	Edith (M 76.3), Rose (M 113.4)
Mrs Loy (M 44.7)	Sophie (M 44.9), Lousse (M 46.9)
Sapo (MD 9.21)	Macmann (MD 55.31), Hairy Mac (MD 91.27)
Moll (MD 85.19)	Sucky Moll, Sucky Molly (MD 91.18, 27); also (French edition) Poupée Pompette
Basil (U 13.23)	Mahood (U 29.2), Worm (U 69.24)
Marguerite (U 74.10)	Madelaine (U 75.5)
Ptomaine (U 41.32)	Ptoto (U 44.3), Isolde (U 50.10)

Beckett's practice of renaming characters reflects the idea that language obscures the reality it is attempting to depict. A name brings with it a superficial sense of a person's identity. But as Molloy says, even his own identity seems 'wrapped in a namelessness often hard to penetrate' (M 41.7).

One way of countering the tendency of names to obscure the reality of what they denote is to avoid using them consistently. Hence, Beckett's narrators often change the characters' names, at times expressing themselves in the same way when they do so:

> M 46.9   Sophie—no, I can't call her that any more, I'll try calling her Lousse
>
> MD 55.31   Sapo—no, I can't call him that any more. . . . So then for, let me see, Macmann

In a passage linked to these by a repeated interjection ('—no'), the narrator of *The Unnamable* indicates his unwillingness to repeat the names of his predecessors:

> U 53.10   I am neither, I needn't say, Murphy, nor Watt, nor Mercier, nor—no, I can't even bring myself to name them, nor any of the others whose very names I forget, who told me I was they, who I must have tried to be

The narrator of *The Unnamable* sees the naming activity as something that belongs to the outer world and resents the characters with names who claim to represent him. As he says of Basil, 'Is he still usurping my name, the one they foisted on me, up there in their world, patiently, from season to season?' (U 13.28).

Proper nouns, common nouns, pronouns – all of them are unsatisfactory because they involve enshrouding the idea of the self in language, which obscures its deeper reality. Beckett's narrators finally accept the fact that they can't get along without names; but they do introduce them grudgingly, knowing that their understanding of the deeper self is weakened when a sense of permanence becomes attached to a name.

MOTIVATION

Beckett's narrators are also reticent about motivation, for reasons that are related to those that lead them to give the characters new names. Often, explaining a character's motives communicates ideas that are distorted when they are expressed in denotative language. In addition, giving reasons for a character's decisions implies that human motives are in general knowable – in Beckettian terms a presumptuous assumption. Hence these narrators may give very detailed accounts of a characters' actions while remaining silent about his motivation.

The description of Moran's pursuit of Molloy is an example. Moran sets out on his quest after receiving a directive from his employer, Youdi; this is delivered by a messenger called Gaber. Moran's assignments always consist of two charges: tracking a person down and then carrying out some task involving that person. As Moran carefully explains, 'My particular duties never terminated with the running to earth. . . . But I had always to deal with the client in one way or another, according to instructions.' This dealing with the client is the essential part of the charge: 'establishing contact', says Moran, 'was the least important part of my work' (M 187.6ff.).

After setting out on his journey Moran realises that he has forgotten the essential part of his assignment: what his duties are once he had found Molloy. This fact is often repeated in passages that contain the word 'found':

> M 187.5   I felt he must have told me what to do with Molloy once he was found
> M 189.5   if, having found Molloy, I still did not know what to do with him
> M 216.24   I still did not know what I was to do with Molloy, when I found him.
> M 199.21   I tried again to remember what I was to do with Molloy, when I found him.
> M 188.20   I could not determine therefore how I was to deal with Molloy, once I had found him.
> M 203.22   But I also tried to remember what I was to do with Molloy, once I had found him.

Moran never does remember the missing instructions concerning Molloy; even so, he does not abandon his quest.

In a sense then, Moran's behaviour is unmotivated. Still, it might be argued that he is merely carrying out the first part of Youdi's directive without for the moment concerning himself about the other. But towards the end of his quest Moran begins to question whether Youdi and Gaber are the sources of his motivation. At this point Moran begins to describe an inner voice that seems to be the real source of his directives:

M 233.7   I have spoken of a voice giving me orders
M 241.17   I have spoken of a voice telling me things

By the conclusion of the novel Moran seems persuaded that the inner voice is important and that he should make an effort to understand it.

The sources of Molloy's motivation are also obscure: he journeys to his mother's house without revealing why he wants to see her. However, he does mention possible motives and then rules them out:

M 22.18   In any case I didn't come to listen to her.
M 23.14   In any case I didn't come for money.

Molloy's reasons for going to see his mother are never made explicit. This fact is emphasised by a series of passages where the word 'settle' is repeated:

M 87.2   if I should soon find my mother and settle the matter between us
M 87.8   I had been bent on settling this matter between my mother and me
M 87.12   soon it would be too late, was perhaps too late already, to settle the matter in question
M 106.10   wondering sometimes . . . if I shall ever see again . . . my mother, to settle with her

Molloy claims that he cannot remember why he decided to see his mother; he also claims that he cannot remember why he needed Lousse:

M 35.8   I had set out to see my mother. My reasons? I had forgotten them.
M 44.25   [Lousse] needed me . . . and I needed her. I've forgotten for what.

There are other instances where Molloy cannot explain his actions: 'Now as to telling you why I stayed a good while with Lousse, no, I cannot' (M 67.32). Molloy says he could try to find reasons for his behaviour, but these would only be another way of saying that he couldn't have done otherwise. Defining one's motives, then, is a form of rationalisation.

Molloy's motives will not or cannot be explained. But, like Moran, he begins to discuss his behaviour in terms of the directives he is given by his 'imperatives', or inner volitional voices. These, he says, mainly 'bore' – even the pun is repeated – on his relationship with his mother:

M 117.6   they nearly all bore on the same question, that of my relations with my mother
M 117.15   they nearly all bore, as I may already have said, on the same painful and thorny question

Molloy finally makes it clear that he went to see his mother because he was directed by an imperative inner voice (M 117.27ff.). This is a more reasonable way of understanding human behaviour than by postulating logical motives for it. We make the choices we do because we are following the directives of mysterious inner voices; our motives are the rational explanations we make up after the fact to pretend we understand the process.

VOICES

Questions about the behaviour of Molloy and Moran are often best resolved by abandoning conventional ideas about motivation. Beckett often indicates that at its deepest level the self is impervious to rational analysis; and he uses the inner voices as images of the mental entities that transmit messages from the self. Beckett's protagonists investigate this process, and an important part of the quest motif is the introspective journey in search of these voices and the source of the messages they transmit.

As the goal of the quests moves inward, the subject-matter of the trilogy changes. Molloy and Moran describe their travels in the outer world; Malone, focusing on himself as he makes up stories, has more to say about his inner life; and the narrator of *The Unnamable* turns away from the distractions of the outer world in order to focus on the inner voice which at times seems to be his own voice and at times that of another. The importance of this issue is stressed in a series of passages with periodically recurring phrases about the voices and the words they utter:

U 52.15 But it's entirely a matter of voices, no other metaphor is appropriate.

U 83.17 But it is solely a question of voices, no other image is appropriate.

U 66.19 It all boils down to a question of words, I must not forget this, I have not forgotten it.

U 66.24 It's a question of voices, of voices to keep going

U 81.8 It must not be forgotten, sometimes I forget, that all is a question of voices

U 136.23 Unfortunately it's a question of words, of voices, one must not forget that, one must try and not forget that completely

Such voices cannot be defined in literal language or be analysed in a logical way. Hence the narrator of *The Unnamable* often speaks about them in paradoxical terms:

U 26.15 this voice that is not mine, but can only be mine, since there is no one but me

U 153.10 the voice which could not be mine, since I had none left, and yet which could only be mine, since I could not go silent

Even when he claims the voice as his own, the source of the words uttered by the voice remains mysterious. The narrator of *The Unnamable* refers to a deeper entity that controls the content of what he expresses:

U 81.10 I say what I am told to say

U 133.24 I say what I'm told to say

The hunt for this deeper entity continues through the trilogy. But no matter where the inquiring self searches, the ultimate self remains hidden.

REPORTS AND STORIES

Beckett's characters use another method of pursuing the deeper self, by seeking the source of the creative impulse. This issue is often framed as an inquiry into the reasons why the narrators write accounts about their experiences.

It seems at first that Moran's report was written in response to requests from Gaber and Youdi. As he says,

>   M 240.17   One day I received a visit from Gaber. He wanted the report.
>   M 240.14   A letter from Youdi, in the third person, asking for a report. He will get his report.

The second remark, about Youdi's request, resembles a comment Moran made on earlier occasions:

>   M 164.10   He asked for a report, he'll get his report.
>   M 165.23   He asked for a report, he'll get his report.

It seems likely, at first, that the pronoun 'he' in these passages refers to Youdi. But Moran makes it clear at the very end of the novel that his inner voice told him to write the report: 'I have spoken of a voice telling me things. . . . It told me to write the report' (M 241.24). In addition, Moran says that although he is 'still obeying orders', they are different from those he received in the past: 'the voice I listen to needs no Gaber to make it heard' (M 180.23).

Molloy is visited by a man who resembles Gaber; this person pays for his writing: 'So many pages, so much money.' But Molloy explains that this isn't why he writes: 'Yet I don't work for money. For what then? I don't know' (M 7.6, 18). This comment resembles two that Molloy makes about visiting his mother:

>   M 23.14   In any case I didn't come for money.
>   M 24.13   But I didn't come for money.

Like his motives for visiting his mother, Molloy's reasons for writing are mysterious. But what finally emerges is that the Gaber-like figure who collects his completed pages may be a personification of his inner voice.

Malone is at first reluctant to record stories in his exercise book or to compile an inventory of his possessions; for reasons that are not made clear he changes his mind. The phrase 'resign myself to' is echoed in passages that refer to this topic:

MD 32.17   I did not want to write, but i had to resign myself to it in the end.

MD 105.6   This exercise book is my life, this big child's exercise book, it has taken me a long time to resign myself to that.

MD 3.35   But can I really resign myself to the possibility of my dying without leaving an inventory behind?

The inventory also refers to Malone's creative efforts, since at times he uses the word to refer to his stock of stories: 'Present state, three stories, inventory, there' (MD 4.35).

Malone often speaks about his stories:

MD 2.7   I shall tell myself stories if I can

MD 54.36   I'll tell myself stories . . . if I can

Malone's stories seem at first to be about other people, but it soon becomes clear that they are attempts at self-definition. This emerges in a passage where Malone speaks about 'the old story, my old story': the old story he tells in different versions about others is ultimately about himself (MD 63.4).

The narrator of *The Unnamable* makes a similar comment about 'my old stories, my old story', stressing the underlying unity of all the stories (U 20.6). This leads him to believe that a description of the essential self is somehow buried in the stories the narrators have told: 'the attempt must be made, in the old stories incomprehensibly mine, to find his, it must be there somewhere, it must have been mine, before being his' (U 177.25).

SELF-REFLEXIVENESS

One reason Beckett's protagonists find it difficult to define the essential self is that their investigations blur the distinctions between subject and object. In ordinary circumstances the self acts as a subject, the agent that examines objects in the world. Such a process, difficult enough to understand, becomes even more complex during introspection, when the self must play a double role as both subject and object. Beckett's narrators act as both subjects and objects when they have roles as the investigators of selfhood and the investigated. Usually Beckett does this with self-reflexive comments that break down the objective level of the fiction (the narrative) and focus on the subjective level (the concerns of the narrator).

The quests of Molloy and Moran take place on both subjective and objective levels. Each part of *Molloy* opens with a glimpse of the writer as subject, followed by the description of a journey in which the protagonist is presented on the objective level. The focus seems to be mainly on the journey, but from time to time the narrative is interrupted to bring the subjective level to the foreground. For example, Molloy the traveller, standing miserably in the rain after a suicide attempt, is momentarily forgotten when Molloy the writer looks at his legs: 'My knees are enormous, I have just caught a glimpse of them when I got up for a second' (M 83.1).

In *Malone Dies* a series of self-reflexive correspondences serves to call attention to the subjective levels of the story. Often, soon after Malone experiences an event, a similar event finds its way into one of his stories. Thus Malone describes people in a nearby house making love and then introduces a scene where Macmann makes love; he is beaten for no reason and then describes how Macmann is beaten, also unreasonably; he thinks of the two thieves crucified with Christ and shortly afterwards depicts Moll telling Macmann that her earrings represent the two thieves.

The narrator of *The Unnamable* undermines the objective level in another way: he suggests that the characters who preceded him lack authenticity. Indeed, he claims that Molloy, Moran, Malone and Mahood are unrealistic versions of himself created in his many attempts to define himself. These narrators are associated with the more objective portions of the trilogy: they describe journeys in the world and make up stories about its inhabitants.

To emphasise this process, Beckett introduces still another type of repetition, as the narrator of *The Unnamable* uses a variety of descriptions, usually derogatory, to refer to his predecessors. Here are some examples:

U 118.32	the same gang	U 127.23	a congener
U 113.14	dirty pack of fake maniacs	U 70.31	fomentors of fiasco
U 28.7	chronicle of moribunds	U 37.23	this caricature
U 52.1	miscreated puppets	U 38.21	my avatars
U 89.26	my purveyors	U 71.8	wretches
U 27.17	my troop of lunatics	U 145.29	old buffers
U 25.2	my mannikins	U 12.14	my delegates

U 37.16 my next vice-exister	U 145.18 these bran-dips
U 147.26 this latest surrogate	U 131.6 renegades

As the narrator of *The Unnamable* says in a related example, 'all these stories about travellers, about paralytics, are all mine' (U 176.29).

An even more predominant type of self-reflexiveness is introduced when a narrator interrupts his account to comment on the writing. This acts as a reminder of activities taking place on a subjective level. Beckett emphasises the importance of such comments by repeating them:

M 8.22 Here's my beginning. . . .	MD 8.24 Here it is.
M 8.27 Here's my beginning. . . .	MD 8.29 Here it is.
MD 98.34 Here is the pro-gramme. . . .	MD 99.1 Here it is.

M 39.13   there you have Molloy, viewed from a certain angle
MD 72.33   such then seems to be Macmann, seen from a certain angle
MD 96.21   such was this Lemuel, viewed from a certain angle

M 172.22   I hope I'm not forgetting anything
U 78.2   I hope I'm not forgetting anything

M 207.27   I am sorry I cannot indicate more clearly how this result was obtained, it would have been something worth reading.
M 228.7   I would have described them once, not now, I am sorry, it would have been worth reading.

U 48.11   Let us rather consider what really took place, if Mahood was telling the truth.
U 49.7   let us consider what really took place, if Mahood was telling the truth

In many instances, this type of self-reflexive comment is self-mocking:

MD 26.1   That's it, reminisce.
MD 26.4   That's it, babble.

MD 74.26   That's the style, as if I were sweet and seventy.

MD 76.23   That's the style, as if I still had time to kill.

MD 100.33   There's reasoning for you.
MD 103.9   There's feeling for you.

U 70.2   That's soon said.
U 70.20   That's soon said.

Some comments of this type recur with some frequency. Thus Malone repeats the sentence, 'What tedium' five times.[19]

At times the self-reflexive comments come in the form of revisions, as the author persona, struggling to set down the details of his narrative properly, repeats himself: 'his front, no, his back, white with, no, front was right, his front white with dust . . .' (MD 66.15). In other instances reiterated phrases are used to mark revisions:

MD 106.7   no, that won't work
U 131.10   no, that won't work

M 37.26   no, that doesn't work
U 36.21   no, that doesn't work

Descriptions are similarly interrupted by interjections beginning with 'no' that mark the narrator's refusal to complete them:

M 196.13   No, I can't.
MD 93.30   No, I can't.

M 15.2   no, I can't do it.
MD 19.32   no, I can't do it.

M 67.32   as to telling you . . . no, I cannot.
M 112.8   to say . . . no, I cannot.

Another example of this kind of rewriting comes in Molloy's attempts to find the word that best describes the place where he attempted suicide:

M 81.25   recesses, no that's not the word
M 81.31   alcoves, wrong again
M 82.5   chapel, that's the word

Such comments interrupt the flow of the narrative and refocus the reader's attention on the author's quest, to get on with the writing.

Another type of interjection is a self-reflexive statement where two recurring words or phrases are adjacent:

MD 13.1   Well, well. (Also at M 78.14, MD 84.22, MD 99.19, U 132.9, U 139.9, U 168.14.)

U 61.4   Wrong again, wrong again

M 231.29   Enough, enough. (Also at M 213.21, M 214.16, MD 109.11, MD 65.26, U 91.10.)

MD 118.22   We're getting on, getting on. (Also at MD 16.25.)

U 72.30   weave, weave

U 104.32   Calm, calm (Also at U 165.31.)

At times a series of these interjections will appear on the same page:

U 91.8   Bait, bait.

U 91.10   Enough, enough.

U 91.16   Agreed, agreed.

The self-reflexive remarks seem to be reactions to the deficiencies in the writing, but this may not always be true. Thus in the following example the self-reflexive interjection ('whatever that means') ostensibly suggests that the narrator himself doesn't understand what he's talking about:

MD 63.25   Then back here to me, whatever that means.

MD 70.15   the skull and its annexes, whatever that means.

U 36.11   I have to speak, whatever that means.

In fact, such interjections indicate that readers are being encouraged to explore the different ways the idea in question can be interpreted.

That the narrators know very well what they are talking about is indicated in the following series:

MD 18.32   I know what I mean

MD 22.5   I know what I mean

U 40.17   I know what I mean

U 67.22   I know what I mean

Beckett's writing is fixed neither to the objective nor to the subjective level: it includes both. The sense of a creative self permeates the idea of the creation until the narrative is active on both levels at the same time. The best way of approximating the inexpressible self is as an entity that exists simultaneously as subject and object, the inventor of the story and also its hero.

CONCLUSION

Beckett introduces many stylistic innovations in the trilogy. Traditional ideas about plot, setting, chronology, characterisation, and motivation are abandoned and new versions of these devices are developed. The repetition often plays an important role in this process. The plot that always centres on the same underlying story, the cyclical time scheme, the settings designed to evoke *déjà vu*, the recurring traits that link different characters, the repeated refusals to discuss motivation – all of these incorporate some form of repetition. When his innovative techniques are difficult to detect or understand Beckett uses repetition to stress and elucidate them.

Each new reading of the trilogy brings with it a deeper understanding of the pattern of repetition and the ideas associated with it. This encourages readers to review passages, to compare recurring details, and ultimately to go back to the first page and start again. This process of rereading is still one more repetitive activity evoked by the trilogy's cyclical quest metaphor.

Some readers, lulled by the narrators' self-critical comments, may persist in believing that the trilogy rambles on aimlessly about 'any old thing'. But it contains hundreds of passages, many of them hundreds of pages apart, with verbatim repetitions. This is the very antithesis of aimless rambling. Even the phrase 'any old thing' is repeated, at times in contexts where its initial sense is qualified:

U 36.21   For any old thing, no, that doesn't work
U 37.1   So not any old thing.
U 37.2   Even Mahood's stories are not any old thing
U 153.4   perhaps it wasn't any old thing, the thing I was saying

The novels of the trilogy are painstakingly organised and meticulously crafted; they are imbued with the kind of grace that bespeaks endless hours of rewriting. This process of revising is still one more repetitive activity evoked by the trilogy's cyclical quest metaphor.

Notes

1. Samuel Beckett, *The Unnamable* (New York: Grove Press, 1970), p. 143, lines 21 and 23. References to the other novels of the trilogy will also be to the Grove Press single-volume editions: Samuel Beckett, *Molloy* (New York: Grove Press, 1970) and *Malone Dies* (New York: Grove Press, 1970). Titles are abbreviated in most citations: M stands for *Molloy*, MD for *Malone Dies*, and U for *The Unnamable*. Page and line locations are given as a number (for the page) followed by a decimal point and a second number (for the line). Quotation marks are omitted after page references of this type. The letter 'v' after a citation indicates that the quoted passage is a variant: similar to, but not exactly the same as an example that was quoted. Ellipses are omitted when it is obvious that passages are fragments. Thus, in the following citation

   U 143.21   any old thing
   U 143.23   any old thing

   indicates that the fragment 'any old thing' appears in *The Unnamable* on p. 143, lines 21 and 23.
2. For example, there is a good deal of repetition in *Murphy*, including some 500 sets of recurring items which involve about 1500 separate elements. Lists of these sets and a discussion of their significance are given in my study of Beckett's earlier fiction; see Rubin Rabinovitz, *The Development of Samuel Beckett's Fiction* (Urbana: University of Illinois Press, 1984), pp. 71ff., 185ff. and 200ff. A number of critics have noted the many reiterated elements in the trilogy and commented on them. See, for example H. Porter Abbott, *The Fiction of Samuel Beckett* (Berkeley: University of California Press, 1973), pp. 99–100; Ruby Cohn, *Back to Beckett* (Princeton, Princeton University Press, 1973) pp. 88–92, 95; John Fletcher, *The Novels of Samuel Beckett* (London: Chatto and Windus, 1964), 131–2, 157; David Hayman, 'Molloy or the Quest for Meaninglessness', in Melvin J. Friedman, *Samuel Beckett Now* (Chicago: University of Chicago Press, 1970), pp. 140–45; Philip J. Solomon, *The Life After Birth* (University of Mississippi: Romance Monographs, 1975), pp. 26, 103.
3. Recently I compiled a catalogue of the significant sets of reiterated elements in the trilogy based on a computer-generated concordance of the trilogy. The concordance was developed in collaboration with my colleague, Professor Michael Preston; I am very grateful to him for his help. One benefit of working with a computer-generated concordance is the ability to claim with some assurance that the word 'ambulance' appears in the trilogy only three times.

4. This is a very conservative estimate; I have included only significant examples in this count. In addition, one-word repetitions are excluded from the total, although some of these are significant (for example, the five appearances of the word 'dream', U 179.5–7).

5. Beckett collaborated in the translation of *Molloy* and translated *Malone Dies* and *The Unnamable* by himself. In a few instances recurring elements in the French original are not entirely preserved in the English translation. For example, the following passages

> M 37.35   Quel pays rural, mon Dieu
> M 211.6   Quel pays pastoral, mon Dieu.

are translated as

> M 38.20   Good God, what a land of breeders
> M 217.10 What a pastoral land, my God.

The translation obscures some of the recurring elements in the original. Even so, the common elements in the English set can easily be recognised. The French versions are from Samuel Beckett, *Molloy* (Union générale d'éditions, 1963), pp. 37, 211.

6. References to corncrakes, M 21.8, M 123.32, M 208.16; M 208.14; to owls or eagle-owls, M 208.14, MD 105.29, U 148.18; to gulls, MD 107.13.

7. Difficulty with speech, M 37.10, M 41.3, M 218.5; questioning the shepherd, M 37.12, M 218.8, 15; the reticence of the shepherds, M 37.23, M 218.9, 15; shepherd and dog watching the hero, M 36.25, 27; M 217.13, 14; 'perfect silence', M 36.17, 'the silence was absolute', M 217.20; black sheep, M 36.30, M 217.9.

8. Molloy wants to go in a straight line in order to get out of the forest, but realises that his hope of doing so is probably futile; this idea is emphasised by repeated phrases like 'going forward in a straight line' (M 115.13, M 122.19) and 'go in a circle' (M 115.14, 19). Eventually Molloy describes his travels as 'spirals' (M 92.3). The trilogy's protagonists often speak about moving in circles, circuits, cycles, and spirals, as in these representative examples: circles: M 112.21, M 115, M 199.3, U 158.10; circuits: U 71.9, 173.7; cycles: 'within each cycle taken separately' is repeated, M 98.25, M 99.1, 18; spirals: U 39.25, U 54.16.

9. Beckett discusses this idea in his comments on habit in *Proust*; see Samuel Beckett, *Proust*, 1931 (New York: Grove Press, 1957), pp. 7–12.

10. 'You must go on' (U 152.6, 6, 7; U 166.22; U 179.10, 14, 15, 17, 23); 'I can't go on' (U 138.32, U 148.26, U 179.15, 24), 'I'll go on' (U 148.27, 29; U 151.16; U 179.15, 24), 'I'll go there now, I'll try and go there now' (U 172.16, 30; 173.29v).

11. I discuss this idea in my essay 'Molloy and the Archetypal Traveller', *Journal of Beckett Studies*, No. 5 (Autumn, 1979), pp. 25–44.

12. Molloy's shelter: M 80.26, 30; Moran's shelter, M 186.30, 197.17, *et*

passim; the narrator of *The Unnamable* describing a 'vertical shelter', U 98.11.

13. The narrator of *The Unnamable* on never having been born, U 91.21, U 128.24, U 129.15; 'this place was made for me', etc. (U 11.6).

14. See MD 87.7ff. and M 56.22ff. There are other parallel ideas in these scenes, such as the possibility that the hero's clothes may have been destroyed. The *Molloy* episode contains the recurring passage, 'The valet came back with the news my clothes . . .'; see M 57.1, M 57.18, M 56.23v. The episode in *Malone Dies* contains a sentence with repeated phrases, 'he cried, My things! My things!, over and over again . . .'; see MD 87.2.

15. Molloy's crutches, M 17.12, M 25.15, etc.; Moran's, M 240.26; Malone's, MD 76.3, MD 81.1; Mahood's, U 46.1.

16. Molloy refers only to one earlier character, Watt (M 103.10). Moran's references to earlier characters: Murphy, Watt, Mercier (M 188.15); Murphy, Watt, Camier (M 230.17). Malone's references to earlier characters: Murphy, Mercier, Molloy, Moran (MD 63.11). The narrator of *The Unnamable*'s references to earlier characters: Malone (U 5.8, 12); Molloy, Malone (U 5.28 etc.); Murphy, Malone (U 6.4, 11, etc.); Malone (U 7.16, 28); Malone (U 9.15); Malone (U 10.11, 18); Mercier, Camier (U 11.17); Malone (U 11.12, 21); Malone (U 14.13, 17); Malone (U 15.9); Malone (U 16.5); Murphy, Molloy, Malone (U 21.5); Murphy (U 23.3); Youdi (an indirect reference: he says, 'Moran's boss, I forget his name'; U 33.8); Malone (U 44.18); Murphy, Watt, Mercier (U 53.10); Malone (U 79.16); Murphy (U 145.17, 28); Watt (72.12); Murphy (U 85.18); Murphy, Molloy, Malone (U 163.28); Mercier, Moran (U 163.32).

17. Malone refers to a story about a boy who looks at the sky, asks his mother a question about it, and receives a sharp reply; see MD 98.17 and 'The End', in Samuel Beckett, *Stories and Texts for Nothing* (New York: Grove Press, 1967), p. 50. 'They clothed me and gave me money' is the opening sentence of this story; the narrator of *The Unnamable* quotes it at U 33.6. This reference was first noted by Brian Finney; see '*Assumption* to *Lessness*: Beckett's Shorter Fiction', in Katherine Worth, *Beckett the Shape Changer* (London: Routledge & Kegan Paul, 1975), p. 72.

18. In *Murphy* the passage 'eyes, cold and unwavering as a gull's' is repeated twice: Samuel Beckett, *Murphy* (New York: Grove Press, 1957), pp. 2, 39; cf. 'eyes as pale and unwavering as a gull's', MD 15.27; Malone's comment at MD 16.5 indicates that he recalls the source of this description. On the same page he quotes Democritus's 'Nothing is more real than nothing', which is alluded to in *Murphy* (p. 246). References to studying astronomy: M 52.11, M 80.24, MD 7.3. References to London, MD 7.5, MD 63.18; to caged owls in Battersea Park (London), *Murphy*, p. 106; U 148.18. The last reference was noted by John Pilling; see his *Samuel Beckett* (London: Routledge & Kegan Paul, 1976), p. 63, where he notes Beckett's other references to this image.

19. 'What tedium': MD 9.32, MD 12.6, MD 41.30, MD 44.18, MD 81.35.

4

The Figure in Beckett's Carpet: *Molloy* and the Assault on Metaphor

Kevin J. H. Dettmar

As a tissue tolerably intricate it was a carpet with a figure of its own; but the figure was not the figure I was looking for.

Henry James, 'The Figure in the Carpet'

'Everyone wanders around having his own individual perceptions. These, like balls of different colors and shapes and sizes, roll around on the green billiard table of consciousness . . .'. Kevin stopped and began again. 'Where is the figure in the carpet? Or is it just . . . carpet?'

Donald Barthelme, *Snow White*

In order to prove its mettle, a critical ideology wishing to make a place for itself on the contemporary scene must wrestle with one of the oldest problems in literary theory – the description and treatment of figurative language in general, and of metaphor in particular. The 'problem' of metaphor is inscribed in the oldest critical text of the western literary tradition: 'Metaphor', Aristotle tells us, 'is the application of an alien name by transference . . .' (*Poetics*, 99). Nearly every subsequent commentator has found Aristotle's terse definition in some way inadequate; as Karsten Harries has written, Aristotle views metaphor as 'an improper naming' (74), a definition which provokes more questions than it answers.

In the twenty years since it appeared on the scene, deconstruction has attempted, not to articulate a theory of the metaphor, not to expound a position concerning metaphor, but rather to illustrate as thoroughly as possible its inability to formulate a theory of the metaphor from outside of metaphor, a 'meta-metaphorics'. Besides receiving attention in such central deconstructionist texts as *Of Grammatology* and *Allegories of Reading*, the 'problem' of metaphor has been the occasion of several important (and, in Derrida's case, rather entertaining) essays, among them de Man's 'The Epistemology of Metaphor' and Derrida's 'White Mythology' and 'The *Retrait* of Metaphor'.

Like critical 'schools', literary movements must 'take a stand' on metaphor. The modernists, in their attempt to 'make it new', sought to reinvigorate metaphor by increasing the 'distance' between tenor and vehicle; one immediately thinks of Eliot's evening – 'a patient etherised upon a table'. But of course, this metaphoric terrorism was strictly speaking nothing new; the metaphysical poets, whom Eliot was later to help resurrect, had three hundred years earlier rejuvenated the conceit in which, as Dr Johnson would have it, 'the most heterogeneous ideas are yoked by violence together'. Both were attempts to make literary language new and enable it to create meaning in the contemporary world.

Postmodernism, in keeping with its thoroughgoing critique of the machinery of modernism, has shown a profound distrust of metaphor. Suspicious of modernism's recuperation of metaphor, postmodern writers have largely rejected it. In the extreme case of a writer like Pynchon, the assertion of resemblance implicit in metaphor merely serves to reinforce paranoia.[1] Jean-François Lyotard's definition of 'postmodernism', in his postscript to *The Postmodern Condition*, stresses this scepticism regarding the efficacy of art:

> The postmodern would be that which, in the modern, puts forward the unpresentable in presentation itself; that which denies itself the solace of good forms, the consensus of a taste which would make it possible to share collectively the nostalgia for the unattainable; that which searches for new presentations, not in order to enjoy them but in order to impart a stronger sense of the unpresentable. (81)

Lyotard defines postmodernism not strictly as a reaction to modernism, but as an impulse within modernism; his definition is without fixed historical reference, but rather the description of an impulse,

and in this respect akin to de Man's conception of modernism.[2]
The postmodern writer, in denying himself 'the nostalgia for the
unattainable', has *de facto* committed himself to writing in as 'literal'
a style as possible. According to Harries, it is this very 'sense of
the unpresentable' that metaphor sets out to conquer.

I

In the few interviews he has granted, and in his early writings on
aesthetics, Samuel Beckett has repeatedly voiced his opposition to
that art which attempts to impose 'meaning' on raw experience.
'Confusion', he told Tom Driver, 'is all around us and our only
chance now is to let it in. The only chance of renovation is to open
our eyes and see the mess. It is not a mess you can make sense
of' (Driver 218). Rather than trying to find some comforting
message *in* or 'making sense' *of* the chaos, Beckett strives to present
his characters' chaotic experiences exactly as they would apprehend
it – a style which Harold Pinter calls 'remorseless' (Pinter 86).

One stratagem for dealing with the chaos of contemporary
experience, without in the process contaminating it with false
artistic 'meaning', is for the writer to restrict his scope to the 'plane
of objects'. In 'A Future for the Novel', Alain Robbe-Grillet outlines
something approaching a manifesto for the kind of fiction that
Beckett had been writing for nearly ten years.[3] One of the themes
which Robbe-Grillet repeats throughout his essays is his call for
an 'objective literature'. In place of a literary tradition which turns
all objects into symbols, Robbe-Grillet insists that the New Novel
must concern itself with objects in and of themselves, with no
ulterior motive:

> Around us, defying the noisy pack of our animistic or protective
> adjectives, things *are there*. Their surfaces are distinct and smooth,
> *intact*, neither suspiciously brilliant nor transparent. All our
> literature has not yet succeeded in eroding their smallest corner,
> in flattening their slightest curve.   (19)

The real world of objects, like the rock Dr Johnson kicked in
refutation of Bishop Berkeley, serves as a necessary reminder of
the humble estate of man, the very ground of his existence.

In *Proust*, Beckett describes the narrative point-of-view employed in *A la recherche du temps perdu*, which the New Novelists would later adopt as their own:

> when the object is perceived as particular and unique and not merely the member of a family, when it appears independent of any general notion and detached from the sanity of a cause, isolated and inexplicable in the light of ignorance, then and then only may it be a source of enchantment. (22–3)

Alongside this emphasis on the object, Robbe-Grillet and Beckett share a preference for a narrative style which does not fix the 'meaning' of these objects, these bits of raw data, before they reach the reader. In 'A Future for the Novel' and the other essays collected in *For a New Novel*, Robbe-Grillet examines the lies that the traditional novel takes for truth, and is nostalgic for a more elementary sort of fiction, one which would 'construct a world both more solid and more immediate' than the world of the traditional novel (21). In the Proust study Beckett posits what he calls literary 'impressionism' as the only viable alternative to the dead-end the novel had come to: 'for the artist, the only possible hierarchy in the world of objective phenomena is represented by a table of their respective coefficients of penetration, that is to say, in terms of the subject' (84).

Beckett does not wish to do away with realism, but rather to substitute a subjective, 'impressionistic' realism for the manipulative realism which both he and Robbe-Grillet associate with Balzac. He goes on to describe in more detail Proust's impressionism, especially as it affects narrative form:

> By his impressionism I mean his non-logical statement of phenomena in the order and exactitude of their perception, before they have been distorted into intelligibility in order to be forced into a chain of cause and effect. The painter Elstir is the type of the impressionist, stating what he sees and not what he knows he ought to see. . . . And we are reminded of Schopenhauer's definition of the artistic procedure as 'the contemplation of the world independently of the principle of reason.' (86–7)

This artistic strategy, when employed in narration, is called in Jakobson's nomenclature 'metonymic'. Jakobson's well-known model says in part that 'the development of a discourse may take place along two different semantic lines; one topic may lead to another either through their similarity or through their contiguity' (*Fundamentals* 94–5). These 'two different semantic lines' correspond to two different narrative orientations – one characterised by metaphor, the other by metonymy. According to Jakobson, any given text will be dominated by one or the other of these processes:

> under the influence of a cultural pattern, personality, and verbal style, preference is given to one of the two processes over the other. . . . In manipulating these two kinds of connection (similarity and contiguity) in both their aspects (positional and semantic) – selecting, combining, and ranking them – an individual exhibits his personal style, his verbal predilections and preferences. . . . A competition between both devices, metonymic and metaphoric, is manifest in any symbolic process . . . . (94–9)

Many later theorists and critics have found Jakobson's nomenclature useful for the description of style in different authors. David Lodge has taken Jakobson's terminology and created from it a taxonomy of the modern novel, one which is useful in describing the purely technical aspects of modern writing.[4] Although it is clearly inadequate to an exhaustive description of Beckett's work, Jakobson's model is a useful taking-off point in discussing the narrative strategies of the postwar novels.

II

Jakobson has characterised prose as 'forwarded essentially by contiguity', and Lodge finds this to be 'consistent with the common-sense view that prose is the appropriate medium with which to describe logical relationships between concepts or entities or events' (88). But among different prose fictions the relative proportion of metonymy and metaphor varies greatly, and Beckett's trilogy is stridently metonymic. The narrators of Beckett's trilogy, with the notable exception of Moran, keep themselves to a rather 'literal' style; 'realistic' description of objects is privileged, and tropes, especially metaphor, are renounced. The eschewal of metaphor, in the first half of *Molloy* at least, is nearly complete.

Moran's 'report' is a somewhat different matter, metaphors rearing their ugly heads from time to time, and will be dealt with in detail below.

Seemingly, the only pattern that Molloy imposes on 'raw' experience is the inevitable distortion introduced by the presence of an observer – the narrative version of the Heisenberg uncertainty principle. Beckett's narrative of 'impotence' and 'ignorance' is structured around metonymic detail, according to the 'order and exactitude' of Molloy's perception. The natural 'plot' organisation for such a narrative is a locomotive/loco-descriptive one – a metonymic one. By choosing this narrative predilection for his protagonist, setting him on the road and having him relate his experiences in a modified stream-of-consciousness fashion, Beckett constructs a text having little apparent structure other than that imposed by narrative time and space.

After a page-long prologue, the reader is regaled with the ninety-page long paragraph which 'speak[s] of the things that are left' (*Molloy* 7). Molloy's narrative is above all about *things*; he constructs his narrative from whatever is at hand, reporting (seemingly without design) a bit of landscape or the state of his rapidly deteriorating body, or amusing himself with permutations of common objects (such as 'sucking stones'). The isolated details set out in a narrative are necessarily surrogates for the mass of detail which assaults the narrator; but when our narrator perceives only chaos with no apparent form, no 'figure in the carpet', the selection of the details that will make up his narrative appears, in the eyes of readers trained to find pattern, to be without rhyme or reason. Molloy is mastered *by* rather than the master *of* his material. When the diversity of experience is perceived as nothing but chaos, the metonymic narration of experience in the text is likewise chaotic.

In his discussion of metonymic narrative, Lodge comments that non-logical deletion 'would seem to correspond to what we commonly refer to as a novelist's "selection" of details in narrative description' (93). In the first half of *Molloy* we are presented with metonymic narrative filtered through the consciousness of a '*bricoleur*', who has structured a discourse from the data available to him. The organisational principle is, as Beckett calls it in *Proust*, 'the non-logical statement of phenomena *in the order and exactitude of their perception*'. As such, rather than 'describ[ing] logical relationships between concepts, or entities, or events' (Lodge), Beckett's metonymic narrative has just the opposite effect – it reflects a radical disjunction in the chain of logical relationships. Molloy, like the third of Eliot's Thames daughters, 'can connect nothing with nothing'. The overwhelming difference between Eliot's character and Beckett's, however, is that while Eliot seems to hold the Thames daughters responsible for their inability to make connections, Beckett does not blame his characters for what their author sees as the inexorable condition of being human. As he said to Israel Schenker, 'I think anyone nowadays who pays the slightest attention to his own experience finds it the experience of a non-knower, a non-can-er' (Schenker 148).

In his role as narrator, Molloy finds himself torn between two irreconcilable influences. His natural predilection, as he tells us countless times, is to talk of things, and things only; he tries 'to pay attention, to consider with attention all those dim things . . . what magic in those dim things' (8). But his writing masters, whoever they may be, have other plans for Molloy. On the book's opening page Molloy speaks of his dual allegiance: 'What I'd like now is to speak of the things that are left, say my goodbyes, finish dying. They don't want that. Yes, there is more than one, apparently. But it's always the same one that comes. You'll do that later, he says' (7). What 'they' want instead of Molloy's inventory of his possessions is a traditional story, complete with a beginning, middle and end, with characters and a plot. Molloy tries to create such a fiction early on in his writing, but continually gets bogged down in realistic detail, so that the story itself never really gets moving:

> So I saw A and C going slowly towards each other, unconscious of what they were doing. It was on a road remarkably bare, I mean without hedges or ditches or any kind of edge, in the country, for cows were chewing in enormous fields, lying and standing, in the evening silence. Perhaps I'm inventing a little, perhaps embellishing, but on the whole that's the way it was. They chew, swallow, then after a short pause effortlessly bring up the next mouthful. A neck muscle stirs and the jaws begin to grind again. But perhaps I'm remembering things.   (8)

Molloy's 'story' is off to a very slow start. The names 'A' and 'C' serve only to call attention to the fact that these two are not characters but ciphers; motivation is similarly undercut, for both were 'unconscious of what they were doing'. But Molloy no sooner names them than his attention is diverted by his fictional landscape, and he lavishes description on the road and cows.

Molloy's labour, imposed upon him by his mysterious writing-masters, is contrary to his deepest literary impulses. Whenever an opportunity for prolonged description of an object presents itself, Molloy is eager to describe lovingly, at length:

> Dear bicycle, I shall not call you bike, you were green, like so many of your generation, I don't know why. It is a pleasure to meet it again. To describe it at length would be a pleasure. . . . What a rest to speak of bicycles and horns. Unfortunately it is not of them I have to speak, but of her who brought me into the world, through the hole in her arse if my memory is correct. First taste of the shit.   (16)

To describe his green bicycle would have been a pleasure; but Molloy is compelled instead to speak of his mother, the one responsible for his *'premier emmerdement'*. Although Molloy desires to describe objects lovingly, he is careful to make his choices appear spontaneous and without motive. Molloy chooses to dwell on things and observations which do not seem to fit into any larger pattern of meaning. He announces quite explicitly that this is the reason for his lengthy description of his knees: 'That my knees are enormous, that I still get up from time to time, these are things that do not seem at first sight to signify anything in particular. I record them all the more willingly' (62). Rather than describing objects as a technique for escaping the banality of his world, as Beckett and Robbe-Grillet accuse Balzac of doing, Molloy instead holds fast to these *Dinge an sich*, seeking not to transcend but merely to caress them.

III

When Molloy uses phrases which sound metaphorical, we are surprised to find out that they are not figural, but literal. For instance, quite early in the novel Molloy describes his observation of the man he has called 'C': 'But in spite of my soul's leap out to him, at the end of its elastic, I saw him only darkly, because of the dark and then because of the terrain . . .' (11). Two metaphors in this remark recommend it to our attention. First, Molloy describes

his soul as 'leaping out' toward this fellow; but the figural quality
of his language serves only to confuse Molloy, who next describes
his soul as tethered with a piece of elastic, in the same manner
that his hat is attached to the buttonhole in his lapel. Further,
Molloy curiously expects that his soul's leap will somehow afford
him a better look at 'C'; the result is either a mixed metaphor or a
metaphor which Molloy mistakenly interprets literally. The phrase
'saw him only darkly' also hovers on the edge of figural language.
Understood figuratively, Molloy's description suggests a profound
awareness of the distance between himself and 'C'; but in Molloy's
mouth, the phrase does not support such a reading. This is not
the 'darkly' of the King James Bible's 'through a glass, darkly', a
metaphor for partial knowledge; this is the 'darkly' which occurs
at night, in the dark.[5]

This same play on words, juxtaposing the physical and epistemological import of the word 'dark', occurs again just a few pages
later; speaking of his mother, Molloy tells us that 'As to her
address, I was in the dark, but knew how to get there, even in the
dark' (22). Molloy's repetition of the phrase 'in the dark' calls its
rhetorical status into question; the expression, which we take at
first glance for a metaphor, is rendered suspect through its
repetition in a literal context.[6]

Surely this is part of the reason for Molloy's penchant for
metonymy – because it makes more modest claims than does
metaphor, its potential to delude is diminished. Molloy often
confuses figurative and literal language, even in his own speech,
but that's not so remarkable – after all, it's the basis of many old
vaudeville gags. But Molloy's hermeneutic situation is ours, and
his confusion is our confusion as well. When we cease to question
the duplicity of rhetorical figures, we begin to take them for truth –
a process which Molloy refers to as 'the principle of advertising':

> But it is useless to dwell on this period of my life. If I go on long
> enough calling that my life I'll end up by believing it. It's the
> principle of advertising. This period of my life. It reminds me,
> when I think of it, of air in a water-pipe.   (53)

Metaphor comforts, for it gives the author the illusion that he is
shaping, making sense of his experience, and reassures the reader
that he is in the presence of a master. But this dream of invention
and escape is pure fantasy:

Saying is inventing. Wrong, very rightly wrong. You invent nothing, you think you are inventing, you think you are escaping, and all you do is stammer out your lesson, the remnants of a pensum one day got by heart and long forgotten. (32)

Molloy's solution to the problem of telling the truth in language, then, is to attempt to restrict himself to purely literal language. Such a project, it may be objected, is surely doomed to failure, and Molloy himself is aware of its shortcomings. While denying the efficacy of any principle which would organise his world, Molloy is forced to assume the existence of just such a principle in order to communicate: for an absolutely 'literal' critique of figurative language, if such a project could indeed be carried out, would not communicate anything to anyone.

Molloy is therefore compelled to posit a unity behind the chaos: 'And if I speak of principles, when there are none, I can't help it, there must be some somewhere' (46); 'For all things hang together, by the operation of the Holy Ghost, as the saying is' (41). In a moment of crisis, Molloy falls back (so to speak) on a metaphor ('hang together'), on the notion of a transcendental signifier, holding everything together, providing a solid base or a still centre (choose your metaphor) for his seemingly chaotic experience. Molloy is courageous, but not fearless; he is a loner, but he does still have a desperate need to communicate.

IV

Ruby Cohn has written that 'After Molloy, Moran is a pygmy, as he is meant to be' (86). Moran has no qualms about the distortions of figurative language; while Molloy disdains the false coherence that metaphor asserts, Moran is partial to its totalising, escapist properties. Discussing *Malone Dies*, John D. Erickson maintains that

Ordered and ordering thought . . . plays little part in the creation of the Beckett character. The direction Malone, Sapo, and Macmann take, in the same novel, is not that leading to intellectual formulation but to a formless sensing. (115)

Erickson's description of 'the Beckett character' is largely accurate when applied to Molloy, as well. But Moran – at least at the beginning of his journey – is an obsessively orderly individual. Unlike the private investigator in a traditional detective novel, Moran's rage for order is a form of weakness; his organisational mania betrays a deepseated fear of losing control, and metaphor provides a ready means of asserting his power over the world:

> Warmth, gloom, smells of my bed, such is the effect they sometimes have on me. I get up, go out, and everything is changed. The blood drains from my head, the noise of things bursting, merging, avoiding one another, assails me on all sides, my eyes searching in vain for two things alike, each pinpoint of skin screams a different message, I drown in the spray of phenomena. It is at the mercy of these sensations, which happily I know to be illusory, that I have to live and work. It is thanks to them I find myself a meaning. So he whom a sudden pain awakes. He stiffens, ceases to breathe, waits, says, It's a bad dream, or, It's a touch of neuralgia, breathes again, sleeps again, still trembling. And yet it is not unpleasant, before setting to work, to steep oneself again in this slow and massive world, where all things move with the ponderous sullenness of oxen, patiently through the immemorial ways, and where of course no investigation would be possible.   (111)

Nietzsche has called the drive toward the formation of metaphors 'the fundamental human drive' ('On Truth' 88), attractive because it claims to obtain access to the unknown and uncontrollable in man's experience through something familiar and non-threatening. When Moran claims to *'drown* in the *spray* of phenomena', he has in fact brought those unruly phenomena under the rule of metaphor; he, the metaphor-maker, sits comfortably at his desk, master of all he surveys.

When presented an occasion for detailed description, the kind of situation in which Molloy delights, Moran instead creates a figurative description; in the following description of his unnamed assailant, for example, no feature is described on its own terms, but all with reference to some other image:

> But all this was nothing compared to the face which I regret to say vaguely resembled my own, less the refinement of course, same little abortive moustache, same little ferrety eyes, same

paraphimosis of the nose, and a thin red mouth that looked as if it was raw from trying to shit its tongue.   (151)

Moran's narrative situation is the exact converse of Molloy's. Molloy desires only to talk of things, but is forced to weave a fiction; Moran, who has literary aspirations, is forced by his employer to write an unadorned report. Where Molloy is frequently tempted from his task by the opportunity to indulge in description, Moran is constantly 'embellishing' his prosaic report with excursions into the 'poetic'. While trying to decide between the names 'Molloy' and 'Mollose', Moran tells us that the idea that

> there may have been two different persons involved, one my own Mollose, the other the Molloy of the enquiry, was a thought which did not so much as cross my mind, and if it had I should have driven it away, as one drives away a fly, or a hornet. How little one is with oneself, good God, I who prided myself on being a sensible man, cold as crystal and as free from spurious depth.   (113)

In his role as professional investigator, Moran prides himself on being 'cold as crystal'; but his investigatory task is constantly in conflict with his literary pretensions, so that one is never quite sure whether Moran desires to be a real-life detective, or rather the protagonist of a detective novel. Surely the overwritten, 'literary' opening paragraph of his report makes clear the stylistic clash that will characterise his narrative:

> It is midnight. The rain is beating down on the windows. I am calm. All is sleeping. Nevertheless I get up and go to my desk. I can't sleep. My lamp sheds a soft and steady light. I have trimmed it. It will last till morning. I hear the eagle-owl. What a terrible battle-cry! Once I listened to it unmoved. My son is sleeping. Let him sleep. The night will come when he too, unable to sleep, will get up and go to his desk. I shall be forgotten.   (92)

Moran is acutely aware of himself as both character and writer; the melodramatic tone of this opening scene makes it clear that our narrator's desire for recognition will not allow him to assume his role as dutiful report-writer without a fight. Youdi requires Moran to report 'just the facts', but the gathering of those facts requires detection, meaning-making, the imposition of logical order.

Aristotle tells us that of all the intellectual gifts of man, 'the greatest thing by far is to have a command of metaphor. This alone cannot be imparted by another; it is the mark of genius, for to make good metaphors implies an eye for resemblances' (*Poetics* 104). In an unguarded moment, Moran admits to his predilection for metaphor, as if a confession were really necessary: 'And at the sight of the blue flesh, between the knickerbockers and the tops of my boots, I sometimes thought of my son and the blow I had fetched him, so avid is the mind of the flimsiest analogy' (170). Conversely, as he says in reference to the wheels of his son's bicycle, 'As soon as two things are nearly identical I am lost' (156). Moran depends on a clear difference between signifier and signified, between the vehicle and tenor of his metaphors; under such conditions, he can exercise his 'eye for resemblances', and yoke seemingly disparate concepts into unity – he becomes something of a modernist or metaphysical poet. Failing such an obvious gap between signifier and signified, between prosaic object and metaphysical conception, however, his mind is paralysed; vast generalisation, rather than precise discrimination, is Moran's forte – and a rather strange one it is for a professional investigator. Moran's motto, too, is an unusual one for a private eye: 'Let us be content with paradigms' (172).

Although Moran desires to master the phenomenal world through metaphor, the objects of the real world thwart him at every turn. Objects are stubborn; as Moran says, 'The inertia of things is enough to drive one literally insane' (119). When Moran here says 'literally', he of course means 'figuratively', as does Lily, the caretaker's daughter who is, in the first sentence of 'The Dead', 'literally run off her feet'.

John Erickson points out that 'the gradual diminution of the characters' physical capacity throughout Beckett's works brings them on the one hand closer to the state of an object and on the other hand to a concrete confrontation with objects' (117). This is most dramatically true of Moran, and his 'fall' into the world of objects is a momentous one. As Moran's journey progresses, his stylistic bent changes; by the end of his journey his writing has become much more literal, involving greater detail and less figurative language. Although he begins his report in a tone of high seriousness and decorum, Moran, as his health steadily declines, necessarily becomes more and more concerned with the contingencies of daily life. In stark contrast to the grandiose manner in which he opens his report, its ending is quite prosaic:

> When it rained, when it snowed, when it hailed, then I found myself faced with the following dilemma. Was I to go on leaning on my umbrella and get drenched or was I to stop and take shelter under my open umbrella? It was a false dilemma, as so many dilemmas are. For on the one hand all that remained of the canopy of my umbrella was a few flitters of silk fluttering from the stays . . . (171).

The steady decline in Moran's life circumstances is mirrored in the decline of the level of his diction, the loosening of his syntax, and the progressive lengthening of his paragraphs. The Moran of the beginning of Part II would never have said 'flitters'; his high style has descended to a level he finds threatening. The anal-retentive tendencies of Moran, so evident at the outset of his report, have given way to a more primal, disorderly personality in the search for Molloy. Starting out a man with a rage for order, 'cold as crystal and as free from spurious depth', Moran is in the end reduced to squatting 'on all fours shitting out [his] entrails and chanting maledictions' in the forest of Turdy (166). This movement from anal-retention to anal-expulsion is also seen in his use of language – precise and fastidious prose at first; free, superabundant, disjointed 'wordshit' near the end. Moran begins his narrative as a metaphorical writer; by the end of his 'report', however, he has come to be, like Molloy, a metonymic writer. Where his opening style is a high one, a language of ideas and ideals, the language of the narrative's end is the language of things – umbrellas, bees, flowers, stockings – *disjecta membra* in search of a strong author. But in the end, Moran no longer has the strength left to wrest from them the secret of their implicate pattern.

After he has been living in the forest for a good while, Moran develops a delight in description which rivals Molloy's; when Jacques Jr returns to camp with the bicycle, Moran, in his much degenerated condition, is only too eager to describe the bicycle with veneration:

> He was pushing a bicycle which, when he had finally joined

me, he let fall with a gesture signifying he could bear no more. Pick it up, I said, till I look at it. I had to admit it must once have been quite a good bicycle. I would gladly describe it, I would gladly write four thousand words on it alone. And you call that a bicycle? I said.   (155)

At the very nadir of his existence, when all the pretensions and shabby gentility are stripped away, Moran's impulse is to return to the most 'basic' kind of narrative. Once the mask falls, so too apparently do the tropes; all ostentation has been banished, and Moran returns to the metonymic foundation of all prose.

The most striking evidence of the change that has come over Moran surfaces just a few pages from the end of his report, a passage which reads suspiciously like a parable. Before setting out on the quest for Molloy, Moran had been something of an amateur naturalist, studying the intricate dances of the bees he kept; he has made, he tells us, a systematic study of the dance performed by the bees upon returning to the hive. 'I had investigated this phenomena very fully', Moran says, and classified the 'great variety of figures and rhythms' (168). But his research, it would appear, had come to an impasse: 'in spite of all the pains I had lavished on these problems, I was more than ever stupefied by the complexity of this innumerable dance, involving doubtless other determinants of which I had not the slightest idea' (169).

Moran's reaction to this frustration, however, strikes us as strangely out of character. Just four pages earlier, he has told us that 'when a thing resists me, even if it is for my own good, it does not resist me long' (165); but when his mind drifts back to the enigma of the bees' dance, Moran joyfully surrenders:

And I said, with rapture, Here is something I can study all my life, and never understand. And all during this long journey home, when I racked my mind for a little joy in store, the thought of my bees and their dance was the nearest thing to comfort. For I was still eager for my little joy, from time to time! And I admitted with good grace the possibility that this dance was after all no better than the dances of the people of the West, frivolous and meaningless. But for me, sitting near my sun-drenched hives, it would always be a noble thing to contemplate, too noble ever to be sullied by the cogitations of a man like me, exiled in his manhood.   (169)

One is reminded again of Oedipa's surrender at the end of *The Crying of Lot 49*; another hermeneutic knight has withdrawn from the quest. The crucial difference, of course, is that Oedipa resigns because she *does* sense the pattern, and fears becoming 'the true paranoid for whom all is organized in spheres joyful or threatening about the central pulse of himself' (95); Moran, on the other hand, comes to believe all such patterns, discerned or imposed, as essentially false, and genuinely longs to 'drown in the spray of phenomena'. To surrender to phenomena is to write in the metonymic mode; metaphor asserts mastery over those phenomena, distorting them 'into intelligibility in order to be forced into a chain of cause and effect'. In the end, Moran comes around to Molloy's vision of the universe; and both become spokesmen for Beckett's utopian dream of a literature which might not *mean*, but *be*.

V

Historically, our literary tradition has privileged metaphor over metonymy as the 'trope of choice' for 'serious' literature. Indeed, Jakobson himself, once having made the distinction between the metaphoric and metonymic poles, has conspicuously little to say about the latter mode of writing: 'when constructing a metalanguage to interpret tropes, the researcher possesses more homogeneous means to handle metaphor, whereas metonymy, based on a different principle, easily defies interpretation' (Jakobson 95).

In *Molloy*, Beckett performs a critique of the primacy traditionally afforded to metaphor. By replacing metaphor with metonymy as the 'trope of choice', Beckett hopes to realise his 'dream of an art unresentful of its insuperable indigence and too proud for the farce of giving and receiving' ('Three Dialogues' 112). In his fiction, Beckett illustrates the same attitude toward metaphor that Robbe-Grillet later professed in his essays:

> Metaphor, as a matter of fact, is never an innocent figure of speech. To say that the weather is 'capricious' or the mountain 'majestic', to speak of the 'heart' of the forest, of a 'pitiless' sun, of a village 'huddled' in the valley, is, to a certain degree, to furnish clues as to the things themselves: shape, size, situation, etc. But the choice of an analogical vocabulary, however simple,

already does something more than account for purely physical data, and what this *more* is can scarcely be ascribed only to the credit of belles-lettres. The height of the mountain assumes, willy-nilly, a moral value; the heat of the sun becomes the result of an intention. . . . In almost the whole of our contemporary literature, these anthropomorphic analogies are repeated too insistently, too coherently not to reveal an entire metaphysical system.   (53)

In one sense, then, the project of *Molloy*, of the entire trilogy for that matter, is a polemical one: to force the reader to accept the text in all the poverty in which it is presented, without recourse to a comforting metaphorical meta-reading which makes sense of the chaos.

This kind of project is often erroneously referred to today as deconstructive. Beckett's project is to examine the rhetorical pair metaphor/metonymy, to explore the philosophical implications of both modes of writing, and ultimately to turn that hierarchical pair on its head, making metonymy the privileged term of the pair. But Beckett does not go so far as to deconstruct the opposition between metaphor and metonymy; rather, at the point of his greatest insight, having revealed with stunning force the metaphysical assumptions behind the use of metaphor, Beckett reinscribes the hierarchy, merely reversing the terms. Strikingly, this reinscription is done, in the climactic 'Parable of the Bees', in the form of an allegory: an extended metaphor. Beckett's procedure is polemical, to be sure; but it is not deconstructive. A deconstructive treatment of the metaphoric and metonymic 'poles' of language would not simply elevate the beleaguered metonymy to the position formerly held by metaphor, but rather would invert the hierarchical pair in order to question the existence of a sharp distinction between the two tropes.[7]

As Nietzsche was at pains to argue, and Heidegger after him, all language is in its essence figurative, and when we start to take our own lies seriously we run into trouble. Although somewhat fanciful, Nietzsche's story of the beginnings of language points to the figural nature of all language:

To begin with, a nerve stimulus is transferred into an image: first metaphor. The image, in turn, is imitated in a sound: second metaphor. And each time there is a complete overleaping of one sphere, right into the middle of an entirely new and different one. . . . It is this way with all of us concerning language: we believe that we know something about the things themselves when we speak of trees, colors, snow, and flowers; and yet we possess nothing but metaphors for things – metaphors which correspond in no way to the original entities. ('On Truth' 82–3)

The distinction between metaphor and metonymy for Nietzsche, then, is not a difference of kind but merely of degree:

> there is no 'real' expression and *no real knowing apart from metaphor*. But deception on this point remains, i.e. the *belief* in a *truth* of sense impressions. The most accustomed metaphors, the usual ones, now pass for truths and as standards for measuring the rarer ones. The only intrinsic difference here is the difference between custom and novelty, frequency and rarity. . . . *Knowing* is nothing but working with the favorite metphors, an imitating which is no longer felt to be an imitation. Naturally therefore, it cannot penetrate the realm of truth. ('Philosopher' 50–51)

Such a conception of language, of course, puts into question the possibility of a language which 'tells the truth'; but Beckett never allows his narrators to entertain so radical a scepticism. Behind all Molloy's distrust of artificial, 'poetic' language lies an unshakeable faith in the ability of the 'proper' kind of language – poor, honest, 'literal' language – to tell the truth. For Nietzsche, because our knowledge of truth is inextricably bound up with our ability to express that truth in language, the very notion of truth becomes problematic in the extreme:

> What then is truth? A movable host of metaphors, metonymies, and anthropomorphisms: in short, a sum of human relations which have been poetically and rhetorically intensified, transferred, and embellished, and which, after long usage, seem to a people to be fixed, canonical, and binding. Truths are illusions which we have forgotten are illusions; they are metaphors that have become worn out and have been drained of sensuous force, coins which have lost their embossing and are now considered as metal and no longer as coins. . . . To be truthful means to employ the usual metaphors. ('On Truth' 84)

Anyone who would perform a critique of metaphor *from outside of metaphor*, be it Molloy or Beckett himself, will find himself, much to his chagrin, in the rather comic position dramatised by Jacques Derrida in 'The *Retrait* of Metaphor':

> The drama, for this is a drama, is that even if I decided to no longer speak metaphorically about metaphor, I would not achieve it, it would continue to go on without me in order to make me speak, to ventriloquize me, metaphorize me. Other ways of saying, other ways of responding to, rather, my first questions. What is happening *with* metaphor? Well, everything: there is nothing that does not happen with metaphor and by metaphor. Any statement concerning anything that happens, metaphor included, will be produced *not without* metaphor. There will not have been a meta-metaphorics consistent enough to dominate all its statements.   (8)

As Nietzsche was at pains to show, even 'Being' itself is a metaphor;[8] and for Beckett's characters, *this* metaphor is surely the most fantastic of all:

> ESTRAGON: We don't manage too badly, eh Didi, between the two of us?
> VLADIMIR: Yes yes. Come on, we'll try the left first.
> ESTRAGON: We always find something, eh Didi, to give us the impression we exist?
> VLADIMIR: Yes yes, we're magicians.   (44r)

Notes

1. So that, for instance, Oedipa Mass starts out her job as executrix trying to sort out the tangled assets of Pierce Inverarity; she discerns in both circuit boards and Southern Californian communities 'a hieroglyphic sense of concealed meaning, of an intent to communicate'. But in the end, Oedipa gives up the hermeneutic quest: 'Oedipa settled back, to await the crying of lot 49' (*Crying* 13, 138).
2. In 'Literary History and Literary Modernity'.
3. Strangely enough, in a book subtitled 'Essays on Fiction', Robbe-Grillet devotes an entire essay to Beckett's drama, and mentions the fiction only in passing.
4. See *The Modes of Modern Writing: Metaphor, Metonymy, and the Typology*

of *Modern Literature* (Ithaca: Cornell University Press, 1977).
5. Beckett's play on the language of the Authorized Version is absent in the French, where Molloy says merely '*je le voyais mal, à cause de l'obscurité et puis aussi du terrain . . .*' (14).
6. Again, the wordplay is lost in the French: '*Pour ce qui était de l'adresse de cette dernière, je l'ignorais, mais savais très bien m'y rendre, même dans obscurité*' (33).
7. See, for instance, de Man's discussion in 'Reading (Proust)', *Allegories of Reading: Figural Language in Rousseau, Nietzsche, Rilke, and Proust*, 57–78.
8. In *Greek Tragedy During the Tragic Age*.

Works Cited

Aristotle, *Poetics*, trans. S. H. Butcher, Intro. Francis Ferguson (New York: Hill and Wang, 1961).

Beckett, Samuel, *Molloy* [English], trans. Patrick Bowles in collaboration with the author. *Three Novels by Samuel Beckett: Molloy, Malone Dies, The Unnameable* (New York: Grove Press, 1955. New York: Black Cat Books/Grove Press, 1965), pp. 7–176.

——, *Molloy* [French] (Paris: Les Editions de Minuit, 1951).

——, *Proust*, 1931. *Proust and Three Dialogues with Georges Duthuit* (London: Calder & Boyars, 1970), pp. 7–93.

——, 'Three Dialogues with Georges Duthuit', 1949. *Proust and Three Dialogues with Georges Duthuit* (London: Calder & Boyars, 1970), pp. 95–126.

——, *Waiting for Godot* (New York: Grove Press, 1954).

Cohn, Ruby, *Back to Beckett* (Princeton: Princeton University Press, 1973).

De Man, Paul, *Allegories of Reading: Figural Language in Rousseau, Nietzsche, Rilke, and Proust* (New Haven: Yale University Press, 1979).

——, 'The Epistemology of Metaphor', *Critical Inquiry*, 5 (1978): 13–30.

——, 'Literary History and Literary Modernity', *Blindness and Insight: Essays in the Rhetoric of Contemporary Criticism*, 2nd edn (Minneapolis: University of Minnesota Press, 1983), pp. 142–65.

Derrida, Jacques, *Of Grammatology*, trans. Gayatri Spivak (Baltimore: Johns Hopkins University Press, 1976).

——, 'The *Retrait* of Metaphor', *Enclitic* 2, No. 2 (1978), 5–33.

——, 'White Mythology: Metaphor in the Text of Philosophy', *Margins of Philosophy*, trans. Alan Bass (Chicago: University of Chicago Press, 1982), pp. 207–71.

Driver, Tom, 'Beckett beside the Madeleine', *Columbia University Forum*, Summer 1961, 21–25. *Samuel Beckett: The Critical Heritage* (London: Routledge & Kegan Paul, 1979), pp. 217–23.

Erickson, John D., 'Objects and Systems in the Novels of Samuel Beckett', *L'Esprit Créateur*, VII, No. 2, Summer 1967, pp. 113–22.

Harries, Karsten, 'Metaphor and Transcendence', *Critical Inquiry*, 5 (1978): 73–90.

Jakobson, Roman and Morris Halle, *Fundamentals of Language* (The Hague: Mouton, 1971).

Lodge, David, *The Modes of Modern Writing: Metaphor, Metonymy, and the Typology of Modern Literature* (Ithaca: Cornell University Press, 1977).

Lyotard, Jean-François, *The Postmodern Condition*, trans. Geoff Bennington and Brian Masumi (Minneapolis: University of Minnesota Press, 1984).

Nietzsche, Friedrich, 'On Truth and Lie in an Extramoral Sense', 1873. *Philosophy and Truth: Selections from Nietzsche's Notebooks of the Early 1870s*, trans. & ed. Daniel Breazeale (New Jersey: Humanities Press, 1979), pp. 77–97.

—, 'The Philosopher: Reflections on the Struggle between Art and Knowledge', 1872. *Philosophy and Truth: Selections from Nietzsche's Notebooks of the Early 1870s*, trans. & ed. Daniel Breazeale (New Jersey: Humanities Press, 1979), pp. 1–58.

Pinter, Harold, 'Beckett', *Beckett at 60: A Festschrift* (London: Calder & Boyars, 1967), p. 86.

Pynchon, Thomas, *The Crying of Lot 49* (New York: Bantam Books, 1966).

Robbe-Grillet, Alain, *For a New Novel: Essays on Fiction*, trans. Richard Howard (New York: Grove Press, 1965).

Schenker, Israel, 'Moody Man of Letters', *New York Times*, 6 May 1956, Sec. 2, Pt X, 1 & 3. *Samuel Beckett: The Critical Heritage* (London: Routledge & Kegan Paul, 1979), pp. 146–9.

5

'Babel of Silence': Beckett's Post-Trilogy Prose Articulated

Barbara Trieloff

The declarative element of Beckett's narratives derives from his increasingly telegraphic and minimalist style, a style found in narratives that are stripped of traditional, 'sense-making'[1] forms – such as sequential progression of plot, character development, and ordered fictional worlds with space–time[2] coordinates. When the text's language itself is then denied syntactical and grammatical consonance, the text defies the reader's impulse to organise these unpunctuated, subverted and asyntactical sentences, leaving him/her confronted with a rhetoric of abstraction (through enantiomorphism, hyperbaton, anastrophe, ellipsis, anacoluthon, annomination, parataxis and incremental repetition).

The accumulated effect of these devices is to disrupt the syntactical sequence of the prose. This textual rupture, or, more precisely, this hermeneutic[3] rift in the reader's grammatical expectations, promotes a sense of syntactical freedom, or anarchy. Meaning, therefore, which should come with the natural progression of both the language and narrative, continually dissolves, losing its form and substance. Consequently, frustrated, the reader comes to listen to, to entertain, other sense-making patterns: sound, rhythm, tone.

It is here that we see the narrative language of the post-trilogy prose qualitatively approaching its aural/oral counterpart, functioning in ways different from those expected of narrative and suggesting, therefore, a different level of intelligibility, one which gives primacy to the oral/aural text over the written. The reader is enjoined to overlook the printed text and to listen, instead, to the phonetic patterns within the language. Thus these literary texts seem Janus-faced, pointing away from their status as written literary artifacts, while indicating their aural/oral dimension.

To begin to see this in operation, we might look at 'Lessness'[4] where Beckett clearly undermines both the referential and syntactical nature of language. For example, the phrase, 'Ruins true refuge long last towards which so many false time out of mind' (p. 51), is devoid of normal, syntactic relationships. The word sequence is aleatory. There is neither a proper and clear subject, nor a verb. Each word stands isolated, distanced from a meaningful context, because it has not been anchored to the hierarchical chain of meaning normally inherent in logical syntax.

Here, instead of normal syntax, Beckett offers a non-logical, non-formal discourse, whereby narrative language is not presented as a chain of clauses, a sequence of cause and effect out of which meaning develops. Instead, we are confronted with a dystaxic series of word-groupings, a series of discontinuous utterances:

No sound no stir / ash grey sky / mirrored earth mirrored sky / grey air / timeless earth / sky as one / same grey / as the ruins / flatness endless. / In the sand / no hold / one step more / in the endlessness he will make it. / It will be day and night again / over him the endlessness / the air heart will beat again.   (p. 49)

Here, the inversion of expected word-order, the lack of an apparent, clearly identified subject governing the first sentence, the elliptical fragments (note the stress on *less*, in words like 'end*less*', and on *ness*, in words like 'flat*ness*'), all these suggest linguistic pandemonium. This apparent freedom of verbal association within the post-trilogy prose arises from what I will call a rhetoric of abstraction, which engineers the de-forming or de-constructing of the structures of language. Freed from fixed meaning, language becomes semantically fluid, thereby miming Beckett's conception of an indeterminate universe and consciousness:

Never was but grey air timeless no sound figment the passing light. No sound no stir ash grey sky mirrored earth mirrored sky. Never but this changelessness dream the passing hour.   (p. 47)

Here, for example, Beckett further reinforces this asyntactical style with other rhetorical devices such as gerund phrases, ablative absolutes, and dislocated modifiers: 'Never but imagined the blue in a wild imagining the blue celeste of poesy. Light white touch close head through calm eye light of reason all gone from mind' (p. 51). The gerund phrase, 'a wild imagining', in the first sentence, is not qualified in the succeeding sentence. This passage also lacks the modifiers needed to clarify the semantic relationship between 'light white touch', 'close head' and 'through calm eye'. The deletion of operative verbs and connectives confuses the relationship between subject, object, qualifying adverbs and adjectives. Clearly, in Beckett's later prose style, precedence and priority are given to each single word and phrase: 'light of reason' and 'calm eye' are of equal semantic weight, whereas conventionally, emphasis is placed on a specific part to give direction and tone. The directionless reader is left to his/her own devices.

Similarly so, in the fragment 'Sounds',[5] we can clearly see various rhetorical devices employed by Beckett to elicit from the reader an awareness of a certain rhythmic, textual fluidity that arises from such a style:

> or if none hour after hour no sound of any kind than he having been dreamt away let himself be dreamt away to where none at any time from here where none come none pass to where no sound to listen for one of any kind' (p. 155).

This unpunctuated, parataxic passage is free of the constraints of traditional English syntax. Through enantiomorphism (emphatic repetition of words), and anacoluthon (change of construction, leaving the first part of the sentence broken), Beckett undercuts the normal, logical construction/progression of subject-verb-object that is otherwise found in the traditional language and narrative form of – at its simplest – 'Once upon a time, there was . . .'.[6]

Traditionally, the reader of narratives has come to expect that the text will provide him/her with a location and a time in which to fix the plot and characters,[7] and that it will do so according to normal linguistic conventions. But in Beckett's *Residua*,[8] as 'Sounds' illustrates, linguistic and fictional form are both denied. The reader enters the inverted linguistic syntax via the preposition and conjunction 'or': 'or if none the hour'. Here, we encounter difficulty, since we are denied information as to both the exact function of the word 'or', and the situating in place or time that are usually crucial to the reader's sense-making faculties. Moreover, 'if none the hour' – which follows 'or' – does not seem to fulfil any explanatory role, though it parodically points to the dimension of time expected. In this context, the word 'or' is not logical: it neither presents a second of two alternatives, nor is it indicative of quality or quantity (as in five or six). It does not designate whether or not there has been an indirect question or conditional protasis; nor does it seem to denote a condition or a comparative sense. In fact, it seems functionally useless – or at liberty.

Thus the impression we receive is that of some sort of delayed clause, without true coordinating conjunctions or subordinating phrases. The use of epizeuxis, in the repetition of 'to where', does little to enlighten the reader as to the direction or intention of the passage; in fact, it parodically mocks our need for spatial situating. Brachylogy (telegraphic, over-concise language) and the deletion of operative words denoting an active subject only add to the confusion.

As the passage from 'Sounds' demonstrates, traditional, narrative coherence is here denied the reader. Yet despite this lack of *syntactical* order, there is another type of order, one which manifests itself in the vowels of words such as 'sound', 'hour', 'or', 'of', 'come' and 'no', and which works to create a certain phonetic rhythm. Thus what happens in Beckett's texts is that certain sound patterns[9] come into prominence, and these patterns follow more an aural than an expository progression.

How It Is[10] also reveals similar rhythms: the repetition of words such as 'unless', 'before', 'after', 'various times', 'no', 'one', 'wrong', 'vast tracts', 'Pim', 'end of part', 'this voice', 'how it is/was' and 'quaqua' creates verbal echoes throughout the text:

> of this old tale quaqua on all sides then in me bits and scraps try and hear a few scraps two or three each time per day and string them together make phrases the last how it was after Pim how it is something wrong there end of part three and last this voice these voices no knowing not meaning
>
> on all sides   (pp. 106–7)

These words and phrases attract further attention because the persistent use of them would seem to hint at a hidden message formed in some cryptic substratum of language. Whatever logical message we might hope to construct, however, tends to founder. Moreover, the 'quaqua' echo, which recalls Lucky's seemingly nonsensical speech in *Waiting for Godot*, prompts us to consider the voice – whose natural order (it claims) is changed because of 'want of memory' – as the emitter of an inane, self-conscious, narcissistic babble of words. Meaning, as the voice also informs us – 'but quaqua meaning' – disintegrates continually.

Evolving out of this deconstructing of meaningful sentences is our awareness of the paradoxical, 'prison-like' quality[11] of this disclosed prose, a quality which makes it similar to the sort of 'topos' Stanley Fish found in John Donne's sermon *Death's Duell* (1630). Although Fish does not deal with Beckett, his explanation of seventeenth-century prose as a 'self-consuming artifact' provides an interesting analogue to the view presented here of the effects of Beckett's rhetorical devices on the reader, effects which eventually prompt the reader to reject the written text and to entertain the text as an aural work.

In the written text, repetition demonstrates, as in *Malone Dies*,[12] 'an art liable to consume itself on its own pyre', or, as Fish describes it, a style that is '*de*progressive, or retrogressive' (p. 56). This prose refuses to move to a conclusion; it continually short-circuits, 'calling attention to what it is not doing . . . proclaiming not only its own insufficiency, but the insufficiency of the frame of reference from which it issues' (p. 42). The denial of meaning in Beckett's texts – the refusal to arrive at a satisfactory conclusion – is made overt as the prose alerts the reader to its inability to create, or to identify, value and identity in fiction. As a result, says Fish, 'the topos has become a prison' and the reader is held under 'the arc of suspension' (p. 62).

It should be noted, however, that the comparison between Donne's text and those of Beckett cannot be an exact one. In Beckett's fiction, there is no latent meaning to which to return. Donne's parishioners may be enjoined to recall God's meaningful creations and to reject man's artificial, confounding substitutes; but in Beckett's world, the reader finds no meaningful frame of reference lying behind the text; s/he has only the lies of our human-made, formal fictions of consonance.

What is happening here, to use Fish's[13] terminology once again, is that the reader becomes involved in a game in which s/he searches for 'meanings that subvert, or exist in a tension with the meanings that first present themselves' (p. 327). Such patterns of expectations and counter-expectations, reversals of directions, traps, invitations to premature conclusions, textual gaps, delayed revelations, and temptations (pp. 344–5) – all of which are strategies designed either to educate or to confound the reader – result in an active interrogation of the text, of its 'latent ambiguities' and also – as we have seen – of the 'presence of alliterative and consonantal patterns'.

Beckett uses these same stylistic devices, though not to the same end as Donne, to enjoin the reader to reject comfortable, human forms, and to look elsewhere, which for Beckett is nowhere. Thus, the epistemological complexities in these texts urge the readers, or listeners, to seek an alternative version of meaning through the rejection of traditional, expected, linguistic and narrative structuring. And, as is readily apparent, Beckett's syntax is anything but conventional, as the text 'Imagination Dead Imagine'[14] reveals:

> But whatever its uncertainties the return sooner or later to a temporary calm seems assured, for the moment, in the black dark or the great whiteness, with attendant temperature, world still proof against enduring tumult. . . . Externally all is as before and the sighting of the little fabric quite as much a matter of chance, its whiteness merging in the surrounding whiteness. (pp. 36–7)

The first part of this passage is syntactically logical. Although we are not given information about the subject, we do know that the self's situation vacillates between 'uncertainties' and 'temporary calm'. The initial clarity of the passage is undermined by the next piece of information, presented in dystaxic language: '[B]lack dark', 'whiteness', 'attendant temperature', 'enduring tumult', 'the sighting of the little fabric'. These terms all suggest someone's perception and an awareness of tensions within the rotunda. However, as in 'Sounds', we are not given a clear enough subject as a point of reference on to which to anchor meaning. Hence, these qualifying words float around 'it', arbitrarily qualifying whatever else is there.

In this way, the reader is forced to reject as sense-less, as unamenable to normal linguistic form, what is literally presented on the page before him, and is asked to devise, instead, an 'implied' version of the text, one that s/he has, imaginatively, both extracted and abstracted from the language. 'Imagination Dead Imagine' acknowledges this need for imaginative interpreting response:

'Rediscovered miraculously after what absence in perfect voids it is no longer quite the same, from this point of view, but there is no other' (p. 37). Beckett's texts continually demand this hermeneutic response. Meaning, we discover, lies in the relationship between the text and the interpreter. It is not latent in the text, but only constructed from this 'implied' text. With the confusion and distortion of the reader's normal sense of the teleological form of fiction – a distortion repeated in the lack of syntactical and grammatical concordances – the structural and formal contours of the work become as indeterminate as the consciousness depicted.

As mentioned at the start, in addition to questioning the legitimacy of syntactical structuring, the post-trilogy fiction subverts our concepts of the *written* text. There is, as previously mentioned, an aural quality to the language, which is created by an intra-linguistic resonance established by the reiteration of certain verbal rhythms and phrases.[15] This aural resonance implies a language of infinite regression, or, as Douglas Hofstadter[16] describes it, 'Canon per Augmentationem, Contrario Motu': a literary fugue on the language of infinite regression. This linguistic recession, along with such a compact, concise, function within the prose to create a retroactive pattern moving toward silence. In *Ping*, the relentless repetition of the following words and phrases expresses this movement: 'All known', 'light heat', 'never seen', 'bare white body', 'traces blurs', 'head haught', 'unover', 'hands hanging', 'fixed elsewhere', 'ping', 'given rose', 'front legs joined', 'second', 'joined like sewn', 'heels', 'memory', 'a meaning', 'almost never', 'no sound'.

As in non-verbal music, repetition and echoing can be said to suggest aesthetic, intra-textual representation: references and relations do not point to phenomena outside of the music or text itself. In *Ping*, the number of repeated vowel sounds, as in 'Head haught eyes light blue almost white silence within' (p. 41), is reduced to a minimum (here emphasising the various 'i' sounds). Like other compositions in the *Residua* and in *For to End Yet Again and Other Fizzles*, *Ping*[17] offers a paradoxical conception of Beckett's universe of sound and silence, oral and written.

These fictions thus highlight the aural quality of Beckett's work, a quality which demands that the reader recognise and recall, through memory, earlier resonances. *Ping*'s explicitly repetitive quality suggests, on the one hand, the notion of the literary fugue discussed by Hofstadter and, on the other, that the text goes nowhere, that there is no end to this formal principle, that there is only echoing sound.

Moreover, although any individual segment of Beckett's 'open' texts might be neatly and intelligibly made to conform to a pattern, the seemingly arbitrarily placed repetitions warrant examination. These repetitions disrupt the text's impulse toward linear narrative and in so doing involve the text in those processes of infinite regress. Any progressive movement offered in the text is automatically curtailed by the refrain. This refrain, or echo-chamber effect, also creates a chiasmic pattern throughout the fictions, and therefore reinforces the more localised recursive structures of the prose style. Hofstadter refers to this as the 'Strange Loops' process, the visual counterpart of which can be seen in the Escher lithographs.

The echo-chamber effect in Beckett's fiction creates a sense of flux, of verbal elements incessantly connecting and fracturing and then disconnecting again. The reader, in his/her unrequited need for form, makes certain chiasmic alignments within the text. But the newly-organised wording of the text, in the reader's mind, does not correspond with its original, printed order. As we saw earlier, when the reader/listener recalls a former use of a similar word, that word is then freed from its fixed, spatial context on that particular printed page. It is recalled from that location and, by being freed from its space and transported into the reader's/listener's temporal memory, the text itself, in a sense, loses its material concreteness in print. Instead, it too becomes fluid, eliciting readings that are both anachronistic (readings based on recall of the past) and anticipatory. The text, therefore, opens up, 'dis-closes' directions and readings other than those first found in the reader's normal, sequential progression, page by page.

This same hermeneutic freedom can be created through punning (paronomasia), so that ultimately, instead of linear plots presented in normal sentences, we find that the micro-structure of Beckett's fiction is indeed conceivable in terms of Hofstadter's 'Strange Loops' process of infinite regress. The phonetic association between words and parts of words demands a regrouping other than that imposed by the normal, syntactical structure of language. Moreover, syllabic similarities – assonance, alliteration, and onomatopoeia (*Ping*, for instance) – create a quasi-musical beat, one which allows us to experience, directly, the aural, rhythmic aspects of language. One of the clearest examples of this emphasis on sound is in the text *Ping*:

Traces blurs light grey eyes holes light blue almost white fixed front ping a meaning only just almost never ping silence. Bare white one yard fixed ping fixed elsewhere no sound legs joined. . . . Ping elsewhere always there but that known not. Ping perhaps not alone one second with image same time. . . . (p. 43)

Most of the words here are monosyllabic, and contain short vowel sounds which, in turn, create a distinct staccato rhythm. This rhythm is further emphasised by the similarity of the consonants 'p', 'b', 'd' and 't'. The clipped, abrupt delivery that would necessarily result (in an oral form) is counterpointed by the longer vowel sounds in 'blurs', 'bare', 'elsewhere' and 'known'. Consequently, the sound emitted by the vowels has a rhythmic, marked cadence in relation to the consonants.

Beckett's emphasis on phonetic structures and on the rhythm of language demonstrates an imposition of an inward focus and autorepresentational structure on his work; that is, he imposes form, but it is, for fiction, a totally unconventional form. That is not to say that Beckett's language does not 'signify', but rather, that words function in different, alternative ways, that their intra-linguistic qualities (in repetition and in punning) also suggest another level of intelligibility: that of music, as in the medieval, antiphonal chants. In becoming part of a musical structure, the function of language is other than a purely signifying one. Meaning yields, temporarily, to tone and rhythm. Reading aloud, then, the reader as speaker and listener moves beyond the confines of the role ascribed to him through his contract with the printed page and comes to experience, actually, the immediacy normally granted only with oral speech. This overcoming of the distance between the printed page and the reader is clearly related more to the dynamics of script and theatre than to fiction. In fact, Beckett's post-trilogy prose uses techniques that resemble dramatic strategies and forms, emphasising language as an event, and thereby turning fixed, written form into something closer to a performance of rhythmic sound and movement.

If we reconsider, then, the reader's role in these texts, we see that this need to create coherent, meaningful structures out of the text can obviously be exploited by an author like Beckett who deliberately writes texts that force us to make 'premature closures'. Moreover, because of the openness of Beckett's syntax, his texts deliberately tease us with 'closures' that can never happen.

Yet the very process involved in our making 'anticipatory adjustments' and 'partial closures' is, in fact, a mediation between the texts' potentialities of meaning and those of meaninglessness. The result of this 'game-playing' with the reader's need or desire to construct meaning is our actual experiencing of Beckett's world as one that is indeterminate, chaotic, and seemingly devoid of a *primum mobile*. It is, therefore, secret, mysterious, and inexplicable. As Beckett said in 'The Lost Ones',[18] 'inside the cylinder alone are certitudes to be found, and without nothing but mystery' (p. 70). Only when we are given the certitude of form can we usually claim knowledge of a thing. Yet it is this very expectation of living that is denied us in Beckett's world. We only have the mystery, the unfathomable world Frank Kermode[19] considers the 'secret' text.

Thus Beckett destroys the architectural framework found in traditional narrative. When any written text is transposed from the printed page to the mind of the reader, what Fish calls the 'active and activating consciousness of the interpreting reader', the result of such hermeneutic transaction, according to William Spanos,[20] is as follows: the reified text, a 'graspable icon', emerges explicitly as verbal text, a text to be heard. Transformed into an 'event', and experienced hermeneutically as event, the fiction comes to be entertained within the atemporal mind of the reader, within the reality of his/her inner voice. Annexed to the reader's/listener's cerebral process, it exists there as a reality.

This fiction, then, which ultimately destroys its own sustaining forms and conventions, and which attests to its own duplicity, is characterised by an arbitrary – or at least unconventional – structure, a structure which parodies its own form. Beckett's rhetoric of abstraction – the 'tattered syntaxes'[21] (*All Strange Away*) – works to make us aware that, as Linda Hutcheon[22] says in another context, this fiction is both 'self-conscious, and self-critical': 'It is process as well as product; both transitive and intransitive, it is itself the paradox facing the reader. It attempts representation while discarding the myth of representation' (p. 141). Finally, 'this fiction tries to transcend its own textual limitations while never forgetting that this is impossible'. Here, the reference to parody is important since Beckett's self-plagiarism (found in the complex, intricate, intra-inter-textual references) does involve – what Hutcheon calls – a 'trans-contextualisation' in which elements are 're-functionalised'. According to Hutcheon, parody can be a personal act of supersession, an inscription of literary-historical continuity, a constructive principle.

In Beckett's prose and drama, imitation, repetition and self-plagiarism indeed serve as parody, but with a different emphasis. On the one hand, self-referentiality in Beckett expresses the relentless eternity of the self condemned to speak forever. On the other hand, however, such self-plagiarism, or parody, does not so much refurbish the fiction (as Hutcheon suggests is the role of modern parody) as exhaust it, through attrition, so that we have, as Beckett says, the same old thing, where nothing changes.

Notes

1. Frank Kermode, *The Sense of an Ending* (London: Oxford University Press, 1967).
2. Mikhail Bakhtin, *The Dialogic Imagination*, edited by Michael Holquist; trans. Caryl Emerson and Michael Holquist (Austin, Texas: University of Texas Press, 1981). Bakhtin employs the label 'chronotope' (literally 'time space') to express 'the intrinsic connectedness of temporal and spatial relationships that are artistically expressed in literature' (p. 84). Although originally a mathematical term coined by Einstein, 'chronotope' exemplifies the type of terminology that has been used by literary critics, but that Beckett's fiction forces us to re-evaluate. Chronotopes fuse 'temporal and spatial indicators' into 'one carefully thought out, concrete whole' so that time 'thickens, takes on flesh, becomes artistically visible', and space, likewise, 'becomes charged and responsive to the movements of time, plot and history' (p. 84).
3. Since I will be using the term 'hermeneutics' throughout this paper, some clarification as to its use is needed. For classification, I refer to Richard Palmer's book, *Hermeneutics: Interpretation Theory in Schleiermacher, Dilthey, Heidegger, and Gadamer* (Evanston: Northwestern University Press, 1969). In his explanatory chapter, 'The Origins and Three Directions of The Meaning of *Hermēneuein-Hermēneia*', Palmer says:

> The Greek word *hermeios* referred to the priest at the Delphic oracle. This word and the more common verb *hermēneuein* and noun *hermēneia* point back to the wing-footed messenger-god Hermes, from whose name the words are apparently derived (or vice versa?). Significantly, Hermes is associated with the function of transmuting what is beyond human understanding into a form that human intelligence can grasp. The various forms of the word suggest the process of bringing a thing or situation from unintelligibility to understanding.

> Moreover, says Palmer, 'something foreign', 'separated in time,

space, or experience is made familiar, present, comprehensible'. In terms of literary interpretation, although the text may be 'separated in its subject from us by time, space, [and] language', the task of interpretation is to transform the text into something intelligible' (pp. 13–14).

Important here is the hermeneutical emphasis on language as the spoken word:

> Saying and oral recitation as 'interpretation' remind literary people of a level too many of them tend to discount or even forget. Yet literature derives much of its dynamism from the power of the spoken word. From time immemorial the greater works in language have been meant to be spoken aloud and heard. The powers of spoken language should remind us of an important phenomenon: the weakness of written language. Written language lacks the primordial 'expressiveness' of the spoken word. Admittedly, the writing down of language fixes and preserves it, gives it durability, and is the foundation of history (and literature), but at the same time it weakens it.   (p. 15)

See also Jacques Derrida *Of Grammatology*, translated by Gayatri Chakravorty Spivak (Baltimore and London: Johns Hopkins University Press, 1976). Derrida discusses the relationship between 'phon-ocentrism' and '*logo*centrism', believing that the 'first and last things are the Logos, the word' (Translator's preface, p. lxviii).

4. Samuel Beckett, *Lessness*, first published as *Sans* (Paris: Editions de Minuit, 1969). Trans. by the author (London: Calder and Boyars, 1970). Also published in *Six Residua* (London: John Calder, 1978). Henceforward, all further page references are to this edition and will be in parentheses, in the text.

5. Samuel Beckett, 'Sounds' in *Essays in Criticism*, 28, 2 (April 1978), pp. 156–7. Henceforward, all further page references are to this edition and will be in parentheses, in the text.

6. See Edwin Muir's *The Structure of the Novel* (London: The Hogarth Press, 1957). According to Muir, 'the imaginative world of the dramatic novel is in Time, the imaginative world of the character novel is in Space'.

7. See Alain Robbe-Grillet, *For a New Novel*, trans. Richard Howard (New York: Grove Press, 1965). According to Robbe-Grillet, the nineteenth-century realist novel 'tended to impose the image of a stable, unequivo-cal, entirely decipherable universe' (p. 32). The 'intelligibility' of the world was assumed and elements of fiction followed its logic: 'unconditional adoption of chronological development, linear plots, regular trajectory of passions, impulse of each episode toward a conclusion' (p. 32). In this more traditional fiction, objects formed the *significant* 'fabric of the plot' (p. 20). In opposition to this sort of '*significant*' fiction stands the New Novel. It denies narrative chron-ology and linear progression, and emphasises a time that is in the present indicative, a perpetual present in which 'space destroys time,

and time sabotages space'. As Robbe-Grillet notes: 'Description makes no headway, contradicts itself, turns in circles. Moment denies continuity' (p. 155).

8. References to Beckett's residual fiction do not relate specifically to the *Six Residua*, but to that corpus of short fiction subsequent to *How It Is* and *Texts for Nothing*.

9. See Marilyn Rose, 'The Lyrical Structure of Beckett's *Texts for Nothing*', *Novel*, 4, 3 (Spring 1971), pp. 223–30.

See also Eugene Webb, *Samuel Beckett: A Study of His Novels* (Seattle and London: University of Washington Press, 1973). Webb is concerned with the form of Beckett's post-trilogy prose, and in his discussion of the composition of Beckett's novels, he takes into account the form of Beckett's recent short fiction: 'Imagination Dead Imagine', 'Enough', 'Ping' and the then untranslated 'The Lost Ones'. Webb suggests that the composition of *How It Is* is 'something very close to music', resulting in a work patterned on the sonata.

See also John Mood, '"Silence Within": A Study of the *Residua* of Samuel Beckett', *Studies in Short Fiction*, 7 (1970), pp. 385–401.

See also John E. Grant, 'Imagination Dead?' *James Joyce Quarterly*, 8, 4 (Spring 1971), pp. 336–62.

See also Paul St-Pierre, '*Comment c'est* de Beckett: Production et déception du sens', *Ecrivains de la modernité*, ed. Brian T. Fitch (Paris: Minard, 1981), pp. 89–114. St-Pierre, in his analysis of *Comment c'est* says: '*le texte moderne reste un jeu – jeu de mots – et Comment c'est s'inscrit pleinement dans cette modernité*' (p. 90). Moreover, '*[l]a modernité s'oppose à ce monde (dé)fini et s'installe dans l'infini du jeu*' (p. 90). St-Pierre also notes that Beckett's texts deny '*un signifié unique*' in favour of a '*pluralisation des signifiés*' (p. 91) – the French title, *Comment c'est*, becomes phonetically '*comme on sait/commençait.*' The result of such pluralisation of meaning, though, is paradoxically semantic evacuation: '*ces textes se mettent perpetuellement en abyme. . . . Ces textes correspondraient à une nouvelle définition du signe – le signe comme renvoi . . . la désintégration du signe*' (pp. 89–90). This game or play is created through quotation and repetition: '*l'opposition entre la parole et l'écriture, le statut de Je*' (p. 92).

See also Marike Finlay, '"Foirades" de Beckett: métonymie à la lettre, métaphore à l'oeuvre, embrayage du discours dualiste', *Ecrivains de la modernité*, ed. Brian T. Fitch (Paris: Minard, 1977). According to Finlay:

> *Il semble que Beckett y joue et déjoue la thématique et la structure de sa prose qui s'y retrouvent en miniature. Étant aussi une sorte d'exercice philosophique, les [("Foirades")], dans un style volontairement paradoxal et moqueur, peuvent être prises dans le sens d'un catalyseur critique qui par association et par superposition des structures, permet d'aller du plus petit au plus grand, du plus grand au plus petit. Entrons dans ce cercle herméneutique.* (pp. 65–6)

10. Samuel Beckett, *How It Is* (New York: Grove Press, 1964). First

published as *Comment c'est*, trans. by the author (Paris: Editions de Minuit, 1960). Henceforward, all further page references are to this edition and will be in parentheses in the text.

11. Stanley Fish, *Self-Consuming Artifacts: The Experience of Seventeenth-Century Literature* (Berkeley: University of California Press, 1972). Henceforward all further page references are to this edition and will be in parentheses, in the text.

12. Samuel Beckett, *Three Novels* (London: Calder, 1959). This edition contains *Molloy, Malone Dies* (first published as *Molloy* and *Malone Meurt* in Paris: Editions de Minuit, 1951. *Molloy* trans. by the author. *Malone Meurt* trans. Patrick Bowles in collaboration with the author). *The Unnamable* (First published as *L'Innomable* in Paris: Editions de Minuit, 1953, trans. by the author).

13. Stanley Fish, *Is There A Text in This Class? The Authority of Interpretive Communities* (Cambridge, Mass.: Harvard University Press, 1980). Henceforward, all further page references are to this edition and will be in parentheses, in the text.

14. Samuel Beckett, *Imagination Dead Imagine* (first published *Imagination morte imaginez* in Paris: Editions de Minuit, 1965). Trans. by the author; reprinted in *Six Residua* (London: John Calder, 1978). Henceforward, all further page references are to this edition and will be placed in parentheses, in the text.

15. See also Elizabeth Bregman Segrè, 'Style and Structure in Beckett's *Ping*: That Something Itself' in *Journal of Modern Literature*, 6, 1 (February 1970), pp. 127–47. According to Segrè, there are 'endo-linguistic' and 'exo-linguistic' associations in Beckett's language. The term 'exo-linguistic' means that the content of words is 'based on associations exterior to language, to those objects and actions to which words refer'. 'Endo-linguistic', however, means that the content of words is 'based on associations interior to language, on its syntactic, rhythmic, and phonetic relations' (p. 133). For further reference, see William Bright, 'Points de contact entre langage et musique', *Musique en jeu*, 5 (1971), p. 71.

16. Douglas Hofstadter, *Gödel, Escher, Bach* (New York: Basic Books, 1979), p. 9.

17. Samuel Beckett, *Ping* (first published as *Bing* in Paris: Editions de Minuit, 1966). Trans. by the author; reprinted in *Six Residua* (London: John Calder, 1978). Henceforward, all further page references are to this edition and will be in parentheses, in the text.

18. Samuel Beckett, *The Lost Ones* (first published as *Le Dépeupleur* in Paris: Editions de Minuit, 1970). Trans. by the author; reprinted in *Six Residua* (London: John Calder, 1978). Henceforward all further page references are to this edition and will be in parentheses, in the text.

19. Frank Kermode, *The Genesis of Secrecy: On the Interpretation of Narrative* (Cambridge, Mass.: Harvard University Press, 1980).

20. William Spanos, 'Breaking the Circle: Hermeneutics as Dis-Closure' in *Boundary 2*, 5 (Winter 1977), pp. 423–53.

21. Samuel Beckett, *All Strange Away* in *Journal of Beckett Studies*, 3 (Summer 1978), pp. 1–9.

22. Linda Hutcheon, *A Theory of Parody: The Teachings of Twentieth-Century Art Forms* (New York and London: Methuen, 1985). Henceforward, all further page references are to this edition and will be in parentheses, in the text.

Bibliography

Primary sources
Beckett, Samuel, *Three Novels* (London: Calder, 1959).
——, *How It Is* (New York: Grove Press, 1964).
——, *Six Residua* (London: John Calder, 1978).
——, *Sounds, Essays in Criticism*, 28, 2 (April 1978), 156–7.
——, *All Strange Away, Journal of Beckett Studies*, 3 (Summer 1979), 1–9.

Secondary sources
Bakhtin, Mikhail, *The Dialogic Imagination*, trans. Caryl Emerson and Michael Holquist, ed. Michael Holquist (Austin, Texas: University of Texas Press, 1981).
Derrida, Jacques, *Of Grammatology*, trans. Gayatri Chakravorty Spivak (Baltimore and London: Johns Hopkins University Press, 1976).
Finlay, Marike, '"Foirades" de Beckett: Métonymie à la lettre, métaphore à l'oeuvre, embrayage du discours dualiste', *Ecrivains de la modernité*, ed. Brian T. Fitch (Paris: Minard, 1981, 65–88).
Fish, Stanley, *Is There A Text in This Class? The Authority of Interpretive Communities* (Cambridge, Mass.: Harvard University Press, 1980).
——, *Self-Consuming Artifacts: The Experience of Seventeenth-Century Literature* (Berkeley: University of California Press, 1972).
Grant, Gerald, 'Imagination Dead?' *James Joyce Quarterly*, 8, 4 (Spring 1971), 336–62.
Hofstadter, Douglas, *Gödel, Escher, Bach: An Eternal Golden Braid* (Vintage Books; New York: Basic Books, 1979).
Hutcheon, Linda, *A Theory of Parody: Teachings of Twentieth-Century Art Forms* (New York and London: Methuen, 1985).
Kermode, Frank, *The Genesis of Secrecy: On the Interpretation of Narrative* (Cambridge, Mass.: Harvard University Press, 1980).
——, *The Sense of an Ending* (New York: Oxford University Press, 1967).
Mood, John, '"Silence Within": A Study of the *Residua* of Samuel Beckett', *Studies in Short Fiction*, 7, 3 (Summer 1970), 385–401.
Muir, Edwin, *The Structure of the Novel* (London: The Hogarth Press, 1957).
Palmer, Richard, *Hermeneutics: Interpretation Theory in Schleiermacher, Dilthey, Heidegger, and Gadamer* (Evanston: Northwestern University Press, 1969).
Robbe-Grillet, Alain, *For a New Novel*, trans. Richard Howard (New York: Grove Press, 1965).
Rose, Marilyn, 'The Lyrical Structure of Beckett's *Texts for Nothing*', *Novel*, 4, 3 (Spring 1971), 223–30.

Segrè, Elizabeth B., 'Style and Structure in Beckett's *Ping*: That Something Itself', *Journal of Modern Literature*, 6, 1 (February 1970), 127–47.

Spanos, William, 'Breaking the Circle: Hermeneutics as Dis-Closure', *Boundary 2*, 5 (Winter, 1977), 423–53.

St-Pierre, Paul, *'Comment c'est* de Beckett: Production et déscription du sens', *Ecrivains de la modernité*, ed. Brian T. Fitch (Paris: Minard, 1981), pp. 89–114.

Webb, Eugene, *Samuel Beckett: A Study of His Novels* (Seattle and London: University of Washington Press, 1973).

6

Fizzles by Samuel Beckett: The Failure of the Dream of a Never-ending Verticality

Paola Zaccaria

It is very difficult to give an account of the genesis and chronology of the short stories collected in the volume *Fizzles* (Fr. *Foirades*).[1] The five *Fizzles*, written between 1950 and 1960, were published in the French magazine *Minuit* in 1973; in 1976 four editions in volume of the *Fizzles* were published: *Pour finir encore et Autres Foirades* (Paris: Editions de Minuit), *For to end yet again and Other Fizzles* (London, Calder), and two American editions by Grove Press and Petersburg Press respectively. Each of the four editions arranged the stories in a different order, with the result that there can be countless readings of the text.

In this paper, I will discuss the short stories following the order of the Grove Press edition, namely:

1 *He is barehead*	5 *Closed space*
2 *Horn came*	6 *Old earth*
3 *Afar a bird*	7 *Still*
4 *I gave up*	8 *For to end yet again.*[2]

In the Petersburg Press edition, which collected only the original five *Fizzles/Foirades*,[3] the text, published both in French and in the English versions, are enriched with thirty-three etchings by Jasper Johns. The back cover gives some information about the collaboration between the two artists:

The French texts first appeared in 1972; the English texts were written by Samuel Beckett in 1974 for this collaboration. The

etchings were made by Jasper Johns and proofed and printed at
the Atelier Grommelynck in Paris in 1975 and 1976. . . . Each
book is signed by the author and the artist: two hundred and
fifty numbered 1 to 250 . . . French text © Editions de Minuit
1976. English text © Samuel Beckett 1976.

Foirades/Fizzles, Beckett/Johns, text/engravure, text/etching: this
bilingual, bi-textual, bi-medial edition re-doubles the frustration
effect experienced by anyone who wants to trace *a* meaning in
Beckett's work. The fact that he does not opt for *one* language tells
us about his refusal of a language which he, like Joyce, seems to
feel as a nationalistic net, as a limit;[4] the inclusion of another form
of art, etching, in his own text, tells us about his refusal of
separation, his will to elide bounds, to mix the verbal with other
signs: here with painting, in the theatrical works he very often
erases the verbal sign to substitute it with *the* sign – the gesture,
which can also be non-gesture, absolute stillness.

The interwoven play of double texts, double readings, double
textures and double writings of signs discloses both Beckett's and
Johns' intention of emitting multiple and contradictory signals.

Fizzles/Foirades is considered by Beckett himself as being a work
with a modular structure[5] since each story can be arranged in
different, endless orders. As a work which can be discomposed
and recomposed, in the Petersburg Press edition *Fizzles* widens its
possibility of arrangement because the reader can place a story in
English near one in French and then look at one of the etchings;
or the English version of the French text can be read after a different
French text and a different etching, and so on.

Contradiction and permutation, typical features of the Beckett
microtext (stories), are also at the basis of his macrotext (*Fizzles*):
linguistic permutation (French/English), artistic permutation
(stories/etchings in the Petersburg Press edition), intratextual permutation (different arrangement of texts), extratextual permutation
(segments of previous texts are inserted in the stories).[6] Permutation
as a way out of repetition, as novelty but also as underlining of the
repetition itself. Permutation also as a denouncing of the void in
which contemporary art operates: no longer a microstructure which
has a logical relation to the macrostructure, but fragments to be
arranged in endless possible ways by the author himself, by the
editor, by the reader.

A text without binding, or with innumerable bindings, *Fizzles* puzzles the reader because of its appearance of an unfinished work. Each section or single story can be interchangeable, the 'character(s)' of each story can be exchanged: they, or rather the 'unnamed' – actually pronouns – are, deep down, endless reflections of the first pronominal entity described in the first story of the Grove Press edition, *He is barehead*:

> He is barehead, barefoot, clothed in a singlet and tight trousers too short for him, his hands have told him so, again and again, and his feet, feeling each other and rubbing against the legs, up and down calves and shins. To this vaguely prison garb none of his memories answer, so far, but all are of heaviness, in this connexion, of fullness, of thickness.[7]

His semanteme is lack: nameless, ageless, sightless, 'barehead' and 'barefoot', without memories (he finds difficulty in reconstructing the past, with the exception of the remembrance of the narrowest sideways and the noisiest falls), this creature is the most complete portrait Beckett sketches in *Fizzles*. This essential sketch-wandering-in-a-labyrinth has the same fragmented body as the entities inhabiting the other stories, the same blindness ('Do his eyes, after such long exposure to the gloom, begin to pierce it? No, and this is one of the reasons why he shuts them more and more', p. 26). Blind, he cannot see other people/himself/*in*-self, though he always hopes that

> some day he'll see himself, his whole front, from the chest down, and the arms, and finally the hands, first rigid at arm's length, then close up, trembling, to his eyes. (p. 25)

Unable to see himself, he needs someone who, from without, *seeing him, describes him*: the narrator who, most of the time, in this story, observes 'he' from a distance and describes his movements, using the camera from a short distance, sometimes the seeing eye offering unmerciful close-ups, sometimes offering the camera to the reader thus making use of the phatic function, while acting as a directorial narrator.[8]

By offering the reader an interlocutory function as regards the object of the discourse (*he*), the narrator reduces *he* to a thing which can only be portrayed, to the victim of a pitiless, indifferent, ironic eye/I.

If we take into account the text *Fizzles* according to the arrangement of the Grove Press edition, we witness a 'progressive sliding' of the narrator-role, a continuous readjustment of the narrator-object-of-the-narration relationship.

In *Fizzle 2* (*Horn came*), there is the introduction of the narrating *I* who, at night, receives Horn-*he*, listens to him speaking in the dark after having consulted his notes by the light of an electric torch: 'Then he switched it off and spoke in the dark. Light silence, dark speech' (p. 33). But since in the dark the narrator/*I* cannot see Horn, one night he begs him to 'light his face', thus marking the shifting from being a detached narrator, one who can see his character even in the dark ('He is barehead'), to the intradiegetic narrator who, besides being able to see 'the other', loses his characteristics of 'pure' narrator, outside narration, to become one of its subjects. As a matter of fact, his difficulty in seeing the other man both hides and is associated with the greater difficulty of seeing himself and of allowing himself to be seen:

> It was five or six years since anyone had seen me, to begin with myself. I mean the face I had pored over so, all down the years. now I would resume this inspection, that it may be a lesson to me, in my mirrors and looking glasses so long put away. I'll let myself be seen before I'm done.   (p. 33)

He has hidden himself from other people and from himself, but now he decides to re-enter the hall of mirrors, specular writing, the *I* who narrates. In this way, Horn, by offering the vision of 'a waning face disclosing, more and more clearly the more it entered the shadow, the one I remembered' (p. 34), functions as a Narcissus-effect. By the light of a torch, surrounded by mirrors and looking-glasses, interrupting Horn's words, though he 'did not like anyone to interrupt him' (p. 34), *I* sees *he*, his like, his peer. When he raises his eyes from the place of signs and sheds light on the darkness from which the words come and, in so doing, silences the words, *I* sees himself in the other, the narrator in the character, he recognises him(self): 'No doubt about it, it is he' (p. 34).

There is a sudden equation between the narrator and the narrated,[9] the eye and the I. Although *I* says that these images organise themselves in the outer space and that if he interposes his hand between the outside and his eyes, if he closes his eyes and takes off his glasses, he cannot see these images any longer, or they become blurred, he has to admit that this is 'a help, but not a real protection, as we shall see' (p. 34).[10] From which images does *I* want to protect himself? The image of himself? Of the other? *I* as it once was? *I* as it is today? Maybe he wants to protect himself from the re-inscription in the text, from seeing himself on the page at a time when *I* believed he was at last outside of it for ever:

> I thought I had made my last journey, the one I must try now try once more to elucidate, that it may be a lesson to me, the one from which it were better I had never returned. But the feeling gains on me that I must undertake another.   (p. 35)

To close one's eyes, to take off one's glasses, is not enough to protect oneself from mirrors. To be tired and confined to bed is not enough to protect oneself from the necessity of the journey (a mental journey, as the verb *elucidate* reveals), from the desire to see clearly. Either one goes to the place of no return – death, silence – or invalidity will not protect one from the compulsion to hold in one's hand the stick for the journey / the pen / the mirror.

—*Dark word, light silence, mirror vision*/CLICK 1/
—*To turn on the light, interrupt the word and in the silence, seeing (oneself)*/CLICK 2/
—*To turn off the light, interrupt the vision and regain the word*/CLICK 3/

since neither darkness nor glasses protect one from the images of the 'other' space.[11] When an image has been fully exhausted and a new failure has been experienced, one starts again on the journey, plays again the same tune.[12]

CLICK 1—CLICK 2—CLICK 3: (*Fizzle 3*)
CLICK 1—CLICK 2—CLICK 3: (*Fizzle 4*).

Other journeys, other intermissions, other maskings–unmaskings of textual subjects and objects. Pro/nominal division (*I/he*) instead of pro-nominal (*I*-Horn). The pro-nominal assimilation shortens distances, smooths the differences that *I* insists on proclaiming.

The vehemence with which the *I* proclaims the differences denoun-ces the interior caesura which cuts *I*.[13] His exaggerated need to deny his existence betrays his disconnection with the self, his blockage of identification, his fear of existing as a body: I, the narrating being, diacritic subjectivity and, as such, bodiless, never born (it is impossible to trace back the birth of the first story), never dead (as long as there is man, there will be stories). The urgency to deny one's existence is so strong that it needs to be reaffirmed in two repetitive short stories (*Afar a bird* and *I gave up*). Endless repetition of the denial which unmasks the feeling of uncertainty of the one who denies (himself). Repetition as regres-sion and stillness – the repetitive syntagmas derive from the compulsion to repeat, from the beating and rebeating of the death pulse. Horizontal repetition (of words) and vertical repetition (as an attempt to reach the core of the words)[14] with the body (*he*) forcing the mind (*I*) into production.

The strenuous fight between *I/He* of *Fizzles* 3 and 4 has been lethal for both fighters or, at least, has been so exhausting that both agents of narrative have, for the time being, been confined to silence and rest.[15] The two opposing forces of the short stories – contradiction and repetition – have produced the destruction of the narrative tissue. Beckett, by means of such devices as opposition, denial, contradiction, has enacted the neurosis of dialectics. At the end there is the discovery that one cannot pose questions or wait for answers, one can only think with an a-categorical thought: weariness, stillness, labour and dumbness are the other side of thought. The philosopher/artist, says Michel Foucault, must let himself be absorbed by '*la bêtise*', the boundless monotony of an ever-returning present.[16]

Repetition destroys, but it can also free the subject: as in the psychoanalytical process, the cure is a journey towards the depths whence the impulse to repetition comes.[17] Sometimes the traveller feels the need to remove the mirrors orientated toward himself, to turn them from the self elsewhere, from within to without. *Fizzle 4* ended with the assertion, 'there is nothing left in his head, I'll feed it all it needs' (p. 46). Since there is nothing left to take from *he*'s head, since *I* has completely dispossessed *he*, *I* allows him(self) the possibility of a truce; he also retires as the narrating voice residing *within* which, like a parasite, feeds on the other's body. He transforms himself into an impersonal entity which is completely absent from the text which, at this point, deals with external closed space:

Place consisting of an arena and a little ditch. Between the two skirting the latter a track. Closed space. Beyond the ditch there is nothing. (p. 49)

In the arena live millions of people, 'Never seeing, never hearing one another. Never touching' (p. 49). In the ditch, which is almost black, whereas in the beginning 'it was all bright' (p. 49), there are millions of bodies. The track, which goes around the circumference,

is made of dead leaves. A reminder of beldam nature. Dead but not rotting. Crumbling into dust rather. Just wide enough for one. On it no two ever meet. (p. 50)

It is a concentric space consisting of three circles: the outer ditch, the track and the arena. Raising his eyes from the closed space of the written text – the hall of mirrors, a body with a mirror *inside* – the writer turns to rest them upon the closed space of life – the arena, a world enclosed by track and ditch.[18] Movement from the asphyxia of personal existence to the asphyxia of public life where, as happens between *I* and *he*, there is no danger of sickness by contagion ('never touching'); on the contrary, people live fearing any contact whatever, they can only run along the track which is only wide enough for one. This narrow, circular track reminds the reader of the labyrinth of the little man in the first *Fizzle*: it is asphyctic, skirts the ditch and is in-between arena and ditch. The dead leaves, a 'reminder of beldam nature', stress the idea that it shares both of death and of life. The man in the labyrinth was threatened by falling masses, the man running along the track is threatened by its contiguity to the ditch. The former risked being crushed, the latter risked crushing himself. The greater freedom of the man on the track – he is *outside*, in the open air, and is not menaced by dangers coming from above – is only apparent. His place is closed, nonetheless: he runs, alone, towards death with no chance of meeting another body, another eye/I.

Moreover, as in *He is barehead*, movement is possible only in a vertical direction: one can climb /up/ the track, or go /down/ the arena, or fall /down/ in the ditch. In the first *Fizzle*, *he* went zigzagging /up/ for the climbing or /down/ the slope. Even the noises were produced by *vertical* falls. Man falls /down/ in life and then falls /down/ in death. Sometimes it seems possible to go uphill – the uphill sideways – but ultimately these chances reveal their deceptive, tricky nature of *fizzles*, because track and climbing are on the edge of the ditch.

Labyrinths, walls, tracks, arenas, ditches: prisons, borders, 'closed spaces'. And also: home, placenta, tomb. Actually, one is never really born in the sense of coming out in the air.[19] From up, down: fall, descent, precipice, even in birth, even in death. From inside, outside (birth), or from outside, inside (death), always on account of a vertical expulsion.[20] The horizontal space is so narrow that nothing can move from right to left, or vice versa. The law of gravity requires masses to fall /*down*/, human bodies to fall /*down*/. The compact falls and produces fragments and splinters (as far as masses are concerned), death and disintegration (as far as bodies), fragmentation of the discourse (as for narration), dust[21] and rotting (as for the word).

Even bodily sensations are felt along the vertical line: *he* in *Fizzle 1* touches, sees, or will see himself, vertically.[22] He does not embrace himself (horizontal movement), the walls do not allow him to touch himself, to touch *in*-self – the *I* which is within him; the walls prevent him from reaching himself, from reuniting his selves. It is a prohibited pleasure for the little man in a singlet, as well as for the writer who has lost his self in the writing labyrinth (he has abandoned the insecure, no-way-out sideways) to reconcile *he* with *I*, body and psyche, the narration and the narrator. But if the writer abandons the labyrinth metaphor and the crushing theme, he falls into the 'closed space' metaphor. This text, which in French is entitled 'Se voir', does not actually tell of any being who sees himself. Dead bodies and living bodies are mentioned, and even if the detailed description of the place presupposes an eye which sees other people and, by ontological transition, himself, nobody assumes the paternity of the voice, nobody says *I*. Pretensions to a-personal narration which the following short story, *Old earth*, immediately belies. Here, the eyes which see are attributed to an *I*:

> Old earth, no more lies. I've seen you, it was me, with my other's ravening eyes, too late. You'll be on me, it will be you, it will be me, it will be us, it was never us.   (p. 53)

The self-vision of *Closed space* was the vision of '(my) other's ravening eyes'; he who sees the earth is an *I* who has borrowed his eyes. That is, most probably, why he could not, in *Closed space*, say whose eyes were the seeing eyes: though they were his, placed in his skull, they also belonged to the 'other'. They were the depersonalised eyes of the ontological vision of the world – they could be anybody's eyes.

Now, *I* has finally seen the earth, though 'too late', when the earth is on the point of re-covering him, of initiating him to the osmotic process of corpse-earth which will finally cancel the otherness ('it will be you, it will be us'), and dust will return to dust. The old game of affirmation-negation is played once again.[23] Once again, but without antithetical asperities, as if the narration were going tiringly on, as if *I* were not aware of the uselessness of opposing himself, of placing himself upright (*I*) with respect to the earth, the old enemy which is awaiting *I* to shift from the vertical posture to the horizontal one. When, tired at last, *I* will lie on it, the earth will swallow the body, slowly, gradually assimilating it to herself.

Oppositions, contrasts, denials, bars, pens belong to the vertical order;[24] to put an end to the *I/he* opposition means to succumb to the horizontal – to death. Actually, the *I* of *Old earth* has just the first symptoms of sinking, he still postpones the end (of the story and of life) as the image of himself 'still, *standing* before the window' (p. 54, the italics are mine), contemplating the sky, suggests. Though he is violently shaken by 'gasps and spasms', *I* succeeds in *standing*, in placing himself against the earth, in continuing to look at the sky, ('a childhood sea, other skies, another body', p. 54). He looks upwards, to something which reminds him of childhood, the beginning, and not downwards, towards the earth which means the end.

This lyrical short story, with a quotation from Dante, '*Tristi fummo nell'aere dolce*', deals with memories which are more consistent and emotional than in the other *Fizzles*:

> For an instant I see the sky, the different skies, then they turn their faces, agonies, loves, the different loves, happiness too, yes, there was that too, unhappily. Moments of life, of mine too, among others, no denying, all said and done. Happiness, what happiness, but what deaths, what loves, I knew at the time; it was too late then.

Though the passage speaks of happiness, deaths, loves, the

emphatic and overcharged tone makes the reader suspicious of some sort of irony.[25]

The lyrical, airy flights of *Old earth* are briskly interrupted by the beginning of the following Fizzle, *Still*. As we have seen, the little bareheaded man of *Fizzle 1* has transformed himself into the narrating *I* at the mirror (*Horn came*), has narrated the impossible fight between he who writes and he who is written down (*Afar a bird* and *I gave up*), has then completely disappeared in *Closed space* where a bodiless voice speaks of the three circles of existence and, finally, has moaned for the pains and joys of life (*Old earth*). After all this, he sits now in a wicker chair, at the window, and becomes again a camera, an eye (though not an *I*): he resumes distance from his self again. The fall into sentimentalism of *Old earth* has left him shameful and with the urge to put an end to his personal life. The idea of end opens the story *Still*:

> Bright at last close of a dark day the sun shines out at last and then goes down. Sitting quite still at the valley window normally turn head now and see it . . .   (p. 19).

Eyes see, arms move, legs go to the window and then back to the chair, a trunk shifts from one position to another, although everything would convey the idea of stillness:

> though actually close inspection not still at all but trembling all over. Close inspection namely detail by detail all over to add up finally to this whole not still at all but trembling all over. But casually in this failing light impression dead still even the hands clearly trembling and the breast faint rise and fall.   (pp. 19–20)

The text entitled *Still* speaks of mobility and tremors, of a being identified only by fragments of body (eyes, arms, wrist, hands, legs, head, trunk), of an entity which is not even a pronoun: there is no *he*, all reference is made impersonally, in the infinitive – perhaps he speaks of himself in the third person or is using the imperative tense.[26] It is the extreme journey toward the killing of any corporeity (of voice) that has been so far accomplished in *Fizzles*; all the movements of the (un)still being are described in detail, but there is no trace of thought. At last out of labyrinths, underground spaces, the creature – though fearing movement – experiments with short syncopated movements and does what he

vaguely remembered in *He is barehead*: he touches a part of the
body – the head – with his hand; at last he can rest the burden of
his head in his hands. Nonetheless, the erasure of the two diegetic
entities – the subject who narrates and the narrated subject – seems
doubtful because of the repetition of the time complement: *now,
this hour*. Now when? And where? In the room with the wicker
chair? And who says 'now'? The still man or he who portrays him?
Now in the writing-room? Now in the reading-room? Here, now,
at this hour, there is just a fragmented body, apparently still,
actually shaken with tremors, who can at last rest his head in his
hands: he makes the head – the place of thoughts, memories,
where writing was born – touch the hand, the agent of writing.
The two parts reach for each other and 'the still' must surrender
to the hand's will ('head to rescue as if hand's need the greater',
p. 21). And it is not by chance that the fingers which hold the
head are the ones used in writing: thumb, forefinger and middle
finger.

The impersonal character of the prose of *Still* is contradicted by
the tremors which make the head shake before the hand comes to
rescue it. Is, perhaps, the (un)still trying to check (himself), to still
(himself), to master (himself and) his need of writing? Could the
mental and physical stillness be only an attempt to stop the hand
from writing and the head from thinking? Anyway, the attempt is
useless: the head, which wants to stand upright, which does not
like to depend on the hand, falls towards this latter, 'as if hand's
need the greater'. Night falls: night is a dark word, 'in the dark
. . . even more than ever necessary . . . the further shelter of the
hand' (p. 21).

To hold one's head in order to think, but also to sustain the
head's words with the hand's transcription: this solution is in fact
chosen in the end, when it is decided that instead of leaving 'it so
all quite still', there will be an attempt at 'listening to the sounds
all quite still head in hand listening for a sound' (p. 21). In the
dark, listening to sounds: all seems to suggest that the sounds do
not come from outside, but from the inside; Beckett himself,
speaking of his search to find the voice of his 'lost self' says
that one must sit in all tranquillity and 'get below the surface,
concentrating, *listening, getting your ear down so you can hear the
infinitesimal murmur*':[27] just what 'the still' man is going to do.

The *in*finite, circular writing presents in a dramatic way the
image of the still man in Act viii of *Fizzles*, 'For to end yet again':

For to end yet again skull alone in a dark place pent bowed on a
board to begin.　(p. 11)

End – skull alone in the dark; closed space – forehead on a board;
to begin: the reader re-encounters in this beginning the topoi
common to the previous seven acts, whereas the internal opposition
'to end/to begin' tells of the interchangeability of the two acts: to
end a text means also to begin another and, inevitably, the
beginning of a text already implies its ending.

Interchangeable contradiction which, being double-faced,
undoes itself; of course, it means to go back to short story 1,2,3,
. . . nth, 'and yet' means also to go on; some steps back 'and yet'
one goes onwards: the acquisition of a new small element justifies
the nth story and, on the other hand, it contributes to stretch the
story towards its ending, to bring the writer toward the word
'end', man toward his end, although the end is never actually
reached because, maybe, both man and narration do not so much
want to come to an end as to escape the condition of stillness or,
as J. Hansford says, nothing can end 'because nothing can be said
to have begun' (op. cit., p. 56; see note 10 above). The illusion of
progression is defeated: 'Progression in time becomes stasis (or
unending progression) in a context of timelessness'.[28] This sensation of 'end' is stressed by the language which speaks of death,
though the Beckettian *persona* does not die: he tiringly moves from
chair to window, switches on his thoughts drawing signs which
speak of an impersonal presence/absence, of human remains.

The true failure of *Fizzles* lies, most probably, in the impossibility
of writing the end, in the impossibility of (writing the story of)
death.[29] Hence, *Fizzles* are stories where the living are unborn (*He
is barehead*) and the dead do not die; the narrator fails to narrate
death and succeeds in representing the degenerative process of
physical and epistemological ageing in a lifeless, deathless and
timeless universe.

The language itself is entirely built around funeral vocabulary
whose task is to call for death (quoting only from the first eight
lines: 'skull . . . , dark place . . . , board . . . , skull in the dark
. . . , void . . . , no neck no face . . . , the box . . . , last place . . . ,
dark . . . , void . . . , place of remains . . . , dark . . . , a remain
. . . , remains. . . .'), though there are hints that, even surrounded
by remains, dust, still air, the 'skull' is not yet without pulp – it
still belongs to a living, though agonising creature. It takes but a

little – the vision of two 'white dwarfs' (p. 12) against the grey – to set the camera to work again, to lengthen the scriptorial tape, to give movement to the scene, matter to thought.

The scene takes place in the skull, cemetery of ruins, remains, falls. But, surprisingly, instead of 'going out of work', this skull goes on again:

(i) Thus the skull makes to glimmer again in lieu of going out (p. 11);

(ii) Thus then the skull last place of all makes to glimmer again in lieu of going out (p. 12).

In the skull is also set the time(lessness) of the happening: in it 'a leaden dawn' first rises then grows 'less dark till final grey' (p. 11). This *grey* immediately colours the landscape, the time, the living being, the story. From the initial black with a few patches of white (the dwarfs, the sheets of the barrow), to grey. The last/first short story is varnished with colour's non-colours, with grey predominating over black and white.[30] *Grey*: the intermediate, the indeterminate, neither black nor white, the *un*-colour which colours also the in(side), the *I*. Grey sky, grey sand, grey body of the living creature who is called 'the expelled'. And then dust everywhere, dust coming from the disintegration of the fallen fragments and which, in its turn, produces other ruins, other destruction. 'Stark erect amidst his ruins the expelled' (p. 12) sees all that greyness, but perhaps cannot see the white barrow carried by the white dwarfs:

Yet to imagine if he can see it the last expelled amidst his ruins if he can ever see it and seeing believe his eyes.   (p. 13)

This confirms that the scene is set in the (grey) skull of the writing being: he has created a grey place, a grey time, a grey body,[31] and has wrapped everything in dust; then, for a change, he has made a fragment fall ('first change of all in the end a fragment comes away and falls', p. 12), has introduced on to the scene the dwarfs, Swiftian freaks, circus memories, who push a wheelbarrow left and right for 'dung litter of laughable memory' (p. 13). But, at this point, something does not work in the skull – too much grey, perhaps – if it repeats 'first change of all a fragment comes away from mother ruin and with slow fall . . .' (p. 12). The third change (the first was the fall of fragments; the second, the vision of the dwarfs) is again first change not simply because it repeats the first, but because the skull seems to have forgotten he has already seen it. This skull tiringly works with worn-out material, and it confuses what he has already seen/written with the new material. The very forgetfulness betrays the fact that consciousness removes experience and that the imagination shapes the present after the past.[32] The similarity to a film-script is almost openly declared towards the last third of the short story:

> Then on so soft the eye does not see them go driftless. . . . Long lifted to the horizontal faces closer and closer strain as it will the eye achieves no more than two tiny oval blanks.   (p. 14)

The skull-with-eyes, at the end, records the last dramatic change:

> Last change of all in the end the expelled falls headlong down and lies back to the sky full little stretch amid his ruins.   (p. 14)

This is the true happening of all the stories: the shift from the vertical position of the various 'living failures' inhabiting all the stories, to the horizontal, oddly human posture of the last expelled who falls 'headlong down and lies back to the sky'. The humanity of the last one to be expelled lies in his 'lapislazuli eyes' (a hint of blue, again), stubbornly open, even after his body looks marble-like. At this point the reader suspects, once again, that the skull with open eyes of the fallen body belongs to the spectator–writer of the scene because, all of a sudden, the relationship between the seing eye and the dying expelled[33] becomes very close, as denounced by the unexpected intrusion of a dialogical relation between the writing skull and the fallen body: 'fall fall never fear no fear of your rising again' (p. 14). The phonetic and lexical redundancy (*fall fall, never fear no fear*) which betrays emotivity, besides the 'you' that the writing eye gives to the fallen body, suggests a relational closeness between the two which nothing said before had suggested. The antithesis without any chance of synthesis of similar situations in other stories[34] disappears here, as if the fallen body, almost dead, had put an end to the old antagonism between *I* and *he*, as if piety had at last touched that skull which persisted in surrounding himself with grey, in stiffening movement, in blocking emotivity, as the rigid, upright position of the living-dying man suggested.[35]

To yield to the horizontal, to erase the antithesis (*I/he*),[36] to lie down, means to lose one's control, to become flabby, impotent. The vertical posture held by the various living beings of the previous stories was the only possible weapon in opposing impotence, scriptural sterility and death.[37]

Once the erection has subsided, once the vertical barriers have fallen, the so far pitiless eye of the cameraman perceives the fallen being as too similar to himself and addresses him with 'you', the pronoun which presupposes a familiar relationship, and discreetly switches off the scene which has been taking place in the skull:

> Sepulchral skull is this then its last state all set for always litter and dwarfs ruins and little body   (pp. 14–15)

The skull-vision room-sepulchre closes on a panoramic image of all the elements of the film/short story which in this way remains stiffened: the vision, when fixed in writing, clots, becomes rigid. The oneiric-diegetic character of the vision is openly stated in the end: it has only been a

> dream of a way in a space neither here nor there where all the footsteps ever fell can never fare nearer to anywhere nor from anywhere further away. No for in the end for to end yet again . . . dark falls there again . . . Through it who knows yet another end beneath a cloudless sky same dark . . .   (p. 15)

And the word 'end', which the narrator had never approached so closely in the previous *Fizzles*, though resounding in the final one, is no longer called for: an end there will be, if there absolutely has to be one. In the meantime, the switch is turned off: dark again. The fact that 'For to end yet again' is the last story in the American edition and the first in the French and English editions, speaks worlds about beginnings and endings of stories and of life: the last story yet, again, a story of a failure of a dream. Last act or first act, what does it matter? From the dark other voices (other's words) will come (dark word; light silence) to end . . . ? To begin . . . ? Again . . . ?

Notes

1. In a previous article of mine on two of the Fizzles, *Afar a bird* and *I gave up*, I tried to establish the genesis of the single texts (see: 'L'*infinito* racconto di S. Beckett', *Annali della Facoltà di Lingue*, Bari, Terza serie, 1984, V, 1–2:133–47).

2. With reference to the Grove Press edition, in the Minuit edition the order is: 8, 1, 4, 2, 6, 3, 5, 7; in the Calder edition, the order is: 8, 7, 1, 2, 3, 4, 5, 6.

3. *Foirades Fizzles*, ed. Véra Lindsay (New York: Petersburg Press, 1976). The order of this edition is: 4, 1, 6, 5, 2.

4. According to Klaus Birkenhauer (*Beckett*, Hamburg, 1971) and Ruby Cohn (*Back to Beckett*, Princeton University Press, 1973), Beckett's fiction since the 1960s is world literature just as Joyce wrote an international language. Beckett's 'syntax of weakness' or 'midget grammar' is penetrated by Nothing; Joyce's language was inclusive of everything.

5. According to Jessica Prinz ('Foirades/Fizzles/Beckett/Johns', *Contemporary Literature*, Summer 1980, XXI, 3:481–510), 'the structure is "modular" because it stands in marked contrast to organic structures in which every element has a purposive, causal or logical relation to the whole' (p. 509).

6. For an analysis of *Fizzles* in the context of Beckett's production, see Rubin Rabinovitz, '*Fizzles* and S. Beckett's Earlier Production' *Contemporary Literature*, Fall 1983, XXIV, 3:307–21; John Pilling, 'Ends and Odds in Prose', in J. Knowlson and J. Pilling, *Frescoes of the Skull* (New York: Grove Press, 1980), pp. 131–91.

7. Though I follow the order of the Grove Press edition, my quotations are from the English edition (London: Calder, 1976). From now on, the page numbers will be directly recorded in the text.

8. For example, 'But see how now, having turned right, for example, instead of turning left a little further on he turns right again. And see how now again . . .' (p. 27).

9. Beckett first used the phrase 'the narrator/narrated' for Molloy, a new kind of character who, as Hugh Kenner suggested, allowed Beckett to bring the 'ambient world into existence only so far as the man holding the pencil can remember it or understand it, so that no omniscient craftsman is holding anything back, and simultaneously bringing into existence the man with the pencil, who is struggling to create himself . . .' (*A Reader's Guide to Samuel Beckett*, New York and London, Thames & Hudson, 1973, p. 94).

10. The following short story, *Afar a bird*, presents the same sudden dismissal of the 'other's' image ('but no more of him, that image', p. 40), of the vision of the other's body because of the narrator's fear of recognising him(self), or of his fear that, if the pronoun which is the object of the discourse is fully portrayed, it can become a noun.

    As James Hansford stated in '*Imagination Dead Imagine*: the imagination and its context', 'imagination cannot be dead; it can only be killed by an act of the imagination' (*Journal of Beckett Studies*, Spring 1982, 7:54). Hansford's is a very interesting essay centred on the discussion of the inside/outside, subject/object, second and third persons oppositions.

11. 'It is in the outer space, not to be confused with the other, that such images develop' (p. 34).

12. Beckett's *Fizzles* have been compared to chamber-music; the repetition of entire passages have been read like codas. For a discussion of the place of music in Beckett's art, see V. Mercier, *Beckett/Beckett* (New York and London: Oxford University Press, 1977), pp. 113–117 and 149–159.

13. Ivan Fonagy (*La ripetizione creativa*, Dedalo, 1982) calls the antithesis 'an ingenious, elegant and rebellious form of repetition' (p. 22) which 'becomes sharper and more explosive when the contradictory aspirations take place in the inside of the same body' (p. 27, my translation). Under this light, the antithetical enunciations of *I* in the Beckettian texts are the expression, on a verbal level, of the violent interior conflict which torments him. A useful essay centred on the role of schizophrenia in *Murphy* and *Watt* rich in suggestions for the reading of other texts is G. C. Barnard's *Samuel Beckett: A New Approach* (London: Dent, 1970).

14. On the idea of repetition and difference, see G. Deleuze, *Différence et répétition* (Paris: Presses Universitaires de France, 1968). According to Deleuze, when repetition takes place, death inspires the language, although by combining an element of a previous work with a new one, the writer allows disymmetry – a sort of 'opening' – to enter the dynamic process of creation.

15. As for the behaviour of the two diegetic subjects of these *Fizzles*, see my previously quoted article 'L'*infinito racconto di S. Beckett'.

16. M. Foucault, 'Theatricum Philosophicum', in G. Deleuze, *Différence et répétition*, op. cit.

17. For a thorough classification of the varieties of repetition in Beckett's trilogy, see Rubin Rabinovitz's 'Repetition and underlying meanings in Samuel Beckett's Trilogy' included in this collection, above pp. 31–67.

18. One can look on this short story as Beckett's hundredth attempt to relate his work to that of Dante. Beckett's Hell, Purgatory and Heaven are here, on this damned closed world, the earth; moreover, there is not much difference between the conditions of the beings inhabiting the three worlds.

    As for geometric shapes and the use of an observing impersonal eye, *Closed space* is strictly linked to *Imagination Dead Imagine* (1965), *Ping* (1967), *Lessness* (1970) and 'The Lost Ones' (1972) (the dates refer to the first English editions).

19. 'The air is so foul that only he seems fitted to survive it who never breathed the other, the true life-giving, or so long ago as to amount to never' (*He is barehead*, p. 29).

    Beckett in an interview claimed that he had a clear memory of his own foetal existence, one of agony and darkness (John Gruen, 'S. Beckett talks about Beckett', *Vogue*, Vol. 127, no. 2031, February 1970, p. 108).

20. Brian Finney in '*Assumption* to *Lessness*: Beckett's Shorter Fiction' (in

Beckett the Shape Changer', ed. K. Worth, London: Routledge & Kegan Paul, 1975: pp. 61–83) gives a list of Beckett's heroes who 'set out to reverse the pattern of growth, to return to the tomb of the womb', but 'conception is irreversible and these heroes are constantly being ejected from their womb-like refuges, and thrown back violently on to the stage of life' (p. 67).

Some of the later heroes spend their time wandering in search of a substitute refuge – the coffin-box, the sitting room, the basement room, the cave or shed – which are doomed to prove hopelessly inadequate.

21. *Grit* is mentioned in *Afar a bird* (p. 40); *dust* in *I gave up* and in *For to end yet again*.
22. Example 1: 'his hands have told him so, again and again, and his feet, feeling each other and rubbing against the legs, *up* and *down* calves and shins' (p. 25).
    Example 2: 'Some day he'll see himself, his whole front, *from the chest down*, and the arms, and finally the hands' (p. 25, italics are mine).
23. Example 1: 'it will be us, it was never us' (p. 53).
    Example 2: 'It won't be long now, perhaps not tomorrow, nor the day after, but too late' (p. 53).
    Example 3: 'it's a cockchafer year, next year there won't be any' (p. 53).
    Example 4: 'I turn on the light, then off' (p. 53).
24. Even the graphic layout, though apparently horizontal – the line – is actually vertical if one thinks of the text as a long ribbon of paper striped with signs: it is decidedly long rather than wide. A curiosity: in 1932, S. Beckett signed a manifesto published in *transition* entitled: 'Poetry is vertical'.
25. According to Marina Mizzau (*L'ironia*, Milano: Feltrinelli, 1984), irony is a complex, pluridimensional, polysemantic figure characterised by semantic inversion and antiphrase (p. 15).

    Irony as antiphrase, verbal inversion, dissimulation, permutation: all these interwoven figures are part of Beckett's style, are the very texture of his work. Being at the same time the ironist and the receiver of irony, the textual subject is here auto-ironic and, as such, he involves the reader in the game.
26. Some examples: (i) 'Sitting quite still . . . turn head now and see'; (ii) 'Even get up . . . and go stand by . . .'; (iii) 'Normally turn head . . . now ninety degrees to watch the sun'.
27. Quoted in: Lawrence E. Harvey, *Samuel Beckett, Poet and Critic* (Princeton: Princeton University Press, 1970), p. 247 (the italics are mine).
28. Brian Finney, 'Assumption', op. cit., p. 74. For an analysis of the tensions between stillness and progression in Beckett's dramatic production, see B. Rojtman, *Forme et signification dans le théâtre de Beckett* (Paris: A. G. Nizet, 1976).
29. All of Beckett's works, for Ruby Cohn, are 'steeped in mortality' although in his 'later work, where being is betrayed by words, nonbeing is temptation' (in: *Back to Beckett*, Princeton University Press, 1973, pp. 5–6).
30. If in previous stories – *How it is* (1964), *Imagination Dead Imagine* (1965), *Ping* (1967) – other colours (blue and rose, associated with eyes and

flesh) were mentioned, in this story, white, grey and black are all that remain; grey is the result of the combination of black and white, the noncolours par excellence.

31. It could be of interest to quote what Beckett had to say about *grey* in *The Unnamable*: 'whether all grow black, or all grow bright, or all remain grey, it is grey we need to begin with, . . . made of bright and black, able to shed the former, or the latter, and be the latter or the former alone. But perhaps I am a prey, on the subject of grey, to delusions.' (*The Unnamable*, London: Calder & Boyars, 1975, p. 17).

32. For a theory of repetition as repression and fixation, see G. Deleuze, *Différence*, op. cit.

33. The following sentence, 'breath has not left him though soundless still and exhaling scarce ruffles the dust' (p. 14) clarifies that the expelled has not yet died.

34. See the relationship between *I* and *he* in *Fizzles 3* and *4*, between *I* and the nightly visitor in *Horn came*.
    According to I. Fonagy, *La ripetizione*, op. cit., p. 94), the idea of negation associated to antithesis is strictly linked to that of annihilation. Beckett, by using repetition, then, paradoxically reinforces the idea of destruction.

35. Commenting on the body's uprightness against the fallen walls and the ruins in *Lessness* (1970), R. Cohn recalls the verse of Ecclesiastes: 'God hath made man upright, but they have sought out many inventions' (*Back to Beckett*, op. cit., p. 264).

36. The *I* (the narrating voice) as the antagonist of *he* (the object of narration) can also be explained in the light of the narcissistic theory described by G. Deleuze, *Différence*, op. cit.: the narcissistic, passive *I* believes the action to be enacted by another form of 'I' seen as 'the other', 'he'. For the narcissistic *I*, time takes the shape of a labyrinth where he loses his memory and is dragged towards a desexualised instinct of death to finally realise that he has lost his power of dying because time has neither present nor past; time is that which never ends: time does not let *I* end by dying.

37. 'I'm working with impotence, ignorance. I don't think impotence has been exploited in the past' (Beckett's statement quoted in V. Mercier, *Beckett/Beckett*, op. cit., p. 8).
    According to I. Fonagy, *La ripetizione*, op. cit., p. 93, the fall of the antithesis favours the birth of nuances. Even though in the non-colour scale, in the black-grey-white graduation there is a mitigation of the contrasts, a small transition toward variety.

7

Worstward Ho and *On-*words: Writing to(wards) the Point

Charles Krance

We are getting on, getting on.

Malone Dies

The pencil on the contrary is an old acquaintance. . . . It is very short. It is pointed at both ends. A Venus.

(Ibid.)

From where she lies she sees Venus rise. On.

Ill Seen Ill Said

Le génie parodique de Beckett nous contraint à ne connaître que l'écrivain écrivant, et non pas la chose écrite, achevée.

J.-J. Mayoux, 'La quête du mal dire'

'Words', observes Eugene Kaelin in *The Unhappy Consciousness: The Poetic Plight of Samuel Beckett* (Boston: D. Reidel, 1981), p. xvii, 'suggest meanings in the images they create.' In Beckett's recent microtrilogy – *Company*, *Ill Seen Ill Said*, and *Worstward Ho* – words persistently suggest meanings in the images they cut short of being created.

The first of these texts, *Company* (1980) is centred about the point of contact, or possibly the hypothetical lack thereof, between the Word transmitted by the voice and the Flesh of its intended receiver. The opening fragment – 'A voice comes to one in the dark. Imagine' – introduces the narrative as an extended metaphor of the word-bearing process, 'imagined' from the vantage point of reader as surrogate recipient. What oozes forth from the creative coupling of the 'one in the dark' with the reader, however, bears only a tangential and often antithetical relationship to what may have been originally intended: 'Only a small part of what is said can be verified. As for example when he hears, You are on your back in the dark. . . . But by far the greater part of what is said cannot be verified. As for example when he hears, You first saw the light on such and such a day' (Fragment 2). Such, of course, is the company that we all keep whenever we put pen to paper: however immediate the conception may appear to be at the moment that the word emerges into meaning, by the time the metaphorical ink dries, the word is often little more than the distanced representation of a gleam gone awry in our conceptual eye.

It is in Fragments 7 and 8, however, that we first receive the full impact of what it means to have meaning and image cut each other off:

A small boy you come out of Connolly's Stores holding your mother by the hand. . . . You make ground in silence hand in hand . . . and after some hundred paces the sun appears above the crest of the rise. Looking up at the blue sky and then at your mother's face you break the silence asking her if it is not in reality much more distant than it appears. The sky that is. The blue sky. Receiving no answer you mentally reframe your question and some hundred paces later look up at her face again and ask her if it does not appear much less distant than in reality it is. For some reason you could never fathom this question must have angered her exceedingly. For she shook off your little hand and made you a cutting retort you have never forgotten. (Frag. 7)

This painful (though certainly not unhumorous) reconstruction of suppressed verbal intercourse with the mother is singularly instrumental in the voice's 'homeward' bound attempts to unsay all that was, and will have been said (to be) – before as well as after this 'ground(ing) in silence'. For his unrepressed response to the tropistic influence of the rising sun, the son is rewarded with the very act the (subconscious) fear of which had led him, in the first place, to stick his neck out from behind the folds of his own censored phallocentricity. This initiatory venture into the discourse of the father leaves him castrated, good and proper, by the mother – at least figuratively. Literally, is another mat(t)er. For what specifically constitutes his infraction is the co-incidence in time of his breaking the silence, or *speaking*, and his looking at the mother's face, or *seeing*. He is in a word, and in a single one at that, guilty of having tried to take *it* all in at a glance, 'asking her if it is not in reality much more distant than it appears'. This breaking of the silence while grounded in the mother's grip creates an unbridgeable gap, cutting him loose and leaving him forever suspended between the literal and the figurative. For the *it*, whose distance, 'in reality', from its 'appearance' is in question, here is at one and the same time the sky, the mother's face, the silence . . . and the sun, whose appearance 'above the crest of the rise' was enough to set the son off on his self-alienating projection into the waywardness of language. Once it (the word) is out, he is left to contemplate the hologram of the unforgotten, and unforgiven, figure of *it all*, turning away in its wholeness from the groundless pattern of its own absent projection.

The very next fragment (8) reopens the hypothesis that 'If the voice is not speaking to him it must be speaking to another. . . . To another of that Other. Or of him. Or of another still', and so on. Much of the tension involved in keeping *Company* from 'lapp(ing) as it were in its meaninglessness (58) is hinged on this particular junction in the text. For in the face of the taciturn mother who held her ground firmly against the son's ill-conceived attempts to engage her in discourse, Beckett puts into question our most deeply-rooted (and commonly repressed) conceptions of linguistic acquisition; namely, the place and status of the word in our psychogenetic world. For it is not dialogue, but the absence thereof that functions as the alienating experience, or mirror stage, of *Company*'s auditor-cum-narratee. The mother's 'cutting retort' is thus both a literal act and a symbolic, verbal gesture, linked forever in his affective memory, and repeated each time another voice is heard from within the matrix of his consciousness. Concomitantly, each time it resurfaces as the voiced presence of a hypothetical (m)other, it reframes the mirrored opposition of self to other in a context of a never-to-be-fulfilled desire. Rather than provide the means of self-inscription within the folds of the (m)Other, the Word in Beckett's late discourse constitutes instead 'a potent tool for repressing knowledge of that gap, the face in the mirror', in a word, 'the Other'.[1] Beckett's auditor is thus left hanging, hungering for that lost locus where there might be constituted the hypothetical 'him' to whom language is spoken as well as the equally hypothetical 'he' who has it speak.[2]

'Headed toward death', writes Foucault, 'language turns back upon itself; it encounters something like a mirror; and to stop this death which would stop it, it possesses but a single power: that of giving birth to its own image in a play of mirrors that has no limits.' This epigraph to Vincent Pecora's recent essay on Joyce's '"The Dead" and the Generosity of the Word' (*PMLA*, 101, no. 2, March 1986, pp. 233–45) connects nicely with the second panel of Beckett's triptych, *Ill Seen Ill Said* (1981). This fragmented text attempts to tell the story of an old spectral figure who, spellbound by the image of her own star rising in the heavens, and unable fully to absorb the spectacle of it all, prepares her exit from 'the inexistent centre' (Frag. 2) of her own mirrored absence:

> Absence supreme good and yet. Illumination then go again and on return no more trace. On earth's face. Of what was never. And if by mishap some left then go again. For good again. So on. Till no more trace. On earth's face. Instead of always the same place. Slaving away forever in the same place. At this and that trace. And what if the eye could not? No more tear itself away from the remains of trace. Of what was never. Quick say it suddenly can and farewell say say farewell. If only to the face. Of her tenacious trace. (60)

Her fate, like that of her appendage, the 'drivelling scribe' who from the beginning of the text spurs her 'on', is to remain in a state of perpetual suspension between the spell of the ill-seen image and its achievement in an equally ill-fated representation: 'Such equal liars both' (38).

'From where she lies she sees Venus rise', as the very first line of the text informs us. (The name of Venus, here, can refer simultaneously to the planet named after the goddess of love and beauty, and to the double-pointed pencil stub with which Beckett's narrator has been inscribing the record of his own demise, ever since *Malone Dies*.) It is *she*, who, as bearer of language for her scribe, is 'headed toward death', encountering 'something like a mirror' as she goes on. What that 'something' is, or rather what form the encounter with that something may take, constitutes the speculative and backsliding progression of the microtrilogy, as it spills over into the third slender volume, *Worstward Ho* (1983).

'Somehow again on back to the bowed back alone. Nothing to show a woman's and yet a woman's. Oozed from softening soft the word woman's' (*W.Ho*, 68). In a textual universe as hellbent on achieving impossible extinction as *Worstward Ho*'s is, it is perhaps not a mere accident that it is precisely in this fragment that the word 'word' appears, or rather oozes – for the first and last time – in its singular singularity.[3] The word 'woman's', which also makes its initial appearance in this fragment, is of course what the word 'word' is meant to designate. But, in the process, the word 'word' is also cut off from its own signified – appended, as it were, to nothing, with 'Nothing to show' for it. The word 'woman's', in all its possessiveness, has thus reduced (indeed emasculated) the signifier to the role of pointless pointer: the oozing by means of which the word 'woman's' finds its way into the text appropriates – by its engulfing absorption with itself – the very sign of the pointer whose only reason for being is to give it body and thereby bring it into focus. We have here an instance of that precise point around which the Beckettian enterprise is structured. The singular Word, having been oozed out, or literally ex-pressed from Nothing ('Nothing to show a woman's and yet a woman's') can only be seen as the result of a deliberately repressed attempt to reinscribe the hypothetical locus of lost speech (abandoned, left hanging by the (m)other, but never quite forgotten) with an internalised phallocentric Verb. The word 'word', in all its unspoken potential, illustrates precisely what Caryl Emerson designates as the 'potent tool' for repressing knowledge not only of the Other, but also of 'the gap between inner and outer speech' ('The Outer Word', op. cit., p. 32). With the word out, on the other hand, we 'Ooze on back not to unsay but say again the vasts apart' (70).

Worstward Ho thus constitutes an attempted project whereby the signifier, left to its abandoned resources, strikes out to charter a new passage through – and, indeed, on the other side of – language. Eugene Kaelin observes, with regard to *Texts for Nothing*, that 'writing as an experience becomes the discovery of finding a way out' of the relationship that binds creator to creature (*The Unhappy Consciousness*, op. cit., p. 296). This notion presents a rather involved problematic: for whatever else enters the relation out of which writing, as an experience, can hypothetically discover a way, accommodation must be made for the act of writing itself. *Worstward Ho* offers us just such a picture of writing, searching for a way to write itself out. The initial difficulty that the reader experiences in the negative progression of this quest is due to 'Beckett's constant concern for getting it right, for making the direct point indirectly, to *show* and not merely to tell.'[4] Which is another way of saying that intrinsic to *Worstward Ho*'s project is its commitment to get it all wrong . . . *it* being the ideal reintegration, from within the writing act itself, of the abandoned signifier with its signified gone awry – an unveiling, as it were, of the very matrix of the *oeuvre*'s mystery.

Fragment 35 makes this direct point indirectly as well – or as ill – as another:

> Whose words? Ask in vain. Or not in vain if say no knowing. No saying. No words for him whose words. Him? One. No words for one whose words. One? It. No words for it whose words. Better worse so.

The underlying strategy of such writing can be traced back to Beckett's famous dictum of 1949: 'There are many ways in which the thing I am trying in vain to say may be tried in vain to be said', at the heart of which lies Beckett's pronounced 'fidelity to failure', whose principle he recognised in the works of Bram van Velde: 'to be an artist is to fail, as no other dare fail.'[5] Failure, as a measure of the success that the writing process may or may not achieve, can only be recognised at the expense of its own project. The reason for this paradoxical quagmire is that writing, as an act, is not only predicated on the occasion that gives it rise – even if that occasion is the commitment to failure itself – but in addition secretes its own endless chain of cause and effect. Beckett's choice of words to express van Velde's heroic stance in the face of the proliferation of the feasible is in itself revealing: 'I suggest that van Velde is the first whose painting is bereft, rid if you prefer, of occasion in every shape and form, ideal as well as material' (ibid., p. 143). To emulate van Velde's heroic standoff, for the writer, is tantamount to submitting to the ineffable appeal of the principle of failure as occasion – hence, as prime mover in the relation between creator and creature (or 'representer and representee' (ibid.)). It is of course this relation itself that Beckett consistently seeks the means of subverting:

> I know that all that is required now, in order to bring even this

horrible matter to an acceptable conclusion, is to make of this submission, this admission, this fidelity to failure, a new occasion, a new term of relation, and of the act which, unable to act, obliged to act, he makes, an expressive act, even if only of itself, of its impossibility, of its obligation.   (Ibid., p. 145)

Thus, 'what Beckett must have seen' in van Velde's pictures, according to a later interpreter, is 'a visible demonstration of forms laboring to achieve formlessness . . . for here creation seems to disarticulate itself into conflict, catastrophe'. And in Beckett's own words, also from 1949, this excerpted description of van Velde's painterly process: 'An endless unveiling, veil behind veil, . . . towards the unveilable, the nothing, the thing again.'[6] The closer such writing comes to the unveiling of its own matrix – as is clearly the point with fragment 45: 'Next the so-said seat and germ of all. . . . skull and stare alone' – the nearer it gets to that 'place of impenetrable nearness', the 'burial in the unique' which Beckett long since sensed was behind the impossible task that the painter Bram van Velde had set for himself (see Albright, *Representation and the Imagination*, op. cit., Plate 8). Fragment 35 thus represents just one of many moments in the Beckett *oeuvre* which openly skirt the issue of zeroing in on the source of it all; for once the final nail is struck, what need remains of the hammer (unless, of course, other 'devisers devising' conjure up additional lids to nail down).

However, unlike countless other attempts before it to get it all said so as to have unsaid it all, *Worstward Ho* commits the initial error of predicating (i.e. grounding) its entire strategy of undoing itself on the projection into beinglessness of nothing less than Being itself. Thus, from its very inception, the opening vocable, *On*, or *being* in Greek, engages the ensuing enterprise upon an endlessly predatory 'gnawing' away at the meaning of being – 'Preying since first said on foresaid remains' (30), 'Gnawing to be gone' (84).[7]

As Eugene Kaelin notes, with regard to 'Beckett's fundamental aesthetic project', 'The expressiveness of the aesthetic context results from the saturation of the linguistic symbols, and is felt as the tense opposition between the negative and the positive held necessarily together as they are forged into synthesis by the author's opening and closing words' (*The Unhappy Consciousness*, op. cit., p. 303). The opening *and* closing words of *Worstward Ho*, however, are already firmly embodied in the opening fragment, thus foreclosing the 'expressiveness' of the 'aesthetic project' by preempting the saturation point of those selfsame 'linguistic symbols' whose 'tense opposition' is already projected as having been resolved: 'On. Say on. Be said on. Somehow on. Till nohow on. Said nohow on.' 'On' already embodies the entire project within the preempted space of its own projectability. It *appears in* the text as *being* itself, while at the same time – and in the same space – foreclosing the need to go on. Whence the negative – the presence of which is essential for the expressiveness to be felt as tension – in such an opener, which avowedly foreshadows its having succeeded to fail? Could the pointlessness of the whole project lie in the very unnegativibility of negation itself? If such is the case, then the writing which endows the project with its dynamism must on the one hand be directed towards the point of pointlessness, while on the other hand it must relentlessly avoid, circle, and skirt the point towards which it is directed.[8] The writing of *Worstward Ho*, in other words, must derive its tension from the incapacity of its words to contain *and* express, in the same breath, the worstwardness of its negative progression.[9]

On is the very word of Being, the sign of which is its utter needlessness of language. Therein, perhaps, lies the greatest impossibility to date that Beckett has (playfully?) set out for himself to undo in the writing of *Worstward Ho*: for the *is*ness of *Being* can only be shown *to be* by the needlessness of linguistic utterance,[10] while the latter, in turn, can only demonstrate, or ex/press *its* needlessness by *de-scribing* itself out of 'the house of Being', namely 'Language' itself (Butler, *Samuel Beckett and the Meaning of Being*, op. cit., p. 178). The 'negativisation' of discourse in this text of Beckett enters a sphere of writing (or literary space) that is not unlike that of Maurice Blanchot. Writing, for both Beckett and Blanchot, is a way out of – or at worst away from – the point of contact between sign and signified. For the one as for the other, writing is 'a kind of clustering of tentative entries into the narrative',[11] while at the same time it traces a process of endless evasion from its own foreclosure, which is always already there, in the thereness of its own, articulated inscription. In a work like *Worstward Ho*, not only is syntax *grounded* on a 'grammar for being elsewhere', its writing project itself, and the *désoeuvrement*[12] which it embodies, constitute a quest for a more fruitful field of failure in which to be inscribed.

Indeed, the entire course that a text like *Worstward Ho* charts out, in its self-proclaimed quest for the place of ultimate failure, seems (as we've already suggested) to encircle the point of its own pointlessness. What's more, its writing makes this point most pointedly, as it reiterates itself to(wards) the point of near-nothingness. The project of this kind of writing, as Blanchot describes it, points in a direction which is diametrically opposed to the premise of its own perfectability. It is a writing away from its own writeability, an inscription begging out of its inscribableness. The kind of true writing to which Beckett and Blanchot have dedicated their lives begins at the threshold of its own undoing; its point of departure lies within its own impetus to write itself out . . . and, in the process, to (re)inscribe itself with the very outwardness of its self-annihilating projection, as it seeks that point where nothing remains to be revealed, short of the point of intimate contact where *here*ness and *nothing*ness meet.

'Whenever art happens' (Heidegger writes) 'i.e. whenever there is a beginning – a thrust enters history, history begins either for the first time or over again.'[13] With the thrust onward of 'On', however, it would seem instead that what happens thereafter is simultaneously breaking new ground *as* it begins all over again: 'All of old. Nothing else ever. Ever tried. Ever failed. No matter. Try again. Fail again. Fail better' (Fragment 4). 'A genuine beginning' (Heidegger goes on) 'is, as a leap, always a leap forward, in which everything to come is already leaped over, even if as something disguised. The beginning [thus] already conceals within itself the end' (Heidegger, 'The Origin of the Work of Art'). *Worstward Ho*, on the other hand, rather than conceal its end within its beginning, openly displays it, as the opening fragment preempts the possibility of its own thrust's inclusiveness within the area of the fiction to come (Heidegger's 'everything to come as something disguised'). Or, to put it another way, the groundlessness of the fiction to come is already grounded – indeed embodied – in Being, whose *On*(e)-ness, once iterated, leaves little room for any activity other than its own reiteration.

The entire project of *Worstward Ho* constitutes a quest for what little remains remain for the creative activity to embark upon as it sees itself being closed in by the embodiment of its own previous ventures towards nothingness. Picking up where *Ill Seen Ill Said* left off, in the self-consuming search for 'the wrong word' with which 'to end yet again', Beckett has perhaps at last lighted upon the right 'wrong word'. *One* right wrong word. *On*. On: the embodiment of Being whose pre-emptive presence casts all else in the shades of Nothingness, a beginninglessness opening on to an endless disclosure of its own beginninglessness. The figure and ground, rolled into one, of hereness and nothingness in endlessly repeated juxtaposition. *On* – 'the so-said seat and germ of all' – is always already there, projecting itself into being through the reiteration of everything the presence of which (and of whom) it preempts.[14] *On* thus provides the hologrammatic outline of absence, which simultaneously besets and is beset by presence: 'On. Say on. Be said on. . . . Till nohow on.' – A more laborious articulation of the loss of the writer's love's labour is indeed hard to imagine. Yet this is precisely what these demanding texts require. Let us not abandon ship, therefore, but instead take another look at the obsessiveness of these reiterations.

'On', the opening vocable in *Worstward Ho*, is a reiteration of the second statement of its predecessor, *Ill Seen Ill Said*, in which it clearly functions as prod: 'From where she lies she sees Venus rise. On. From where she lies when the skies are clear she sees Venus rise followed by the sun. Then she rails at the source of all life. On.' The 'On' which sets the old woman in *Ill Seen Ill Said* off from the outset derives from Beckett's translation of 'Encore' (in *Mal vu mal dit*). As if it were not enough for her to personify figuratively ageless imagination labouring on, in the French text Beckett has her bearing witness, *reflexively*, to her own star rising, and, in the process, to the reiteration of her own embodiment, *in absentia* (as it were), 'At the inexistent centre of a formless place' (*Ill Seen*, Frag. 2): '*Da sa couche elle voit se lever Vénus. Encore. . . . Elle en veut alors au principe de toute vie. Encore.*' It is the reiteration of *Encore* that gives rise to her embodiment, *en corps*, against whose life-source she rails in vain – a fact made explicitly clear (for once) by the time we light upon the beginning fragments of *Worstward Ho*, when from the opening 'On. Say on' we fall under the labouring spell of *Ill Seen*, Frag. 2 ('Quick then still under the spell of Venus . . .'), and follow through, in Fragment 3 of *Worstward Ho*, with 'Say a body. Where none.'

Two beginnings, (col)lapsing towards worstwardness: 'First the body. No. First the place. No. First both' and 'So on . . . Still worse again' (*W. Ho*, Frag. 5). The problem with beginning lies in its very un-iterability; the attainment of an end is therefore always in serious question, held in abeyance, postponed indefinitely, or at least till end and beginning – 'Now the one. Now the twain' (Frag. 14) – join hands. In his introductory comments to his *Dialogues avec Heidegger* (Editions de Minuit, 1973) Jean Beaufret makes the distinction between *commencer* (to enter into question) and *débuter* (to depart from), and adds that it is within the purview of *début* to keep in its shadows the enigma of commencement. Seeking the resolution of the enigma in Greek thought, he concludes with the observation that as concerns the point of departure of all beginning, 'the Greek word, on this point, remains enigmatic' (*'La parole grecque, sur ce point demeure enigmatique'*). We are thus thrown right back to *On*: the embodiment of the place of beginning, 'the so-said seat and germ of all', whose function as *début* is displayed in proportion as what it departs from is kept in the shadows. Its thrust heads nowhere but towards its own goal-lessness, as it casts the ensuing project in a process of *désoeuvrement* (see above, p. 131) whereby the *but*, or goal, of its foregrounded point of departure as embodied *début*, is persistently and systematically forestalled, put off, held in abeyance, left (forever) gaping towards the projected image of its (endlessly) reiterated irresolution.

A quarter of a century ago, Beckett had already almost worked the problematics of beginning to death (his entire *oeuvre*, for that matter, like Blanchot's, is an ongoing *désoeuvrement* of the 'death sentence', or *Arrêt de mort*, with which it is inscribed). For, coming on the heels of 'I can't go on, I'll go on' with which he closed his macrotrilogy, he followed suit, and reopened old wounds, beginning, it would seem, all over again. I am referring, of course, to *Comment c'est* and its re-entry into question of *How It Is* (. . . to begin). Rather than reopen that can of worms here, however, let us return, momentarily, to Heidegger's dictum regarding what happens 'whenever art happens'.

What happens in Heidegger's equation of happening and beginning (see above, p. 132), quite simply stated, is that it states itself into being in and of itself: it *shows* its *being* by *saying* how *it is*. Let us begin to quote him again, with no interruption save his own: 'Whenever art happens – i.e. whenever there is a beginning' (etc.). The triggering mechanism here – explicited to the point of its being 'leaped over, as something disguised, thus concealing within itself the end' – is the 'i.e.', *id est*, the *is*ness of Being displayed in its utterly unadorned, genderless, neuter presence. *Whenever art happens* (in other words), *it is*. Or, to continue through with the chain, 'Whenever art happens . . . is whenever there is a beginning.' Beginning is thus predicated on happening, with *is*ness left alone (i.e. eclipsed?) to bask in the radiance of Being. Being, however, as we know it, and for it to be known, requires the presence of consciousness for it to be *there*, i.e. constituted in the *there*nesss of there is. The (impossible) task that Beckett seems to have set his writing to achieve, in *Worstward Ho*, can now be summarised thus: as writing, its communicative function must be strictly confined within the sphere of its initial happening (the seat and germ of all to which Being is eternally open); at the same time, however, the stakes that it places on its very communicability, even (and especially) if so restricted, are such that its projection, from the initial point onward, cannot allow itself to eclipse that point itself – knowing, all the while, that the consciousness of the Being of the work, the requisite for *its being there*, is precisely that which, though engendered *by* the writing, undermines it. It is a writing, 'pointed at both ends' (*Three Novels*, New York: Grove Press, p. 209), whose reason for being is the reason for Being. No more. No less. *Worstward Ho* shows us more clearly than ever what being Beckett means.

What *being*, on the other hand, *does* Beckett mean? That, of course, is the question which provides the grounds for the on-going quest of the writing and the saying in *Worstward Ho*. As Derrida writes in *Writing and Difference*, 'Meaning must await being said or written in order to inhabit itself, and in order to become, by differing from itself, what it is: meaning.'[15] We should not lose sight – for the writing of *Worstward Ho* certainly does not – of the word for Being with which the text happens to be: the *On*, which goes thereupon (*there*-up-*on*) begging for recognition, differing from itself through its manifestly repeated reincarnations (Encore/en corps – On/Being – No[how] On . . . ?), and deferring the disclosure of the meaning with which it is inhabited until the instance of its having been (said), in order to become what it is (. . . and know happiness to boot?).

—'On. Say on. Be said on. Somehow on. Till nohow on. Said nohow on.'

—'Such thinking, which recalls . . . Being itself . . . tills the ground and plows the soil. . . . But what still appears as ground . . . is presumably something else, once it is experienced in its own terms – something as yet unsaid [. . .]. Such thinking [is said to be] "on its way".[16] Such thinking – *in deed* – such writing provides the very fabric of *Worstward Ho's* regressive progression, 'projected' on its way to(wards) meaning as it 'points the way back' to the ground of Being, repeatedly landing (us), along the way, in pitfalls of 'utter [t]error': 'Something not wrong with one. Meaning – meaning! – meaning the kneeling one' (*W. Ho*, Frag. 36).

'How did it come about,' Heidegger queries, toward the end of 'The Way Back into the Ground of Metaphysics', 'that with Being It really is nothing and that Nothing really is not?' This question, voiced from authorial ground, is heard again and again throughout *Worstward Ho*, as it is experienced, from within the groundlessness of its own figurative projection into the questionable ground of fictional musing (one hardly dare call this 'fiction'). Or, as Lance Butler writes, Beckett's work is indeed 'an attempt to find an objective correlative for being – a parable that will somehow manage to "say" the ontological nature of the world' (*Samuel Beckett and the Meaning of Being*, p. 159). Fragment 35 (which we've already touched upon – see pp. 129, 130) provides a clear instance of this parabolic attempt:

> Whose words? Ask in vain. Or not in vain if say no knowing. No saying. No words for him whose words. Him? One. No words for one whose words. One? It. No words for it whose words. Better worse so.

If such an instance as this illustrates the attempt to find a fitting parable (an attempt whose failure we are primed to accept), it is precisely by virtue of its showing, as well as its saying, what this parable consists of: a placing beside, a juxtaposition of potential objective correlatives – Him? One. One? It – which, if ever singled out would of course bring the whole process to a screeching halt. For (among other things) *One*, as an objective correlative, is a fictional aberration of Being: it barely disguises its likeness to *On*, which, to the bilingual author, beckons the French word for one (*on*), they, people in general – i.e. the Heideggerian '*Das Man*', the configuration of inauthenticity itself, the faceless herd, which Butler describes as 'the indefinite, collective neuter. Something like an impersonal goad, in fact' (*Beckett and the Meaning of Being*, pp. 38–42). Hence the instantaneous (or so it seems) leap on from *One* to *It*: 'One? It. No words for it whose words. Better worse so.'

What might appear to be a mere exchange of one neuter goad for another is in reality an attempt to avoid, or skirt, the pitfall of communicable utterance (engendering *other*-ance), whose very communicability would project the consciousness of Being into the community, and out of its immediate sphere of inarticulable presence. The onwardness (in other words) of the text's reiterations must not allow itself to be disposed of as a representation of its own otherness: this is why, as a parable of ongoing failure, it *must* fail – which also provides the reason for its unprecedented urgency to succeed.

> If I were obliged to name the class of things to which [poetry] belongs, I should call it a secretion.
>
> A. E. Housman, *The Name and Nature of Poetry*

The centre toward which *Worstward Ho* is drawn, in its fragmentary 'voyage outward and return home to self, existing alone and anguished to know how and why' (Kaelin, *The Unhappy Consciousness*, op. cit., p. 145), like that of Blanchot's, is both movable and fixed. It is to be found (concealed) everywhere that the closure of signification beckons words in their onward search for a way out of their vain attempts to get it all said. It is already always *there*. It is its thereness that makes it unattainable while at the same time drawing all activity towards it. It is Being with no knowledge (nor need thereof) of Nothing.[17] It stands for want of Nothing.

It was in Fragment 6 that we saw the first clear sign of what questionable ground this circuitous search for a way out of representation is grounded in: 'It stands. What? Yes. Say it stands. . . . Say ground. No ground but say ground.' From there on in (or is it out?), everything seems to point toward the It and the question which it goads (both of which here make their initial appearance in tandem) as the point around which the book (and the whole Beckettian *oeuvre* in tow) is centred, and away from which the writing – as it proceeds onwards to write itself out – must be directed. It is the Being-there of It – which stands in place of Being – that determines the itinerary of the journey worstward, towards the pointlessness of its reiterations. In Blanchot's *Literary Space* the point toward which the work avowedly seems to direct itself is the gaze of Orpheus. In *Worstward Ho*, the focal point towards which the double-pointed Venus pencil traces its regressive progression is Fragment 58:

> Enough still not to know. Not to know what they say. Not to know what it is the words it says say. Says? Secretes. Say better worse secretes. What it is the words it secretes say. What the so-said void. The so-said dim. The so-said shades. The so-said seat and germ of all. Enough to know no knowing. No knowing what it is the words it secretes say. No saying. No saying what it all is they somehow say.[18]

It is here that the *it* re-*it*erates itself to the point of utter confusion: secreted words uttered forth unknown, oozing back unknowable, into the all-inclusive secret – 'the so-said seat and germ' – of *it all*. Textual here-say based on Nothing to be known. A *per*formative playing to the recesses of consciousness. . . . A *pre*formative plying of remanded memory. A dumbfounded journey through 'shades of void'. An ill-founded attempt to get it all said, expressed, oozed out – while through the back door, other voices creep in, rearranging the movable fixtures as they see fit.

> Not another word. Home at last. Gently gently.
>
> *Ill Seen Ill Said*

'In [Borges's] preferred story', writes Anthony Kerrigan in his Preface to *Ficciones*, 'a man must pick up a knife . . . and go out into the brainless night. . . . Why? He does not know. All our knowledge has led us exactly to this point, just where we started, endless ages ago. We have only been playing a game, an immortal game all along.'[19] I have tried in this essay to make a few pointed remarks concerning the game being played out in *Worstward Ho*: an anything-but-childish game, whose impetus (perhaps) lies in 'the never forgotten' 'cutting retort' with which the mother 'shook off [the] little hand' in *Company* . . . for no apparent reason other than to have raised a pointed question. With all its desperate playfulness, *Worstward Ho* has still not found a way to dislodge 'No's knife' from 'Yes's wound'.

Notes

1. Caryl Emerson, 'The Outer Word and Inner Speech', Gary Saul Morson (ed.), in *Bakhtin* (University of Chicago Press, 1986), p. 32.
2. I have altered the following statement of Lacan (as quoted by Caryl Emerson) with regard to the mirrored *je-moi* opposition which 'gives rise to that permanent hunger for "a locus where there is constituted the *je* which speaks as well as he who has it speak"' (ibid.).
3. No less intriguing is the fact that although this fragment does exist in two typescript versions, it is nowhere to be found in the original manuscript.
4. According to Anna-Teresa Tymienecka, in her introduction to *The Unhappy Consciousness*, p. x. And in the conclusion to his penetrating study behind the surfaces of Beckett's language, Kaelin attributes 'the unhappiness of both projects [i.e. writing and interpreting] to the uncertainty of their results. . . . To write of the poetic plight of Samuel Beckett is to find oneself on the other side of [the] mirror of life' (p. 300).
5. From the third of the 'Three Dialogues' with Georges Duthuit, *transition*, Dec. 1949; reprinted in *Disjecta* (Grove Press, 1984), pp. 138–45. The reader of Beckett's recent, difficult prose can take heart (small consolation!) in the author's admission of nearly forty years ago that his 'inability to do' what he had set out to do 'places [himself], and perhaps an innocent, in . . . an unenviable situation' (p. 145).
6. Daniel Albright, *Representation and the Imagination* (University of Chicago Press, 1981), texts accompanying Plates 7 and 8; see also Plate 6.
7. For further implications of the impossible task that Beckett's consciousness of Being sets for itself, see Butler's discussion of the Heideggerian predicament, whereby the 'forgotten Being', in all its 'indeterminate emptiness' necessitates a reentry into the plenum/void of language, which houses Being, 'but not Being as such', for the latter 'cannot come to be by being *said*' (*Samuel Beckett and the Meaning of Being*, London: Macmillan, 1984, pp. 178–9, and passim). A fruitful comparison might also be made between Butler's account of Heidegger's reentry into the language-house of Being by way of 'The Way Back into the Ground of Metaphysics' (which occasioned a re-working of his *Introduction to Metaphysics*), and Caryl Emerson's account of Bakhtin's projected return (in 1961) to his 1929 study of Dostoevsky, for the express purpose of reinvesting the notion of consciousness with its essential multiplicity by way of the verb *to be* (Emerson, 'The Outer Word', op. cit., pp. 32–3).
8. To align this apparent tautology with Wittgenstein's *Tractatus*, a quick reference to 4.461 should do nicely: 'The proposition shows what it says, the tautology and the contradiction show that they say nothing.'
9. Beckett's comment on *Work in Progress* could surely be applied to *Worstward Ho*: 'The title of this book is a good example of a form carrying a strict inner determination' ('Dante . . . Bruno. Vico . . . Joyce', in *I Can't go on, I'll go on*, New York: Grove Press, 1976, p. 117).
10. 'By recalling the beginnings of history when Being unveiled itself in

the thinking of the Greeks, it can be shown that the Greeks from the very beginning experienced the Being of beings as the presence of the present. When we translate εἶναι as "being," our translation is linguistically correct. Yet we merely substitute one set of sounds for another.' (Martin Heidegger, 'The Way Back into the Ground of Metaphysics', in Walter Kaufmann (ed.), *Existentialism from Dostoevsky to Sartre*, New York: Meridian Books, 1957, p. 215.) 'Linguistically correct' though it may be, this *pre-sumptuous* translation of εἶναι as 'being', rather than as *to be* (which is what it means), already calls into question the ontological status of language itself.

11. Gilbert Sorrentino, 'Language – Lying and Treacherous', *New York Times Book Review*, 25 May 1986, p. 23.

12. This term, which translates as 'idleness', and which in the phrase '*par désoeuvrement*' means 'for want of something to do' (or, as Ann Smock, one of several translators of Blanchot translates it: 'worklessness'), is one of the key concepts in the Blanchotian lexicon; for it literally designates the 'unworking' process which is always at work in the literary act of creating an *oeuvre*. Its kinship with the worstwardness of *Worstward Ho* should not go unnoticed.

13. Heidegger, 'The Origin of the Work of Art', in Albert Hofstadter and Richard Kuhns (eds), *Philosophies of Art and Beauty* (New York: Modern Library, 1964), p. 697.

14. Here, too, Beckett and Blanchot display a similarity of narrative strategies. For it is a trait common to both that the elusiveness of their narratives is largely de/pendent on the paralysing preemptiveness of language itself.

15. Translated by Alan Bass, University of Chicago Press, 1978, pp. 11–12 (quoted in S. E. Gontarski, *The Intent of Undoing in Samuel Beckett's Dramatic Texts*, Indiana University Press, 1985, p. 3).

16. From Heidegger's 'The Way Back', op. cit., pp. 208–9; 212.

17. The absent thereness of Godot comes to mind, but in vain: for Godot cannot show its Being, knowing not (nor needing) where it is that It is not. Being-there is not Godot's Job.

18. It is revealing to note that, by comparison with most fragments of *Worstward Ho*, Beckett set this one down all of a piece, from the outset, with virtually no changes through its three stages of composition (one manuscript, two typescripts).

19. Jorge Luis Borges, *Ficciones* (New York: Grove Press, 1962), p. 11.

8

Beckett's *Company*, Post-structuralism, and *Mimetalogique*

Ed Jewinski

Beckett, in his novels and plays, has constantly questioned the adequacy of the human imagination. In the *Unnamable*, for example, the narrator recognises the possibility that the imagination may soon 'die' and that there will be no more characters with which to while away the time. In *Malone Dies*, Malone voices a related fear: 'perhaps as hitherto I shall find myself abandoned, in the dark, without anything to play with'.[1] In *Imagination Dead Imagine*, the predicted circumstance seems to come true – the imagination is no longer strong enough, or vigorous enough, to do anything more than sustain man at the most elemental level.[2] Finally, the possible death of the imagination seems most fully developed in *Company*, for in this work there is no 'character' who can 'imagine' himself. As in *Not I*, the 'content' of the work is the mere presence of 'voice' reluctantly talking itself into Being, although in *Company* the mouth from which the voice emanates has disappeared into darkness. In his later works particularly, Beckett seems to be playing or toying with the paradoxical questions of what a human might 'imagine' in a world in which no human can successfully give an adequate 'imagine' to himself. In part, then, Beckett's *Company* puts into question one of the most celebrated values of literature – the power of the imagination. This is not surprising, for, as one reads Beckett's works in sequence, one might view this writer's work as a sustained series of efforts to deprive the protagonists of attributes and possessions which are inessential to the core question of *how* Beings imagine themselves.

Company, as this chapter will emphasise, summarises the achievement of Beckett's career: man is the deviser 'Devising figments to temper his nothingness'.[3] Man, Beckett seems to suggest, is a 'product' – possibly a byproduct – of language. In *Company*, Beckett shows mankind to be in a true dilemma. On the one hand, Beckett's 'mankind' unwittingly succeeds at 'Being' in the dark. Because of the power of an unnamed voice which speaks until hearing ends, mankind cannot escape into solipsism – for a voice comes to one in the dark, although one cannot ascertain whose voice it is, or why it is speaking. On the other hand, Beckett's mankind cannot be certain that the world is not wholly of its own making – that the voice is definitely not its own. In this sense, Beckett's mankind fails, for it can never know with certainty whose voice is speaking. In *From an Abandoned Work*, Beckett wrote, 'there never was anything, never can be, life and death, all nothing, that kind of thing, only a voice dreaming and droning all around'.[4] In *Company* he develops this notion fully, adding that it is only the imagination which gives credence and substance and resonance to the words of the droning voice. Despite the seeming richness of the imagination, it fails mankind: it is incapable of creating a completely satisfying sense of 'company'. Ironically, however, largely because of the power of the imaginative faculty, man intensifies his aloneness with every effort to get beyond the small part of what he knows: 'you are on your back in the dark.' (C, p. 7.) As a result, Beckett's mankind is trapped in language, the one tool which gives articulation to his effort to explain what happens in the dark.

In Beckett's *Company*, the particular formulations or words with which man attempts not only to understand his 'self' but also to capture relations beyond his 'self' are inevitably inadequate. For Beckett, the human circumstance is, at best, 'Ill seen, Ill said'. The self is ever receding beyond the verbal expression of the discrete experiences with which man attempts to establish a secure identity. Imagine as he will, man cannot give presence to himself. As the word *imagine* implies: man can only give 'image' or 'shape' to what is *not* 'present'.

Beckett's determination to create literary works which focus upon the problem of 'imagination' mark his central contribution to contemporary literature. Beckett's 'experimentalism' in both the later fiction and drama might best be seen as efforts to organise, for lack of a better term, 'structures of resistance' which counter those dominant forms of conceptualising that give direction to western literature. Words like 'novel' or 'play' seem utterly inadequate in light of Beckett's later work. In particular, Beckett seems wholly discontent with *mimesis*,[5] for such a form of writing, in itself, presupposes that the mere presence of voice grants the imagination the power to give *more* than image or shape to what is not present. The trust in the power of the voice to describe human experience fully and unequivocally is precisely what Beckett's works seem to reject. In the earlier works, such as the trilogy, Beckett seems to be developing what is now called *metafiction*, fiction which self-consciously reveals its fictionality. In the later works, however, the narrators are less intrusively stressing their 'fictional' presence. Now, it is not a mere matter of fiction being less truthful for being a fiction, but a matter of what made traditional fictional works so convincing, so powerful. What cast of mind influenced the acceptance of *mimesis* as the dominant form of recreating mankind's sense of the real? *Company*, if it may be said to have a subject or 'theme', then, has the problematic 'theme' of the mental habit 'underlying' *mimesis*, the habit of accepting 'from the incontrovertibility of the one [known fact of being in the dark and hearing a voice] to win credence for the other [the knowledge that what the voice is saying is accurate about what might be beyond the darkness].' (C, p. 7.) Beckett's fiction, in other words, has broken the bounds, the supposed rules, the unstated conventions of *mimesis*, simply by explicitly exploring the implications of presenting in writing 'how things are'. Beckett, it seems, is primarily concerned with specific, determined effects of literary texts, rather than with simply creating the effects themselves. For that reason, the narrator of *Company* stresses that the work is not about 'life', but about a 'proposition' about life: 'That then is the *proposition*. To one on his back in the dark a voice tells of a past. With occasional allusion to a present and more rarely to a future. . . .' (my emphasis, C, pp. 7–8).

The impact of such fiction is direct, powerful, simple, although never simplistic. Effectively describing what Beckett has achieved, however, is difficult; his narrative technique in this short novel is often so sustained and exacting that it places extreme demands on the reader. Possibly by turning to Jacques Derrida's method of 'deconstruction', one might find a method to help a reader come to terms with Beckett's *Company*.[6]

Derrida is a philosopher, not a literary critic, but his method has often been profitably applied to literary works. 'Deconstructing' a literary text, however, is not an easy enterprise, and therefore a short explication of Derrida's approach to his subject might be helpful here. One cannot do better than begin with Derrida's own explanation of his process. Derrida stresses that 'To "deconstruct" . . . would be to think – in the most faithful interior way – in the . . . concepts [of a discipline], but at the same time to determine – from a certain exterior that is unqualifiable or unnameable by . . . [that discipline] – what . . . it has been able to dissimulate or forbid. . . .'.[7] In simpler terms, Derrida works out a problem in the way that thinkers in a particular case usually do, but at the same time he asks why the 'normal' pattern of thinking in a particular discipline should be accepted.

I try to follow his lead when presenting literary criticism. I try to think in the ways most faithful to literature while, simultaneously, considering the frame of reference which regulates my thinking outside of literary criticism. In the case of *Company*, I believe, such an approach is both necessary and inescapable. When thinking within the concepts of the discipline of literary criticism, I normally expect to read about a character, and I expect a logical sequence of events which will illuminate that character's life. When reading *Company*, however, I find that the 'normal' process does not work. Beckett does everything he can to disrupt the easy flow of character development. As a reader, I can either be frustrated by Beckett's method of hindering my understanding of the major character, or I can simply ask why I *expect* a novel to develop the character of the protagonist? I might even go so far as to ask: 'What in fact is a "character"?' and 'Why do I, as a reader, look for one?'

The moment readers question the validity of their usual expectations, they have arrived at what Derrida calls 'a certain wariness about the motif of "literarity" at the very moment of opposing it to the stubborn authority of the ensemble of . . . *mimetologism* (not *mimesis*, but a determined interpretation of *mimesis*)' (*Positions*, p. 70). Admittedly, Derrida's philosophical phrasing requires clarification, but his point, for the purposes of this essay, can be summarised in the following way: mimetic literature (books like *Tom Jones* or *Emma* or *The Ambassadors*) have virtually conditioned readers to expect characters to be presented in a particular way, a way which makes the character appear to act, think and behave in a world which resembles our ordinary world. The 'logic' of the traditional pattern is so powerful that we, as readers, often forget that 'characters' in fiction are words on paper, not living people – they need not be created to act in accordance with our norms. The reader's goal, Derrida suggests, is to recognise that Beckett may have written *Company* to challenge – even to deny – the traditional conventions and expectations of 'literature'. To feel comfortable with *Company*, therefore, a reader must accept that Beckett, as a writer, recognises that readers expect an author's words to invoke a particular pattern of thinking. By questioning that expected pattern of thought engendered by traditional literature, Beckett questions the adequacy of the mimetic manner of delineating character.

Since *Company* only seems to offer the history of a main character's life, Beckett seems to believe that *mimesis* is inadequate. In fact, the narrative pattern denies, again and again, that a single, main character can be imagined properly. Beckett's narrative technique, therefore, is worth careful analysis.

One way of understanding the narrative pattern Beckett offers his readers is to adapt Derrida's approach to literature. When dealing with *Company*, therefore, I consider one crucial aspect of its 'interior', namely its narrative pattern. However, I also give due consideration to what is beyond or outside of this narrative pattern. That 'outside' is difficult to define in exact terms. Let me simply describe it as a reflection upon a complex habit of mind, a habit best described as the unnamed desire or predisposition to expect that by the end of the book I will have a clear sense of the protagonist. Derrida's term *mimetalogique*, for the purposes of this essay, then, will simply mean that as a reader I not only tend to accept, or give credence to, or even *create* a particular central character, but I also expect that character to have specific features and qualities.

In effect, then, as a reader, I give the protagonist of the novel *presence* or *actuality*, and I all too easily allow myself to forget that I am only reading words in a book. To illustrate the point, I shall ask you to imagine (if I may borrow Beckett's key word here) a blackboard with the following words on it:

THIS IS NOT A VOICE. YET I HEAR IT.

Somehow, chalk on a chalkboard makes me hear what is not heard. When I read 'This is not a voice', I imagine a voice actually speaking, although I know I hear nothing. My very desire to subordinate what is there (chalk on a board) in favour of a presence that is not there (a speaking voice) explicates the effectiveness of Beckett's opening sentence:

'A voice comes to one in the dark. Imagine.'

Derrida's terminology may be exasperating, but his point is appropriate: 'What defers presence . . . [in this case writing] . . . is the very basis on which presence is announced or desired in what represents it, its sign, its trace . . .' (*Positions*, p. 96). Derrida's point is that the mere word 'voice' has the power to make readers imagine a voice, although none is actually heard. In my mind, Beckett, like Derrida, wrestles with this elusive quality of written language, for written language can make something appear to be present, when, in fact, that 'something' is not actually there.

The underlying structure of *Company* rests, I believe, on this dual aspect of language. The unnamed, silent protagonist of *Company*, for example, is 'there', in the book, but only in the same sense that the voice is 'there'. The imagination continually gives presence to what is absent. As readers, as long as we 'hear' a narrator, we expect that someone or something being spoken about must be there. After all, we tend to think – because of the logic of *mimesis* itself – that it is impossible to talk about 'no one'. In traditional fiction, everyone grants that the character is simply imagined, but imagined in such a way that the character resembles people we know. Beckett, however, reverses the method, foregrounding the very conventions which usually allow readers to skim over the problem of how the conventions of *mimesis* allow readers to give to characters a sense of self-presence. For Beckett, it seems, such traditional methods simply invite readers and writers to escape 'How It Is'.

Following Derrida's approach, then, it might be best to begin an analysis of *Company* from the 'inside', that is, by following what we as readers usually expect: a story about the protagonist. The presence of the character, and his knowledge about himself, is achieved in *Company* by the use of two 'voices' which simultaneously describe the experience of the main character, an unnamed figure lying on his back in the dark. The first 'voice' expresses itself in the third person, discussing the main character as 'he'. This 'voice' is the seemingly 'truthful voice' which simply usurps the right to knowingly distinguish the reliability of what it represents. It is a voice of logic and reason, a voice which often examines details with excruciating exactness. This voice is 'reason ridden' (*C*, p. 33), and self-consciously 'cankerous' (*C*, p. 8), often locked into its highly cerebral reflections. It is also a voice which openly and directly asserts that the unnamed listener, at times, 'reasons ill' (*C*, p. 11), although no direct entrance is ever made into the mind of the unnamed, speechless protagonist.

The second voice constantly uses 'you'. It is a dull voice of iteration. It simply describes for the unnamed his past and present experience, without explicit qualification or hesitation: 'A small boy you come out of Connolly's Stores holding your mother by the hand' (*C*, p. 10). This second voice is never self-reflective. It simply describes a scene, or moment, or action or experience without passing judgement or offering explanations. As a result, the reader is trapped between the voice which describes experience as if it were capable of being presented in an immediate, straightforward manner, and the voice which logically and sceptically questions the authority of the other voice's presentation of experience. In the following passage, for example, the sceptical voice discredits the value and force of the content of its opposing voice, insisting that the voice using 'you' may, by the mere force of repetition, tempt the unnamed listener into accepting as his own experience what is being described:

> Another trait its repetitiousness. Repeatedly with only minor variants the same bygone. As if willing him by dint to make it his. To confess, Yes I remember. Perhaps even to have a voice. To murmur, Yes I remember. What an addition to company that would be! Murmuring now and then, Yes I remember. (*C*, p. 20)

The presence of the two voices, however, does not create a dialogue. Rather, the reader discovers only two diametrically opposed assertions of the presence of self: the first is a detached murmur of 'this happened and then this'. The second is one of explicit judgement of the rhetorical force of the 'you' voice. Incapable of choosing between the two voices, the reader is forced into an endless process of questioning. Every word and phrase, by both narrators, becomes ambivalent and enigmatic. Neither voice has any authority beyond its own rhetorical power to convince. Furthermore, the values implied by these voices push the reader to the margins and limitations of the authority invested in disembodied speech.

Of course, it must be remembered that the authority of speech, an authority which seems so overwhelming in this short novel –

'A voice comes to one in the dark. Imagine.' – is based upon an illusion. The opening statement is written, not verbalised. By imagining a voice, the reader immediately gives presence to what is not there. The point is crucial, and needs to be repeated here, if one is to recognise how *Company* immediately thrusts the reader into the very position of the unnamed protagonist himself. As Derrida points out, we are fundamentally a 'logocentric' culture, a culture which is dominated by the word, the *logos*; we give primacy to the voice, to speech, and if speech is heard, we assume someone must be there to speak, and some *thing* must be spoken about. Such a mental habit, however, is mainly a habit of thought, not of fact. Moreover, it is the mental habit that is repeatedly explored in this novel. Rather than being satisfied with examining what is there (a series of words), and what is not (a voice), the reader all too easily projects beyond the text, thereby allowing words on paper to be transformed into the sounds of two voices. Only by restricting the text to 'writing', to rhetoric, to the problem of how words get transformed into 'imagined' sounds, will the novel be a fully satisfying experience.

From this perspective, one can again consider the opening statement of the text. Although the first statement of the novel is 'A voice comes to one in the dark. Imagine' (*C*, p. 7), the reader actually encounters two voices – one using 'he', another using 'you'. Since the main character never achieves enough self-consciousness to articulate his feelings, the reader is left at an impasse. Which voice accurately describes the situation of the protagonist? Is the 'you' voice more accurate than the 'he' voice? Even if one voice is more accurate than the other, on what grounds can one decide such an issue? Possibly, one might suggest, the misleading desire to accept one voice's authority over the other's is the central issue of the book? One could, instead, look to what Paul de Man would call the rhetorical tropes, the rhetorical devices, of this work and realise how one voice cancels out the other's assertions, and thereby perceive that no 'meaningful' statements are made by either voice, and that, furthermore, no choice between the voices is possible. In effect, the reader can acknowledge that *Company* is primarily a reflection on rhetoric, a reflection on how written language deceives readers into believing they are hearing 'voices'. The central test of the book, then, is to read the work with constant attention to the problems of how language creates illusions. The illusions themselves should be ignored, for they cannot be sustained. The process is a difficult one; it resembles the problem of seeing a mirage. The specific things seen in a mirage are of less importance than the explanation of how the mirage is created. The man in the desert who believes he is seeing an oasis rich with water will always be defeated by the sand and air and sun if he allows himself to race to the water. Only by understanding the forces involved in the creation of the illusion might he help himself. So with the language of *Company*: it offers many illusions that a character is there, but a closer examination of the power of Beckett's handling of rhetoric reveals that the image is an illusion motivated by the reader's desire to have fiction recreate an 'image' of man. A book based on such premises demands a radically different type of reading.

If such a reading is possible, one would have to begin with de Man's view that 'No such thing as an unrhetorical, "natural" language exists that could be used as a point of reference; language is itself the result of purely rhetorical tricks and devices.'[8] Or, as Jacques Derrida argues, the reader must be compelled 'to accept into his discourse the premises . . . [of rhetoric] . . . at the very moment when he is employed in denouncing them.'[9] Like Beckett, who might prefer works without words, but who must use writing to express that point of view, the critic must accept that contradiction is the essence of both literature and of literary analysis. Moreover, to make sense of Beckett's work, one must not merely accept contradiction, one must embrace it, particularly if one is to understand how Beckett's *Company* reveals that contradiction is as intolerable as it is inescapable.

In fact, the whole book centres on the contradiction inherent in reflective thinking about and direct description of experience: man either *exists* as a being fully alive to his immediate experience, or he *is* a being locked into self-reflection about experience, and, at least mentally, separated from any sense of direct continuity and continuance. When one faints, for example, what happens to the mind? When one gets so involved with a particular problem that the world all around seems to disappear, what happens to the world? The very duality of man's experience, for Beckett, is the central omission of mimetic literature.

Mimesis should, in a sense, mirror our everyday experience. Such a presentation of our sense of the real, however, excludes, or pushes to the side, the problem of man's dual nature as a thinking and feeling Being. In *mimesis*, one arbitrarily links the two extremes, thereby evading the gap between the two. The assumption of the continuance of identity is made in mimetic art. Somehow man 'is', even though he may not consistently be aware of himself as Being in a physical world. Underlying the assumptions of *mimesis*, then, is a continuous, unquestionable self, which, from childhood to old age, remains the same. The notion, of course, is a metaphysical one, a notion Beckett has his narrators question as early as *The Unnamable*.

> perhaps that's what I feel, an outside and an inside and me in the middle, perhaps that's what I am, the thing that divides the world in two, on the one side the outside, on the other the inside, that can be as thin as foil, I'm neither one side nor the other, I'm in the middle, I'm the partition, I've two surfaces and no thickness . . .[10]

Beckett's concerns here seem strikingly similar to those of Jacques Derrida. Derrida has repeatedly argued that western thinking is fundamentally 'logocentric'. By that he means that our thinking is mainly dualistic, a thinking in terms of oppositions, such as inside/outside, real/fanciful, mind/body, thought/feeling, presence/absence, and so on. In all these oppositions, the 'essence' of man is, initially, either one alternative or the other, as in the notion that although man is a mortal Being, man is immortal, for he has a soul. Derrida has argued that if one accepts the dualism of mind/body, then one can only uphold the supremacy, for example, of the soul by denigrating or belittling the importance of the body. The body becomes reduced to a 'temporary' vessel of the soul. Man, of course, has no absolute knowledge, no transcendent knowledge, about either body or soul, and therefore cannot really answer his own question about the nature of his dual 'existence'. Possibly, and Derrida would say more than 'possibly', man should recognise that he 'is', in effect, a contradiction: a 'Being' composed of incompatible and irreconcilable ideas, values and attitudes attributed to body *and* soul without *Being* (knowing himself to be) either body or soul. He *is*, in a sense, in the gap between them. He is, in Beckett's terms of *The Unnamable* 'outside' his body and 'inside' it, without any 'thickness'. Man is, at best, 'two surfaces and no thickness'.

A similar notion underlies *Company*, and much of Beckett's other work. While Derrida challenges the notions of philosophy, Beckett challenges those of mimetic art. Beckett recognises that *mimesis* is more than a form of art; *mimesis* requires a certain unstated form of thinking about what happens in 'art'. One central assumption in *mimesis* is the acceptance of the continuity of 'self', for without that underlying assumption traditional 'characterisation' could not be possible. Beckett's own 'art', however, is a challenge to both the notion of continuance of self and the possibility of creating 'characters'. Distrusting the assumptions of mimetic art, Beckett can only play against it by exploring where, how and when 'art' requires readers to read with unstated assumptions in mind, rather than with the words of the text. In the case of *Company*, for example, all man knows about the 'self' is again twofold. Either 'man' is the fragments that some unnamable 'you' voice articulates (the words with which this voice offers to describe the world, the enigmatic vignettes which it tells), or he is the exacting and excruciating 'voice' which ruthlessly and logically examines the undecidabilities of linguistic structures, recognising that any address to a 'you' is a direct address to an indeterminate listener. In other words, the 'you' voice might or might not be addressing the one on his back. The one on his back might simply be overhearing a voice speaking to some other Being. And, as the narrator using 'he' points out, the unnamed protagonist would be thinking 'ill' if he supposed that an unidentified speaker were talking about him to someone else, for then the voice would have to use 'he' not 'you'. Either he is hearing about himself or he is hearing about some unnamed other, but he is not hearing a discussion where he is the subject. The point is that Beckett challenges his readers, for no mediation is offered in this work, no reconciliation of narrators takes place. The unnamed remains unnamed. Two voices predominate.

The uncertainty of who is speaking and who is listening is begun with the opening word of the text: 'you'. In the main, pronouns, as Jacques Lacan has argued, are slippery signifiers.[11] Anyone can use 'you', but the word is appropriate for discussions between, at least, any two people. When one hears 'you', one has no way of determining who is being addressed. How often have 'you', for example, whilst walking in the street, heard: 'Hey you, stop!' and stopped, only to find that 'you' weren't being addressed?

In the opening sections of *Company*, the narrator using 'he' wrestles with the ambiguity of the word 'you', wondering if the unnamed main character is being spoken to, or if he is merely overhearing a voice speaking to another. The narrator using 'he' is continually baffled by the disrupting effect of language, particularly its power to evoke a sense of presence in a world where presence is always ambiguous, uncertain and indefinite. For the narrator using 'he', the inevitable fear is this: if the listener were to yield to incessant repetition, then the protagonist would unquestionably be the mere product of the language of an unnamed voice. He could have no assurance of a *presence* outside and beyond the language of the 'you' voice itself.

However, if the protagonist were restricted to the scepticism of the narrator using 'he' (a problem this narrator never recognises), then he would be reduced to asking the unanswerable metaphysical questions resembling those of the scholastics concerned about the number of angels on the head of the pin. In this case, the unnamable crawling in the dark might ask: 'Can the crawling creator crawling in the same create dark as his creature create while crawling?' (*C*, p. 52).

Beckett's well-known use of the 'unnamable' signals an admission that the internal 'Other' or 'self' – a Being which can merge both an absolute sense of itself independent of time and mutability and a sense of itself as a creature defined by change and alteration – cannot emerge into language as a stable identity, but must remain unnamed in the *gap* between the desire to be expressed and the inadequacy of the verbal expression. As Derrida would have it, only a 'trace' of the 'Self' remains. The very sense of Being asked for is contradictory and self-cancelling.

While the narrator using 'he' continually tests all with reason and logic, the narrator using 'you' presents all directly, immediately and forcefully. At first, this voice seems more inviting and hospitable,[12] for it offers a sense of directness that the voice of excruciating logic lacks. The following episode illustrates the point:

It is late afternoon and after some hundred paces the sun appears above the crest of the rise. Looking up at the blue sky and then at your mother's face you break the silence asking her if it is not in reality much more distant than it appears. The sky that is. The blue sky. Receiving no answer you mentally reframe your question and some hundred paces later look up at her face again and ask her if it does not appear much less distant than in reality it is. For some reason you could never fathom this question must have angered her exceedingly. For she shook off your little hand

and made you a cutting retort you have never forgotten. (*C*, p. 11)

The narrator using 'you', initially seems to be inviting a far more immediate sense of reality. Compare the sense of the boy's experience with the following passage by the narrator using 'he':

Or by some successful act of intellection as were he to think to himself, Since he cannot think he will give up trying. Is there anything to add to this esquisse? His unnamability. Even M must go. So W reminds himself of his creature as so far created. W? But W too is creature. Figment. (*C*, p. 45)

The 'he' voice is too wrapped up in 'intellection', and the reader is immediately distanced from him. The narrator using 'you', however, seems warmer and more inviting only because he offers, at first, a presentation of experience on traditional mimetic lines. The scene of the boy's incomprehension, the reader initially feels, at least forcefully conveys how and why a boy might be confounded by the inexplicable actions of adults. However, *mimesis* is not a form of immaculate perception; its version of reality is not innocent. As every one of the mimetic vignettes in *Company* illustrates, the experience leads nowhere. It merely defers complexity, ambiguity and indefiniteness. Be it the scene with the boy and his mother (*C*, p. 11), the boy on the diving board (*C*, p. 18), the couple in the summerhouse (*C*, p. 42) or the old man on the strand (*C*, p. 54), each vignette ends abruptly, stressing the incompleteness of experience. Admittedly, after the difficult reading of the passages of the narrator using 'he', the 'you' passages are a seeming release, until, as with the boy, the expression of the real terminates with an imponderable enigma: a 'cutting retort'; a request by 'many eyes', presumably imploring the boy to be 'brave'; an uncertainty about the woman loved, 'Can it be she is with child without your having asked for as much as her hand?'; and finally, a paradox, 'Were your eyes to open dark would lighten.'

The event or happening or force of Being resonates throughout such brief passages given by the narrator using 'you', but at a distance. That which is – that which is 'really' happening between the son and mother, for example – does not seem to be present. Since the episode occurs distanced from the unnamable main character and the reader, the experience seems doubly puzzling, enigmatic and elusive. What did the boy do? Fail to do? Why did the mother react in such a fashion? Did what happen affect the boy more deeply than what didn't happen? How can one judge? Something has happened, but exactly what is unclear. Although, paradoxically, the reader knows all he requires to understand how mysterious and incomprehensible experience can be, he has no more sense of the boy's world than he had before reading the passage. Throughout the work, the immediate presence of Being, the life lived as described by the narrator using 'you' – whether he describes the boyhood scenes or the scenes of the older man – remains so direct that its force overpowers and dulls the senses. Beckett, in effect, makes the reader see to the point of blindness. What happens is startlingly clear in each individual episode; why it happens remains unanswered.

The disruption in the 'you' sections, moreover, creates a problem for traditional readings. If character is a cumulative process, if character grows and changes and develops because of some causal pattern inherent in these events, the narrators' not making clear exactly what happened in the character's mind prevents the reader from putting the 'pieces' together. Time and time again, the character described by the 'you' voice remains as an unnamable remnant of a striking and captivating single event. How one event leads to the next, or how it is modified by the next, is left indefinite. The normal pattern of character development is not simply modified, but exploded. In an otherwise excellent study of Beckett's *Company*, Eric P. Levy, frustrated by these short enigmatic scenes, argues that Beckett 'expands the *mimetic* project' of western literature.[13] To do so, however, Levy must always bring back an enigmatic scene to one of Beckett's earlier works or to one of Beckett's own experiences.[14] In other words, Beckett's challenge to the mimetic mode has made itself so forceful that the reader adds a necessary supplement – a point of reference or a biographical incident or a critical comment – to the text of *Company* whenever the 'character' of this short novel fails to 'come together' into a satisfactorily full or 'round' character.[15] The repeated disruptions of full character development, it seems, are too intolerable. Since *Company* does not offer relief, readers begin to look for similar scenes in either the Beckett canon or the Beckett biography, or both, to create a chain of causality that adds a clear mimetic coherence lacking in *Company* itself. Granting that *Company* is a work of *mimetalogique*, however, can help clarify *why* Beckettians will continually find themselves adding to the text while Beckett increasingly diminishes from it. The logic of *mimesis*, itself so powerful, underlies western fiction, and Beckett can only increasingly tease the reader into acknowledging that the dominant form of reading literature not only desires, but insists, upon *mimesis*.

Beckett's use of language, his rhetoric, in these sections presented by the narrator using 'he' is, then, to be particularly admired. Here Beckett achieves what Richard Coe describes as Beckett's concern to get beyond language: 'to transmit not ideas but (in his own words) the more elemental "shapes of ideas"; not concepts but the logic of the failure of conceptualization.'[16]

One could conclude, therefore, that a reader may initially react against the overly intellectual voice because of its tendency to overindulge in seemingly minor speculations. Turning to the 'you' voice, however, offers only a temporary respite. What seems so immediate, direct, and all-important – as well as comprehensible, for it seems to mirror our world in such an immediately recognisable fashion – is seen, suddenly, to be marginal, for the reader now desperately wants to know what is the significance of such an experience as the death of the hedgehog. Is the reader, like the boy, doomed to a world of constant enigmas? Can the reader, like the narrator using 'he', only endlessly involve himself in a web of words?

As the reader completes the book, the alteration, which remains a series of disruptive comments by both narrators, becomes oppressive. Neither voice shares its knowledge with the other. No integration takes place, no synthesis. The work is not dialectical. The reader may be shown direct experience, but to evaluate it, he must return to the voice of intellect. From directness, back to abstraction. Once one begins to abstract along with the narrator using 'he', the reader is simply even further removed from the direct answers he seeks. He may be on another plane, even a 'higher' one: 'But no improvement by means of such achieved so far. Or on a higher plane by such addition to company . . .' (*C*, p. 45).

What Beckett achieves in *Company* is the very thrusting of the reader into the 'logocentric' problem of western culture. On the one hand, the unnamed protagonist should be there. He should have a permanence. Yet, at the same time, given his possible history from birth to death, he should also be a creature of growth and coming-to-be. If he is a mere series of discrete enigmatic experiences which never 'add up' to anything, what can one possibly make of him? But that very issue brings the reader back to the opening of the novel. Once Being is reduced to an image, a product of imagining, once Being becomes understood as an idea, then one assumes that the protagonist's Being should somehow be less than the multiplicity, complexity and ambiguity traced in the novel. In other words, the desire to add to company, to move to a 'higher plane . . . [by knowing various things about the protagonist] . . . as a movement of sustained sorrow or desire or remorse or curiosity or anger or so on' (*C*, p. 56) should, ironically, in our thinking *reduce* and *limit* the totality of the Being, rather than add to it, augment it, expand it, develop it, increase it – possibly infinitely, so that no single or complete sense of Being (in this case the protagonist) can ever result. In simpler terms, or at least in a shorter sentence, for both Beckett and Derrida, we pay lip-service to the notion that there is no master-sense, no single all-inclusive sense, of Being. We ask for infinite variety, but are appalled by it when it is revealed to us. Beckett, with his use of minimalism, his use of reduction, his method of carefully circumscribing his paradoxical subject, gives us this fullness, this plenitude, this indeterminate variety of human experience. By limiting himself, he gives us so much that we cannot possibly encompass it all. Like the unnamed silent protagonist of *Company*, we cannot speak to the fullness of Being because we are simultaneously inside it and outside it, part of both its surfaces, but with no thickness. We cannot have a special form of Being which excludes the ambiguous non-present presence we have. In Derrida's terms, there is no *Aufhebung* (no place to stand outside of experience to reflect upon it, for every effort to reflect upon it is experience itself); in Beckett's terms, the unnamed protagonist will always be silent, a trace remaining that suggests, but never proves, that the narrators using 'he' and 'you' are talking about something.

In conclusion, perhaps *Company* is exemplary in that Beckett concentrates on the contradictory, metaphysical (and simultaneously physical) problem of Being in so many images throughout the text: birth, age, rat, hedgehog, journey, seaside, light, dark, and so on. But what is most important about this concentration is that each image – given an immediate but *temporary* sense of unity by the 'you' voice and then a tortured but fractured sense of unity by the involutions of the 'he' voice – points to irreconcilables that can never be unified or integrated. The disunity, bred from the consistent presentation of opposites is, after all, the very definition of *Company* – more than one, or a host, or a group. The unnamable in Beckett's work is shown as an eternal recurrence of all things, but that recurrence resembles an endless chain that will not redeem the unnamable to himself.

Beckett's 'rhetorical method' is one of offering voices which continually distance or lead away from the subject in two manners. The 'you' voice gives an almost microscopic view of an isolated incident. As the scene becomes clearer and sharper, the reader constantly wants to know more and more. Like all microscopic visions, the logic is that something more elemental underlies what is seen. The desire is always for a more powerful microscope, and an even more powerful microscope. What does underlie the father's desire for the boy to jump? Why does the old lady bless the boy? What is going on under the surface? The 'he' voice offers the telescopic view. It looks to the grander vision, twisting itself into a galaxy of possibilities, one galaxy after the other. By the end of the book, however, the reader is completely confounded. Is there one single angle of vision, one point of view which *should* dominate? But a single point of view, again, is a pattern of mimetic representation, the very form of writing which Beckett's work, paradoxically, employs to supplant. In fact, the narrative structure of *Company* seems carefully designed to reveal that the desire for the continuity of a character's experience is so fundamental to the dominant tradition of *mimesis* that readers can barely tolerate any disruption to that form of art. Derrida's term, *mimetalogique*, may add another cumbersome term to literary theory, but it is one which can and does assist in clarifying precisely what creates the confusion about Beckett's fiction and drama. Beckett's subject, in effect, is the dominant mode of perceiving and responding to art itself.

With such a notion in mind, one could conclude that *Company* embodies what one might call Beckett's compassionate pessimism. Beckett realises man is unceasingly 'craving for company' (*C*, p. 55) – be that craving in life or art – but that very notion of 'company', when voiced as independent fragments of the unnamed self, becomes oppressive and divisive. In Beckett's vision, as the last word of *Company* emphasises, once all is said (for nothing can be done), man is 'Alone'; the voices grant a plenitude which can never be entered or lived in from some place outside of it. Beckett's art stresses that when representational art falters, when mimetic art appears impossible, the verbal play of Beckett's storytellers continues in the solitude of unprovable self-contained interiority. When all exteriority is found wanting and the final break with the shared world is accomplished, what is left is the speaker alone with the consciousness of himself, so alone that his consciousness is neither directly confirmed nor directly denied. There, in the solitude, as long as the hearer hears, 'Till finally you hear how words are coming to an end' (*C*, p. 62), the play of language goes on and on. Man, because he is the product of language, becomes the play of language, and he is unable to extricate himself from that play. Man, to summarise the point, discovers himself as the product of a voice insisting 'You are', while, at the same time, questioning the authority of a voice insisting 'You are', without any thickness in between, without any solid frame of reference either to accept or to question the insistent droning of the voice asserting Being.

Notes

1. Samuel Beckett, *Three Novels* (New York: Grove Press, 1965), p. 180.
2. For a discussion of Beckett's view of the imagination, see James Hansford, 'Imagination Dead Imagine', *Journal of Beckett Studies*, Spring 1982, Number 7, pp. 49–70.
3. Samuel Beckett, *Company* (New York: Grove Press, 1980), p. 46. Hereafter citations to this text are parenthetically included in the body of the essay.
4. Samuel Beckett, *First Love and Other Stories* (New York: Grove Press, 1973), p. 49.
5. In an excellent article entitled '*Company*: The Mirror of Beckettian *mimesis*', *Journal of Beckett Studies*, Autumn 1982, Number 8, pp. 94–5), Eric P. Levy also points out that Beckett's work can best be understood in the context of this author's efforts to expand the boundaries of traditional fiction. The argument I offer presents both a vocabulary and an approach for an analysis of Beckett's particular method of altering the forms of traditional fiction.
6. Although Jacques Derrida develops a radically different view of ontology than Heidegger, Sartre or Hegel, Lance St John Butler, in *Samuel Beckett and the Meaning of Being* (London: Macmillan, 1984), has convincingly demonstrated that the notions of philosophers cannot be dismissed if one hopes to get beyond the surface of Beckett's work. Derrida's notions in particular, can assist at those points where Beckett discards or rejects the views of the three principal figures studied by Lance St John Butler.
7. Jacques Derrida, *Positions*, trans. Alan Bass (Chicago: University of

Chicago, 1981), p. 6. Hereafter citations to this text are parenthetically inserted in the body of the essay.

8. Paul de Man, 'Nietzsche's Theory of Rhetoric', *Symposium*, Spring 1974, Number 28, p. 35.

9. Jacques Derrida, 'Structure, Sign, Play' in *The Structuralist Controversy*, ed. by Richard Macksey and Eugene Donato (Baltimore: The Johns Hopkins Press, 1972), p. 272.

10. Samuel Beckett, *Three Novels* (New York: Grove Press, 1965), *The Unnamable*, p. 386.

11. Jacques Lacan, *Speech and Language in Psychoanalysis*, trans. Anthony Wilden (Baltimore: The Johns Hopkins University Press, 1968), pp. 215–18.

12. For a reading of the 'you' narrator as inviting and hospitable, see Enoch Brater, 'The *Company* Beckett Keeps', in *Samuel Beckett: Humanist Perspectives* ed. by Morris Beja, S. E. Gontarski and Pierre Astier (Ohio: Ohio State University Press, 1983), pp. 157–71.

13. I am in strong sympathy with Eric P. Levy's general reading of *Company* (see note 5); however, in my argument I stress that an understanding of *mimetalogique* offers an explication of Beckett's particular method of breaking away from traditional *mimesis*.

14. Eric P. Levy, like John Pilling in a review article of *Company* (*Journal of Beckett Studies*, Spring 1982, Number 7, pp. 127–31), often turns to Beckett's autobiography whenever the lack of *mimesis* disrupts the sense of characterisation in *Company*. The point to be made here, then, is that the desire to see unity, development and causality in character development is so oppressive that even expert readers will supplement the text to ease the tension created by Beckett's work.

15. E. M. Forster, *Aspects of the Novel* (Harmondsworth: Penguin Books, 1963), p. 75.

16. Richard N. Coe, 'Beckett's English', in *Samuel Beckett: Humanistic Perspectives* ed. by Morris Beja, S. E. Gontarski and Pierre Astier (Ohio: Ohio State University Press, 1983), p. 38.

9

Watt: Samuel Beckett's Sceptical Fiction

Michael E. Mooney

As Lawrence E. Harvey pointed out in his admirable study,[1] one of the earliest conversational exchanges in *Watt* (1945; published in 1953) serves to adumbrate the novel's concerns. The speakers in this conversation are Mr Nixon and Mr Hackett; their subject is Watt, who has stepped off a tram one stop before the railway station and proceeded to walk the remaining distance to the terminal. Their curiosity about the Chaplinesque Watt, apparently 'wrapped up in dark paper and tied about the middle with a cord' (16),[2] focuses on who he is and what he is doing. Mr Nixon, who once lent Watt some money, is asked by Mr Hackett to 'describe your friend a little more fully':

> I really know nothing, said Mr. Nixon.
> But you must know something, said Mr. Hackett. One does not part with five shillings to a shadow. Nationality, family, birthplace, confession, occupation, means of existence, distinctive signs, you cannot be in ignorance of all this.
> Utter ignorance, said Mr. Nixon.
> He is not a native of the rocks, said Mr. Hackett.
> I tell you nothing is known, cried Mr. Nixon. Nothing.
> A silence followed these angry words, by Mr. Hackett resented, by Mr. Nixon repented   (21).

The exchange contains a denial of the conventions of 'realistic' fiction, in which we might expect to receive details about a character's 'confession, occupation, means of existence'. But this denial comes as no surprise: Beckett had denounced the cardboard façade of realism in his 1931 study of Proust.[3] What *is* surprising, as Harvey perceptively observed, is the nature of the announcement of the novel's principal theme: 'the need to know and the difficulty and indeed impossibility of knowing.'[4] In his analysis Harvey describes in great detail Watt's unsuccessful search for meaning at Knott's house, drawing example after example from the novel. Where his analysis weakens, and where this essay wishes to begin, is in the extent to which the theme of *Watt* is the utter futility of attempting to know.

The Beckettian view of man as 'a non-knower, a non-can-er' was explicitly set forth in his 1956 interview with Israel Schenker.[5] The philosophical attitude underlying this position, however, has not received the attention it deserves. It has not because critical attention to Beckett has been directed, from its inception in the Fall 1959 special issue of *Perspective*, to the importance the life and thought of Descartes has had for Beckett's art. In that issue, edited by Ruby Cohn, Samuel I. Mintz and Hugh Kenner advanced a similar thesis about the relationship between Beckett and Descartes: for them, Beckett was a writer for whom Descartes's separation of mind and body and pronouncement, *'cogito ergo sum; je pense, donc je suis'* held particular relevance. During the 1960s seven major studies followed the trail blazed by these essays, each in its own way upholding the position articulated by Kenner in 'The Cartesian Centaur': 'The Cartesian Centaur is a man riding a bicycle, *mens sana in corpore disposito.'*[6] So much was this so that critical response to Beckett largely overlooked the primacy of philosophical scepticism in his work.[7]

Even a cursory reading of *Watt* reveals the state of ignorance Watt reaches at the end of the second of the novel's four sections. Appropriately, the language used to express this condition directly echoes the language Mr Nixon used at the novel's opening. His attempts to understand, to comprehend what goes on in Knott's house now exhausted, Watt questions what he has learned during his stay on the ground floor:

Watt was now tired of the ground floor, the ground floor had tired Watt out.
What had he learnt? Nothing.
What did he know of Mr. Knott? Nothing.
Of his anxiety to improve, of his anxiety to understand, of his anxiety to get well, what remained? Nothing.
But was that not something? (148)

Thanks to Harvey, readers now recognised that these are the

precise terms also employed in Beckett's first published novel, *Murphy* (1938), when an equally frustrated Murphy confronts the imperturbable indifference of Mr Endon. After their notorious chess-game, Murphy feels 'the positive peace that comes when the somethings give way, or perhaps simply add up, to the Nothing, than which in the guffaw of the Abderite naught is more real.'[8] But even Harvey fails to explore the full importance this statement has for Beckett. He recognises, as have subsequent critics, that the 'Abderite' referred to is the 'laughing philosopher', Democritus of Abdera, the contemporary of Aristotle and the principal exponent of philosophical atomism. He recognises also that the 'Nothing' represents the Democritean void, filled with atoms so minute that while they are invisible, yet they are 'something'. What he does not realise is that in the New Academy and in the works of Sextus Empiricus, Democritus was generally regarded as a proto-sceptic. For Cicero, and later for Empiricus, Democritean atomism lost its philosophical brilliance as a solution to the perennial problem, first posed by Thales, of what lay behind the sentient world, and became instead an epistemological proposition. A passage in Cicero's *Academica* provides the *locus classicus*. Cicero writes of Arcesilas, the sceptical head of the New Academy, who attacked Zeno the Stoic

> . . . by reason of the obscurity of those things which had brought Socrates to the confession of ignorance, and even before Socrates, Democritus, Anaxagoras, Empedocles, and nearly all the ancients; who asserted that nothing could be ascertained, or perceived, or known: that the senses of man were narrow, his mind feeble, the course of his life short, and that truth, as Democritus said, was sunk in the deep; that everything depended on opinions and established customs; that nothing was left to truth. They said in short, that everything was enveloped in darkness; therefore Arcesilas asserted that there was nothing which could be known, not even that very piece of knowledge which Socrates had left himself. . . .[9]

The double sense of 'nothing' as the void and as learned ignorance should be apparent.

I quote Cicero at length because he supplies a crucial connection between presocratic atomism and philosophical scepticism in Beckett's work. The connection is crucial, because it explains Beckett's conflation of Democritean and sceptical terminology. Near the end of the third part of *Watt*, after Watt has been replaced on the ground floor by Arthur and moved upstairs, one such sceptical term is mentioned prominently. The term is *ataraxy*, and it appears after Watt tells us, through the narrative voice of Sam, that he

> suffered neither from the presence of Mr. Knott, nor from his absence. When he was with him, he was content to be with him, and when he was away from him, he was content to be away from him. Never with relief, never with regret, did he leave him at night, or in the morning come to him again.
>
> This ataraxy covered the entire house-room, the pleasure garden, the vegetable garden, and of course Arthur.
>
> So that when the time came for Watt to depart, he walked to the gate with the utmost serenity.   (207–8)

Ataraxy is the apathetic inner calm that comes from doubt; in the vocabulary given us in the novel, it is the sceptical realisation that 'nothing is known'. As Sextus Empiricus defines it, *ataraxy* is a state of 'contentment' and 'serenity' that the sceptic will achieve once he replaces dogmatic assertion with 'incurious wonder'. It is inevitable that we should shortly learn that 'From Mr. Knott's voice *nothing was to be learnt*' (208, italics mine).

Watt's sojourn in Knott's house teaches him the futility of attempting to impose meaning on events or to concern himself 'with what things were, in reality' (227). It isn't that he doesn't try to understand, even after he leaves Knott: he is, like later Beckett creations, simply burdened by the miseries of conation. In the novel's last section, when Watt tries to determine what figure comes along the road, he falls again 'into this old error, this error of the old days, when, lacerated with curiosity, in the midst of substance shadowy he stumbled' (227). But his experience has modified him, and it affects those around him. The final farcical interlude at the railway station reveals the effect Watt's own apathetic calm has on Mr Gorman, Mr Nolan and Mr Case, the bumbling railway agents. The novel has come full circle, ending where it began in a train depot.[10] While Watt waits for the ticket office to open, he falls into a stupor. Mr Nolan and Mr Gorman come up with the capital idea of trying to rouse him by dousing him with a bucket of slimy water. Unfortunately, they drop the bucket on Watt's head. We are told that 'Blood now perfused the slime' (241). Watt nonetheless awakens, requests a ticket to the end of the line, and then mysteriously disappears. The novel concludes with the three agents looking at each other in stupefied perplexity:

> Mr. Nolan looked at Mr. Case, Mr. Case at Mr. Nolan, Mr. Gorman at Mr. Case, Mr. Gorman at Mr. Nolan, Mr. Nolan at Mr. Gorman, Mr. Case at Mr. Gorman, Mr. Gorman again at Mr. Case, again at Mr. Nolan, and then straight before him, at nothing in particular. And so they stayed a little while, Mr. Case and Mr. Nolan looking at Mr. Gorman, and Mr. Gorman looking straight before him, at nothing in particular, though the sky falling to the hills, and the hills falling to the plain, made as pretty a picture, in the early morning light, as a man could hope to meet with, in a day's march.   (246)

The repeated phrase, 'nothing in particular', serves to conclude the novel by returning us to where it began, in the perplexity of attempting to know 'nothing'.

Each of the four sections of *Watt* ends with an awareness of 'nothing'. But scepticism clearly runs counter to our every rational and analytical instinct, and we are appropriately stupefied by the direction toward which we are led in *Watt*. To get at the novel's 'meaning', however, we must paradoxically get at its very lack of meaning, since that is its principal theme. It is for this reason that Beckett supplies us with non-event after non-event. The visit of the Galls, 'the principal incident of Watt's early days in Knott's house' (72), offers a case in point. Although the Galls, blind Senior and Junior, come to tune Knott's piano, very little actually occurs. All the Galls determine is that the piano, like themselves, 'is doomed' (72). But this *is* the 'principal incident' because, as the narrator tells us, 'In a sense it resembled all the incidents of note proposed to Watt during his stay in Mr. Knott's house, and of which a certain number will be recorded in this place, without addition, or subtraction, and in a sense not' (72). What initially 'distresses' Watt about this incident of the Galls, 'was not so much that he did not know what had happened, for he did not know what had happened, as that nothing had happened, that a thing that was nothing had happened, with the utmost formal distinctness' (76). The problem at this point is that Watt 'could not accept that nothing had happened, with the clarity and solidity of something' (76). 'But', as we learn, 'to elicit something from nothing requires a certain skill and Watt was not always successful, in his efforts to do so.' Here the play upon 'something' and 'nothing' is related to Watt's 'sometimes unsuccessful and sometimes successful' attempts to foist 'a meaning' (77) upon an event, to make conjectures into certain truths. But when his attempts to provide meaning fail, it will be the 'inevitable caprice' (72) of this event that will fascinate Watt; its lingering meaninglessness will comfort him. 'So Watt did not know what had happened. He did not care, to do him justice, what had happened' (74).

The incident with the Galls anticipates subsequent ones, each, like the novel itself, 'of great formal brilliance and indeterminable purport' (74), each involved with 'this pursuit of meaning' in terms of 'this indifference to meaning' (75). To explain or to provide a meaning, as Watt says, is 'to exorcize' (78), to foist a 'meaning . . . where no meaning appeared' (77) – to impose a meaning on events 'that resisted all Watt's efforts to saddle them with meaning' (79). But once Watt fully comprehends his failure to impose meaning, he begins to become tranquil, the dogmatist's fury becomes a sceptic's calm: 'Watt learned toward the end of his stay in Mr. Knott's house to accept that nothing had happened, that a nothing had happened, learned to bear it and even, in a shy way, to like it' (80).

The incidents following the one with the Galls involve us in this same kind of interdeterminacy; each is an exercise in rationalistic circumlocution, and each contributes to the novel's epistemological farce. Watt's attempt to name a pot, as readers note,[11] renders the 'semantic succour' (83) we find in language ineffective. Language turns meaning into a 'pillow of old words', enabling us to turn a 'disturbance into words' (117). Watt of course longs to hear his upstairs-counterpart, Erskine, 'wrapping up safe in words the kitchen space' (83) and all the other objects and events in the house. But Watt's difficulty in 'his efforts to distinguish between what happened and what did not happen, between what was and what was not, in Mr. Knott's house' (126), is precisely the point. And so it is with his attempt to analyse the picture discovered in Erskine's room. Because so many spatial and temporal explanations of the relationship between the circle with the black circumference and the blue dot are possible, Watt feels obliged to consider them all; so perplexing are these possibilities that they lead to tears. But not, we find, of sadness: 'Watt's eyes filled with tears that he could not stem, and they flowed down his fluted cheeks unchecked, in a steady flow, *refreshing* him greatly' (129, italics mine). And so it is with every other incident in the novel, from Watt's initial attempt to enter the house to his final departure from it. In sceptical terms, the obligatory consideration of equally possible meanings (*isothenia*) leads to the *ephetic* suspension of judgement and to the state of *ataraxy*, the apathetic inner calm that comes from doubt (*aporia*).[12]

In fact, the matter goes deeper than this. What occurs (or doesn't occur) on the level of incident is also true of the manner in which *Watt* is written. Readers may tire of Beckett's lists of explanations and his seemingly interminable strings of 'ors', the most famous of which is Molloy's discourse on the sucking stones. In *Watt*, the 'twelve possibilities' for the arrangement made to feed Mr Knott (89) and the solutions (and objections to those solutions) to the problem of the dog(s) who might have eaten Knott's food, or the remnants of that food (91–100), provide other examples.[13] When, after thirty pages of consideration, Watt grasps, 'in its complexity, the mechanism of this arrangement . . . it interested him no more, and he enjoyed a comparative peace of mind, in this connection' (117). Indeed, Watt is himself a member of a series lacking an explicable causal relation among its parts: he has replaced Arsene, who replaced Vincent as Knott's retainer on the ground floor; and he replaces Erskine on the second floor when Arthur takes his place and leaves Knott's when a new retainer arrives in the night. When he thinks, 'in search of rest', of the possible relations between sequential and causal, temporal or spatial effects, 'between . . . "the series of dogs, the series of men, the series of pictures' (136), it is to provide possibilities, permutations. The stylistic function of this enumeration is to admit all possibilities, in true sceptical fashion, so that no one meaning is possible. And to this play with language must be linked the destruction of language itself as a vehicle for signification, seen in Watt's inversion of syntax and of the letters that make up his words.

'I'm working with impotence, ignorance', Beckett told Schenker, 'I don't think impotence has been exploited in the past.' In *Watt*, Beckett works out for the first time the sceptical vision that will occupy him for the next ten years. In doing so, he sets himself the task that the first poem listed in the addenda to *Watt* expresses so clearly:

who may tell the tale
of the old man?
weigh absence in a scale?
mete want with a span?
the sum assess
of the world's woes?
nothingness
in words enclose?

The poem may well serve as an epigraph to all of Beckett's sceptical fictions.

Notes

1. *Samuel Beckett: Poet and Critic* (Princeton, 1970).
2. *Watt* (New York, 1959). All citations are from this edition.
3. See *Proust* (New York, 1931), pp. 57–64, for Beckett's views on 'the grotesque fallacy of realistic art – "that miserable statement of line and surface."' Also see Enoch Brater, 'Privilege, Perspective and Point of View in *Watt*,' *College Literature*, 8 (1981): 209–26, for comment on the way 'the exchange between Hackett and the Nixons, parodying the questions the reader of realistic fiction might ask, introduces a sceptical attitude toward the pursuit of knowledge' (213).
4. *Samuel Beckett: Poet and Critic*, p. 352.
5. 'Moody Man of Letters', *New York Times* (Sunday, 5 May 1956), Section 2, 1, 3.
6. See *Perspective*, 11 (1959); 155–65; 132–41. Also see Kenner, *Samuel Beckett: A Critical Study* (New York, 1961); Cohn, *Samuel Beckett: The Comic Gamut* (New Brunswick, 1962); John Fletcher, *The Novels of Samuel Beckett* (London, 1964) and *Samuel Beckett's Art* (London, 1967); Richard N. Coe, *Samuel Beckett* (New York, 1964); Robert Harrison, *Samuel Beckett's 'Murphy': A Critical Excursion* (Athens, 1968); Michael Robinson, *The Long Sonata of the Dead* (New York, 1969).
7. It is important to remember that Descartes's *Discourse on Method* was an attack upon scepticism and that many of his pronouncements, including his famous statement when he converted doubt into dogma, were defences against scepticism. Two are apposite: 'while I thus wished to think everything false, it was necessarily true that I who thought so was something. Since this truth, *I think, therefore I am*, was so firm and assured that all the most extravagant suppositions of the sceptics were unable to shake it, I judged that I could safely accept it as the first principle of the philosophy I was seeking.' 'I was assailed by so many doubts and errors that the only profit I appeared to have drawn from trying to become educated, was progressively to have discovered my ignorance.' See R. E. Sutcliffe, trans., *Discourse on Method and the Meditations* (Harmondsworth, 1968). Also see Richard

H. Popkin, *The History of Scepticism from Erasmus to Descartes* (Assen, 1960), pp. 197–217; and Michael E. Mooney, '*Molloy*, Part One: Beckett's *Discourse on Method*', *Journal of Beckett Studies*, 3 (1978): pp. 40–55, and 'Presocratic Scepticism: Samuel Beckett's *Murphy* Reconsidered', *English Literary History*, 49 (1982): 214–34.

8. *Murphy* (New York, 1957), p. 246.

9. See *Academica*, I, 12.

10. See Brater, pp. 215–23; and J. E. Dearlove, *Accommodating the Chaos: Samuel Beckett's Nonrelational Art* (Durham, 1982), pp. 42–8, on the manipulation of linear, narrative and novelistic expectation and on the ordering of the chapters in *Watt*. In support of this view, see J. M. Coetzee's earlier essay, 'The Manuscript Revisions of Beckett's *Watt*', *Journal of Modern Literature*', 2 (1972): 472–80.

11. Jacqueline Hoefer's '*Watt*', *Perspective*, 11 (1959): 166–82, is the earliest analysis of this dimension of the novel. Hoefer's suggestion that the source of Beckett's view of language is Wittgenstein has been questioned. See Rubin Rabinovitz, *The Development of Samuel Beckett's Fiction* (Urbana, 1984), pp. 124–50, especially pp. 144–5 n16; and Linda Ben-Zvi, 'Samuel Beckett, Fritz Mauthner, and the Limits of Language', *PMLA*, 95 (1980): 183–200.

12. See R. G. Bury (ed.), *Sextus Empiricus* (Cambridge, 1955), 1: p. 19. For an allied discussion of *aporia* and the *ephetic* suspension of judgement, see Fred Miller Robinson, 'Samuel Beckett: *Watt*', in *The Comedy of Language: Studies in Modern Comic Literature* (Amherst, 1980), reprinted in Harold Bloom (ed.), *Modern Critical Views: Samuel Beckett* (New York, 1985), pp. 147–93.

13. See Dearlove, *Accommodating the Chaos*, op. cit., p. 44, on the care Beckett took to work out these permutations.

10

A New Approach to *Watt*

Gottfried Büttner

d'où
la voix qui dit
vis
d'une autre vie
(Beckett, 1981)

Because of the queer and irritating character of *Watt* – the man as well as the book – we may ask the same question as Mr Gorman does towards the end of that novel: 'Who the devil are you . . . and what the hell do you want?'[1] Beckett finished *Watt* immediately after the Second World War, and in *Mercier et Camier* (1946), his first novel thereafter, written in French, he again refers to the difficulty of knowing Watt. The English translation reads:

I am Watt, said Watt. As you say, I'm unrecognizable. Watt? said Camier. The name means nothing to me. I am not widely known, said Watt, but I shall be, one day.[2]

Compared with the 'utter ignorance' registered at the beginning of the earlier novel, this statement implies that Watt *can* be known.

When I first read *Watt* in 1969, it immediately captivated me; like any other reader, I was puzzled by it, even though it has always been for me the missing link between *Murphy* and *Molloy*, that is, part of a sequence. Like most of Beckett's fiction it provokes questions, and if the author himself is not keen on answering such questions, it is clear that his work does seek adequate responses. Though Beckett is not really willing to answer questions about his work ('No thought . . . as to riddles, solutions')[3] he does concede that 'for such serious stuff we have universities, churches, coffee houses etc.'[4] We may ourselves judge on which level of understanding we should read the novel. There are undoubtedly different

169

levels of understanding and 'Watt' can entertain readers in different ways.

John Fletcher, in his book *The Novels of Samuel Beckett*, finishes his chapter on *Watt*, referring to Ruby Cohn's comparative study on *Watt* and Kafka's *Castle*, with the following sentence:[5]

> Both novels are however similar in that they are myths, the interpretation of which must be a subtle and complex affair, for they have the power of haunting the mind on many levels without being explicit: they fulfil the functions of a symbol of *unassigned* value: it is we who lend the symbol meaning, from our own hopes and fears.

Although Beckett uses mainly ordinary words in *Watt*, the novel gives the impression of verbal richness. There was no question for me but that the true meaning lay *between* the words, in the repetitions, in the pauses, in the rhythms, and that the strange whisper recurring through the work came from beyond space and time, from a realm of existence quite different from our world. Linda Ben-Zvi touches on that question, describing Watt as a 'solitary wanderer' (like Beckett's other protagonists):[6]

> Watt resides for a time under the roof of Knott, or naught, attempting, through close observation, to pierce his secrets.

And a little further, on Watt's attempts to rationalise:

> he is constantly battling to control the phenomena he encounters, to shape them into some form he can examine, then verbalize and, thus, having conquered, forget. The results of his struggle for understanding are deadening, a torture for Watt and for the reader who follows page after page of calibrations, calculations, and repetitions that constitute thinking for this postlapsarian man . . .

Well, I believe the world Watt finds himself exposed to cannot be 'rationalised' in the usual way; attempts to do so are bound to fail.

Watt raises questions which cannot be answered by the techniques of literary criticism alone. Neither is a psychologically oriented interpretation sufficient in itself; it must be supplemented by epistemological and anthropological concepts, constituting altogether a 'spiritual science' or thought. Otherwise we wind up stranded on the level of psychological relativism, which would block our effort to do justice to the stature of the work. The common 'Madhouse theory' is tempting and still common in literary criticism,[7] but it seems to be merely an evasion of the deeper issues. It can be accepted only with certain reservations. Superficially looked at, Part III of the novel (where Sam is told the entire story by Watt) involves a 'lunatic situation'. But this does not mean that the situation should be taken literally. Watt is in a state which can be expressed only by means of an 'asylum' image. That's all. Neither Watt nor Sam is insane. The author creates the suspicion that Watt is a mental patient because he describes separate buildings and little gardens surrounding them. Psychiatric institutions frequently consist of a number of such 'pavilions'. But such phrases as: 'looking about me *like* a mad creature'[8] or: 'continuing my inspection, *like* one deprived of his senses'[9] say only that it appeared to the observer 'as if' . . . .

Beckett's method, as he describes it in his essay on Proust, is the path of internalisation and contemplation. For an artist, 'who does not deal in surfaces'[10] there is only one way 'To the deep – Down, down! . . . Through the cloudy strife / Of Death and of Life . . .' as Shelley said in his poem 'Prometheus Unbound' in 1820.[11] To quote Beckett himself: 'the only possible spiritual development is in the sense of depth.'[12] Beckett has repeatedly stressed that he is incapable of speaking about his work. In a letter to me he wrote: *'Moi je suis tout à fait incapable d'en parler. Je ne le vois et ne le vis que du dedans.'*[13]

Beckett's creative vision comes from the deepest inner levels of the psyche. We may find ourselves thinking of Shakespeare's *A Midsummer Night's Dream* (Act V, Scene 1, lines 13–17):

> The poet's eye, in a fine frenzy rolling,
> Doth glance from heaven to earth, from earth to heaven;
> And, as imagination bodies forth
> The forms of things unknown, the poet's pen
> Turns them to shapes, and gives to airy nothing
> A local habitation and a name.

But Beckett is unique in contemporary literature in the way he creates out of inner experiences of a kind ignored for centuries. Watt may not be much of an initiate and clearly has difficulties in describing what he suffers under, but Beckett deciphers for him. Watt's is a voice which gets its information from the *preverbal world* of so-called nothingness, a nothingness which has become a source of value and inspiration to Samuel Beckett himself.

Eric P. Levy, another Beckett scholar who has written a study of the prose fiction[14] describes Watt's situation adequately: 'Just as Adam was the first man to name the animals, Watt becomes the first man to inhabit a world beyond the reach of language . . .'.[15] The problem we have in following Beckett's – or rather Sam's – description is that our own shrunken horizon of rational thinking, trained to grasp only the world of cause and effect around us, has to be gradually set aside. The outer world has to be eliminated before we can follow Watt's path into nothingness or rather into Mr Knott's house and garden.

The story of Watt begins in a normal way, as Mr Hackett 'turned the corner and saw, in the failing light, at some little distance, his seat',[16] from which vantage-point he observes not only Watt's strange figure but, in a sort of framework story, also receives information about the human sexual behaviour, the pregnancy, and the delivery of Mrs Nixon, and so on. All this focuses the reader's mind on what happens to Watt, who is approaching the station. He is about to start his first journey. At the beginning of this journey there is the strange encounter of Watt with the 'porter', wheeling a milkcan. Watt becoming acquainted with his mother? I presume so. His journey in the train begins, with his back to his destination, as he apparently prefers to travel, and it ends abruptly. On his way to Mr Knott's house, Watt finds himself subsiding into a ditch, listening to a strange chorus or choir.

Subsequently, in a subconscious way, Watt crosses the threshold into Mr Knott's house to start his career on the other side of existence. It's the 'life to come' which he begins on the ground floor. He's now one of Mr Knott's constantly shifted servants and he gets some explanations from one of his predecessors, now leaving. 'What was changed was existence off the ladder'[17] – the ladder was taken away. 'For in truth the same things happen to us all . . . if only we chose to know it.'[18]

We are told that 'the coming is in the shadow of going and the going is in the shadow of the coming'[19] except for the one who is 'eternal' in the sense of not having to come and to go like all his servants: 'And yet there is one who neither comes nor goes, I refer I need hardly say to my late employer . . .',[20] that is, Mr Knott.

'But to go into this matter as longly and as deeply and as fully as I should like, and it deserves, is unfortunately out of the question.'[21]

The hierarchical structure of the realm of Mr Knott is represented in Parts II and III of the novel. 'Mr. Knott was a good master, in a way',[22] the description starts, and it leads through two entirely different parts of the house and garden of Mr Knott. Whilst aspects of the narrator change more than once, there are phases in which the authorial, all-knowing narrator prevails, and there are others, when one figure alone tells a story or pretends to do so. I need not go into detail, but the atmosphere is densely filled with strange events in order to depict the total change from earthly conditions to those which one can only expect to happen in another world: the Galls, the problem of the dogs, Erskine's room on the upper floor, Mrs Gorman, Mr Graves and so on.

We can assume that what Watt reports from Mr Knott's house and garden is qualitatively different from what is said about Watt when he is on his way to the station, in the train and on his way to Mr Knott's house. If we consider the sequence of events on the basis of the revised structural relationships, many irregularities and inversions suddenly become clear.[23]

If we accept the initial hypothesis that Mr Knott's house and garden are to be found in another realm of existence, it is no wonder that in the first section we read of Watt's hope of one day being face to face with Mr Knott. This situation resembles that of *Waiting for Godot* except, as matters proceed, this 'Godot' becomes in certain moments visible, at least in anthropomorphic terms. The hierarchy of numerous servants revolves around Mr Knott; the master nevertheless keeps his distance. Mr Knott, as a lively entity, his 'figure' and behaviour, can only be depicted through Watt's weak capacity of observation.

The whole world of Mr Knott seems illogical. This suggests that the entire concept of 'meaning' has changed, in that events now signify something both while they are happening and as they appear in retrospect. All events reported are only *occasions*, not ends in themselves; that is, they are referential in character: they point to something else, to something other than what they appear to be on the surface. The stylistic features of *Watt* confirm this. Pseudo-logical excesses occur; endless enumerations and the like. These should not be confused with mere poetic effusions, for this would be to underestimate their function. Those passages do not fill page after page simply to display formal brilliance. Rather, they are the expression of an uncompromising effort to obtain clarity and to escape the constraints of external, superficial meaning. The so-called 'series' (mathematical plays) also have an educative effect, in that they exercise the mind. Meaning here is in the 'how', not in the 'what'. The objects discussed – the pot, the food, the disposal of the dog's leftovers – are of secondary importance.

Watt ascends the rungs of this hierarchically-ordered world, beginning his service on the ground floor and moving to the next one where another sudden change takes place. The structure of Part III has puzzled most readers. Its special features do not appear to connect smoothly with Part II. There is a break here. But if we take what has been said about the superficiality of *literal meaning* seriously, that is to say, that words can only approximate to what is really meant, then we can understand where Watt has now arrived, although the scenery has changed into pavilions in little fenced gardens. Watt's move upwards means a separation from the past or even a totally new frame of reference. We realise that Watt is no longer just Watt, but that he now has a partner, Sam, who functions as Watt's alter ego. He represents a consciousness which has separated or split itself off from him. Although this cleavage suggests schizophrenia, the split is not pathological; it is controlled and can be overcome or reversed at any time, as in fact occurs. Here no one is a victim, but there is no doubt that this state of consciousness resembles somehow that of a deranged person.[24]

Beckett's choice of imagery appropriately expresses the two spheres of consciousness which he needs for Watt and Sam: each has his own little fenced-in garden, his separate field of consciousness, and the manner in which each gets about is characteristically different. Two men walking side by side, one forward, the other one backward. And the weather has to be such, so that they both can get together; the spiritual atmosphere has to be sunny and windy at the same time. Bodily movement is equivalent here to *moving about mentally*. We should never forget that. Walking backward is only another image for *talking* backward, and this in turn refers to a reversal of the thinking process. This type of thinking – the mirror image of logical, straightforward thinking – can be learned. It is in fact acquired in stages by practice on the 'second floor'. Thus the process of inversion is in full swing.

At the climax of Part III we discover a striking text if we rearrange the reversed text:

Abandoned my little to find him. My little to learn him forgot.
My little rejected to have him. To love him my little reviled. This
body homeless. This mind ignoring. These emptied hands. This
emptied heart. To him I brought. To the temple. To the teacher.
To the source. Of nought.[25]

Watt thus gives up his 'little' to find Mr Knott, to learn from him,
to have him. He abandons his little, his miserable body and
unknowing mind, and empties his hands and heart to love him.
Watt has brought all this to the temple, to the teacher, to the
source of nothingness. The 'source of nought' – this is a description
of the second floor of Mr Knott's house. The dismembered Watt,
split into two consciousnesses, has entered this timeless sphere,
only distantly related to our world. Movement there is non-
Newtonian, as Beckett suggests in Chapter 6 of *Murphy* where he
states that Murphy's mind after all is the gravamen. There it was
Murphy's, here it is Watt's.

We should not be too puzzled by other changes in the text. All
of a sudden the narrative takes a new turn, the scene shifting to
the garden, where Mr Knott disappears into a huge tree, after he
has been described sitting on a mound at first or disappearing
behind a bush and emerging from behind another. We have to get
used to the fact that in this nowhere Mr Knott can be anywhere.
The region in which Mr Knott lives has the power to recall,
immediately and urgently, anyone who has been forced away from
it. Yet his house is called a refuge. Watt tries to describe Mr Knott's
peculiar nature, his indefinable appearance, his impenetrable
being. But this is only anthropomorphic insolence on Watt's part.
His powers are not equal to the job.

In spite of the fact that the realm of Mr Knott is hard to describe
and in spite of the enormous proliferation of images and events,
this third part of the novel *Watt* is nevertheless a self-contained
whole. This is evident from the way in which this chapter begins
and ends. It ends with the same pavilion with which it has begun,
and with the same image of it. Watt moves backward to his pavilion
and thus becomes separate again from Sam.

Nowhere in *Watt* is there a more concentrated attempt to describe
Mr Knott in all his peculiarities than in Part III. Nowhere is the
narrator hotter on his trail. But transformation is Mr Knott's nature.
However, although the attempt to obtain intimate knowledge of
Mr Knott ultimately fails, we still learn a good deal about him.

Part III is dedicated to the finally unknowable Mr Knott, who thus becomes the most important element, the climactic point of the entire novel. We learn at the same time that our language, especially its logical content, is not equal to the task of describing him. Even imagery fails, metaphors remain incomplete and inaccurate. Watt is not an omniscient narrator.

The whole novel is composed in four movements, like a symphony. Each part leads back more or less to its beginnings, like four successive waves.[26] Parts II and III belong closely together and there are certain similarities, although reversed, between Parts I and IV. The story ends with Watt once again at a railway station, having been released from Mr Knott's house, having returned only to be shut up overnight in a waiting-room which is a kind of uterus from which poor Watt is to be expelled next morning. 'As Watt came, so he went, in the night . . .'.[27] Micks, his successor on the ground floor, crosses the threshold like Watt once he has arrived: 'One moment I was out, and the next I was in.'[28] Another picture for coming down to earth is taken up a few lines later: 'Hyperions Schicksalslied' comes to Watt's mind. Hölderlin's poem refers to suffering mankind, falling like water thrown from cliff to cliff, year after year down into uncertainty. In the waiting room, Watt's position is described in the following way: 'he drooped sigmoidal in its midst'.[29] Whom else could this refer to other than an embryo on its cord? Even the placenta is neatly described: 'an object of some importance' was his chair on one leg . . . .[30] 'It was not part of the ceiling, nor of the wall, nor, though it seemed in contact with the floor, of the floor . . .'.[31] Watt has to take his roll of toilet-paper for a handkerchief because of the smell, exceptionally foul, penetrating from the neighbourhood into the waiting room: the anatomical associations and equations are obvious.

When knocked down on to the floor, hit by the two wings of the swing door, slimy water mixed with blood is splashed across him – all this fits with the picture of being expelled from a mother's womb. Watt starts his new journey by asking for a ticket 'to the end of the line'.[32] 'The long summer's day had made an excellent start. If it continued in the same manner, its close would be worth coming to see . . . life isn't such a bad old bugger.'[33] The noticeable course which Watt's mind takes through the great metamorphoses of life and death, as depicted in *Watt*, happens twice: there are two railway stations, at the beginning and towards the end, through which poor Watt has to go in order to begin a new journey.

The nightmarish story dwells, not entirely, it is true, but most intensely, on Watt's *experiences in death* rather than his experiences in life. The strange educational exercises offered by Mr Spiro, editor of 'Crux'(!), in the train do not elicit Watt's special interest. His first journey (through life) ends all of a sudden after Watt has passed by the racecourse and ended up in the ditch.

Samuel Beckett consciously lives on the fringe of existence. His interest is with the deep dark gap between here and there where any ego becomes lonely. Beckett's searching mind is directed towards this inner world of loneliness, not so much toward the desolate muckball he has never really been unduly fond of. Rubin Rabinovitz describes how Beckett at times withdraws from the world:

> Beckett has said that as a prelude to writing he sometimes engages in long periods of contemplation, and his descriptions of such experiences resemble those he depicts in the novel. When Watt feels himself losing touch with the outer world, he begins to hear faint sounds: 'In his skull the voices whispering their canon were like a pattern of mice, a flurry of little gray paws in the dust' (p. 232). In a conversation with Lawrence Harvey, Beckett spoke about his own sense of 'getting below the surface, concentrating, listening, getting your ear down so you can hear the infinitesimal murmur . . .'.[34]

This reminds us of the description Beckett gives in *Murphy*: how the young Irish fellow can move about in three zones of darkness within him, feeling like 'a mote in the dark of absolute freedom'.[35] Although I do not want to confuse Beckett with Murphy, I believe that this characterises perfectly an explorer's mind face to face with the invisible, a realm we might call the supersensible world. 'A mote in the dark of absolute freedom' is a wonderful picture for a searching I, for a lonely searching human ego. Let me play with words in repeating Shakespeare's line: 'The poet's *eye*, in a fine frenzy rolling . . .'.

In his essay on Proust[36] Beckett's method, as he describes it, presumably as much for himself as for anybody else searching for the truth about man as a spiritual being, has been the path of internalisation and contemplation. At the same time, it should not be overlooked that he transcends the merely subjective realms of experience conveyed in more comprehensible psychological terms by other authors (including Proust) and actually explores virgin territory. In his 'search for the self'[37] Beckett sets aside his everyday ego and advances to the existential thresholds of birth and death. The experience of the void, which reveals itself to him as the womb of the irrational, the 'matrix of surds' (according to *Murphy*, Chapter 6), has become for him a creative source of imagination and intuition. He is capable of seeing into the world of the unborn and the dead.

In *Watt* Beckett succeeds in annulling the temporal aspect of existence. He crosses the borderline or rather pushes the frontier a little further into that spiritual world, which is unknown to most people. He knows that, when the zero-point is passed, the world of the mind undergoes a reversal. It must have been hard for him to express this in literary images because of the difficulty of keeping them properly organised. But with an enormous effort, in a *tour de force*, he has captured his experiences in words. In addition to seeing images, which still depend heavily on previous experiences and on pieces of digested memory, he must have begun to hear 'voices' speaking to him – Watt's voice. Thus *Watt* is a record of actual inner events. All its visual motifs, its words, the rhythms of its language, and its overall composition are subordinated to this spiritual reality of life and death which raises quite naturally the question of reincarnation. Beckett depicts a plane of reality which mankind is prone to forget. This is for me the 'secret' of this text and its fascination, though it ought, I feel, to be perceivable by anyone who makes a serious attempt to understand *Watt*.

Notes

1. *Watt* (London, 1963), p. 243.
2. *Mercier and Camier* (London, 1974; New York, 1975), p. 111.
3. See programme no. 187 of the Schiller Theatre Workshop, Berlin 1967/68, translated into English in: G. Büttner: *Samuel Beckett's Novel* Watt (Philadelphia, 1984), p. 3.
4. Ibid.
5. J. Fletcher, *The Novels of Samuel Beckett* (London, 1970), p. 89.
6. L. Ben-Zvi, *Samuel Beckett* (Boston, Massachusetts, 1986), p. 65.
7. Ibid., p. 66; there we read: 'if we are to believe Sam, the story we read in the pages of the novel *Watt* is a story that a madman dictates to another madman in a garbled language and a broken chronology . . .'. See also J. Pilling, *Samuel Beckett* (London, 1976), p. 42.

8. *Watt*, p. 158.
9. Ibid., p. 159.
10. S. Beckett, *Proust* (New York, 1931; eighth printing, n.d.), p. 46.
11. Quoted from J. Calder (ed.), *Beckett at Sixty* (London, 1967), p. 93.
12. S. Beckett, *Proust*, op. cit., pp. 46–7.
13. Mr Beckett kindly gave permission to publish the entire letter in the publication of the Kassel-Symposium (April 1986) on 'Samuel Beckett und die Literatur der Gegenwart', published in October 1987 by Carl Winter Universitätsverlag, Heidelberg, W. Germany. Beckett's letter is dated 24 May 1963.
14. E. P. Levy, *Beckett and the Voice of Species* (Ottowa, New Jersey, 1980), p. 28.
15. See also S. Kennedy, 'The Simple Games that Time Plays with Space', 'An Introduction to Samuel Beckett's Manuscripts of *Watt*' in *Centerpoint*, Vol. 2, no. 3, Fall 1977, p. 55.
16. *Watt*, p. 5.
17. Ibid., p. 42. See also: L. Ben-Zvi: *Samuel Beckett*, op. cit., p. 69: 'The experience is the central one in the book, the loss of certainty in the physical world and in the language that describes it.' And: 'Arsene . . . describes a similar experience of slippage by employing a ladder image. . . . The imagery is borrowed from twentieth-century philosophers Fritz Mauthner and Ludwig Wittgenstein who employed it to describe a similar situation: the struggle to climb beyond the limits of language . . .'.
18. *Watt*, p. 44.
19. Ibid., p. 56.
20. Ibid., p. 56.
21. Ibid., p. 61.
22. Ibid., p. 64.
23. *Watt* Part IV, p. 215, starts off with the following sentence: 'As Watt told the beginning of his story, not first, but second, so not fourth, but third, now he told its end.' See: Laass/Schröder: *Samuel Beckett*, (München, 1984), pp. 87–104 (containing a thorough analysis of the structure of *Watt*) and G. Büttner: *Samuel Beckett's Novel* Watt, op. cit., p. 84.
24. E. Brater in his study 'Privilege, Perspective, and Point of View in *Watt*', *College Literature*, Vol. VIII, no. 3, Fall 1981, p. 220 states: 'If one assumes the possibility that Sam, like Watt, is mentally deranged, the confusion of persons and pronouns may be explained as the dissociation of a madman.' Authors like A. Alvarez (*Beckett*, London, 1978), R. Breuer (*Die Kunst der Paradoxie*, München, 1976) and H. Breuer (*Samuel Beckett*, München, 1972) refer, in respect to *Watt*, to 'signs of psychosis' but do not sufficiently take into account the spontaneous *reversibility* of the process which speaks against an illness.
25. *Watt*, p. 166.
26. L. Ben-Zvi specially refers to the lyrical passages at the end of Parts III and IV: '*Watt* ends in a lyrical passage rather than in a laugh or a grimace . . . a quietus after the pain of the quest.' (*Samuel Beckett*, op. cit., p. 70.)

27. *Watt*, p. 214.
28. Ibid., p. 215.
29. Ibid., p. 233.
30. Ibid., p. 233.
31. Ibid., p. 234.
32. Ibid., p. 244.
33. Ibid., p. 245.
34. Rubin Rabinovitz, *The Development of Samuel Beckett's Fiction* (Chicago, Illinois, 1984), p. 137.
35. *Murphy* (New York, n.d.), p. 112.
36. S. Beckett, *Proust*, op. cit., p. 46.
37. 'The Search for the Self', title of Martin Esslin's chapter on Beckett in his *Theatre of the Absurd* (Garden City, N.Y., 1969).

11

Conspicuous Absence: *Tracé* and Power in Beckett's Drama

Stephen Barker

Beckett's sparsity of writing[1] demonstrates, throughout his work, a deep sense of the ascetic, the eschatological, the reverential. The humour, the precision and the vagueness, the form, the mechanisms of syntax, Beckett's entire economy of presentation manifest as ascetic *care* that is both Heideggerian, as Lance Butler has pointed out (*Sorge*; care in the sense of self-discovering, the self-centred concern with bringing the whole self forth into the world, but without moral or ethical overtones), and Nietzschean (care as concern and action). Indeed, this may not at first seem to concur with one's impression of Beckett. Lance Butler correctly says that 'Beckett seems to be in violent revolt against the nature of this world' (151). This would hardly seem to engage the kind of care one confronts in these other writers. And yet Butler goes on to give us the key to Beckett's *engagement*: of Beckett's revolt, Butler says that 'it is clearly not something political or psychological that he is revolting against. It is something ontological' (151). Beckett's works, he says, are 'ontological parables'. It is at the level of existence (or of being) itself that Beckett engages the world.

Yet, typically, this seems paradoxical in light of the fact that the first and most abiding sense one has in reading or viewing Beckett's literature is a sense of absence. Whether it be the name of the unnamable, the rest of Winnie's body or Billie Whitelaw's face, or Godot himself, something is perennially absent. Not missing, not non-existent – absent. A truism of contemporary critical theory,

1. In the following essay, Beckett's work will be considered in translation unless the effect of his 'original' French is desired over that of his 'original' English; given that Beckett is his own translator, interpretation of his English is all the more justified.

indeed of contemporary culture in general, however, is that absence is itself dialectical, that to 'introduce' absence is to 'introduce' presence in a 'play' that transcends both – thus are we all the sons of Hegel. It is a function of the bimodality of modern thought: polarity and synthesis as structural ground. This polarity goes as far back as Plato – Nietzsche would say as far as Sophocles. The invocation of these names is significant for a treatment of Beckett: a playwright, Sophocles, and a philosopher, Plato: the meeting of drama and abstract conceptualisation.

But again, how does this apply to Samuel Beckett, who says that he is unaffected by philosophy, that he doesn't read it because he doesn't understand it. Anyone who has read 'Whoroscope' or Lucky's monologue from (quaquaquaqua) *Godot*, or Lance Butler's book on Beckett's relation to Heidegger, Sartre, and Hegel, knows how much to trust this typical Beckettian self-assessment. The question as to whether *Godot* is a very long existential play or a very short metaphysical poem is the same one. Again the polarity, again the play of absence and presence, the fundamental philosophical and eschatological interrogation.

But with deconstruction this question takes a new turn, becomes a new *tropos*. Derrida's formulation of the trace, out of Heidegger but within a Nietzschean genealogy, gives us a new way to look at the pervasive theme of the trace in Beckett. These, then, are the names I want to invoke: Nietzsche and Derrida. My contentions:

—That a review of Derrida's *trace* and *tracé*, in the context of the Nietzschean opening of writing, will provide a new and helpful perspective on Beckett

—That that perspective will consist of an explanation, a placing, a locating of Beckett's ubiquitous absence

—That this topology will demonstrate the basis for Beckett's power as dramatist, poet, thinker.

The issue of presence and absence, and of the Derridean trace in Beckett is raised at every moment by and in the ascetic sparsity of Beckett's writing, and comes through Derrida from Heidegger's *Holzwege*, in which Derrida reads that 'the matinal trace (*die frühe Spur*) of difference effaces itself from the moment that presence appears as being-present.

CONSPICUOUS ABSENCE: *TRACÉ* AND POWER IN BECKETT'S DRAMA

Throughout his work, from his plays to his novels to his poetry, Samuel Beckett is recognised as a manipulator of and commentator on absence. Whether it be Winnie's body, the rest of Billie Whitelaw's face, the younger Mr Krapp, Godot himself, or the name of the unnamable, something is absent in Beckett. Not non-existent, not simply missing, but *absent*. Beckett criticism has focused on this absence and given it many groundings, ranging from cultural determiner (and Beckett as interpreter of a culture in which a thematics of absence is central), to absence as a sign of that favourite Beckett theme, failure, a psychological manifestation of man's 'running down' and the entropy resultant from a (correct) perception of man's world.

I want to reexamine this apparent absence in Beckett, and to provide this reexamination with an anchor, to use an appropriately Derridean image, in writing itself. I want to suggest that Beckett's writing has perceived that its power is in its play *beyond*, that is in the tension of energy between, conceptual rigidities such as 'absence' and 'presence'; further, I want to apply Derrida's strategies of the *trace* or the *tracé* to Beckett to show it (and his work) as a non-concept in which that play of absence and presence *is* the suspended threshold of meaning.

To reach this trace in Beckett one must take an ahistorical route. The concept of the trace, directly so-called, has its roots in Heidegger's discussion of Being and presence, but is only made something of by Derrida in his critique of Heidegger's concept of the difference of Being, of which 'trace' is a part. In Derrida's article *'Différance'* he investigates the Heideggerian coordinates of time and space in the concept of difference, introducing the trace by quoting this passage from Heidegger's 'Anaximander Fragment' in *Holzwege*: 'even the early trace (*die frühe Spur*) of the distinction [between the present and the presencing of Being] is obliterated when presencing appears as something present and finds itself in the position of being the highest being present' (*'Différance'* 24). Although this passage, like many in Heidegger, sounds a great deal like Lucky, it marks Derrida's departure from Heidegger: for Heidegger the trace is a memory of difference, specifically between a distinctive moment and consciousness of that moment, which makes the being of the moment transcendent. The Heideggerian trace is a remnant, a nostalgic focus projecting its *geist* into a present in which it lingers like Shelley's fading coal; trace is a reminder of a past in which *Dasein* no longer speaks for itself but is covered over and lost, leaving only its trace, which is then itself lost and forgotten. And indeed, to further an argument in Lance Butler's book *Samuel Beckett and the Meaning of Being*, the trace presents one with an 'ontological parable' in which language acts as the medium of presence, but in which Being is present only as a trace. In Heidegger, unlike Derrida and Beckett, the nostalgia indigenous to the trace pacifies the revolt against the conundra of being (lower case) and of *Dasein*. For Heidegger, language is 'Being [upper case] speaking', but Being is never spoken by language, only by its imminence.

This is Derrida's point of departure, and the place at which he, under the influence here of Nietzsche, and Beckett reach the *Godot-*esque *carrefour*, the crossroads at which the trace undergoes a radical turn from its Heideggerian origin. Derrida is influenced by Nietzsche's concept of *force* and its application to *written* language in a way Heidegger is not; for Derrida, the trace

> *n'étant pas une présence mais le simulacre d'une présence qui se disloque, se déplace, se renvoie, n'a proprement pas lieu, l'éffacement appartient à sa structure. . . . Le paradoxe d'une telle structure, c'est, dans le langage de la métaphysique, cette inversion du concept métaphysique qui produit l'effet suivant: le présent devient le signe du signe, la trace de la trace.*

> [not a presence but the simulacrum of a presence that dislocates itself, displaces itself, refers itself, it properly has no site – erasure belongs to its structure. . . . The paradox of such a structure, in the language of metaphysics, is an inversion of metaphysical concepts, which produces the following effect: the present becomes the sign of the sign, the trace of the trace.]   (25)

The so-called present, in the realm of the Derridean trace, is itself substantiated only in its inscription: it is the mark of a cipher. The acknowledgement of the trace, like that of a particle in a cloud-chamber or a particle accelerator, infuses writing not with absence but with the force of action. The action of writing, for Derrida, sublimates but cancels the present, as it does the past and the future; indeed, the Derridean trace operates outside of time and can never be appropriated into any Heideggerian 'as such'. The *'différance'* of the trace has no essence and is aconceptual. It is a strategy.

Writing's employment of time and place, like its ability to seem to 'contain' the empty boxes we call 'names', is dramatically a secondary sub-strategy. This describes Beckett's separation of words and things and his mirage of absence. As though he is echoing Beckett, Derrida says of the trace that

> *cet innommable n'est pas un être ineffable dont aucun nom ne pourrait s'approcher. . . . Cet innommable [the trace] est le jeu qui fait qu'il y a des éffets nominaux, des structures rélativement unitaires ou atomiques qu'on appelle noms.*

> [this unnamable is not an ineffable Being which no name could approach. . . . This unnamable [the trace] is the play which makes possible nominal effects, the relatively unitary and atomic structures that are called names.] (*'Différance'* 28)

It is in writing, in the activity of systems and ciphers, that trace enters into play. Thus Derrida puts the trace outside of space and time, and outside the nominal, declaring it to be the *force* 'behind', as Joyce would say, the seeming oppositions of chance and necessity, abstraction and concretion, essence and experience. But this is not Hegelian synthesis nor Heideggerian cooption; no longer is trace the remnant and sign of loss; it has undergone, in Derrida, through an un-Heideggerian rereading of Nietzsche, a radical shift from the experience of *Dasein*. Suddenly, trace is linked not to Being nor to *Dasein* but to textuality. All sign systems, according to Derrida, operate on the basis of intratextual forces of transference and difference such that

> *aucun élément ne peut fonctionner comme signe sans renvoyer à un autre élément qui lui-même n'est pas simplement présent. Cet enchaînement fait que chaque 'élément' . . . se constitue à partir de la trace en lui des autres éléments de la chaine ou du système. Cet enchaînement, ce tissu, est le* texte. *. . . Rien, ni dans les éléments ni dans le système, n'est nulle part ni jamais simplement présent ou absent. Il n'ya, de part en part, que des différences et des traces de traces.*

> [no element can function as a sign without referring to another element which itself is not simply present. This interweaving results in each 'element' . . . being constituted on the basis of

the trace within it of the other elements in the chain or system. This interweaving, this textile, is the *text*. . . . Nothing, neither among the elements nor within the system, is anywhere ever simply present or absent. There are only, everywhere, differences and traces of traces.] (*Positions* 38)

On the grid established by Derrida and within which Beckett's texts occur, writing is a compendium of vectors, forces that operate beyond the horizon of presence/absence, that produce the enabling mirage of presence and absence but that achieve their power through the distancing and deferring of writing, of the trace, itself, undisguised.

What is *taking place*, then, in the positing of the trace, to which Derrida sometimes refers as *la trace*, the sign, the mark, the trace – or, as we shall see, *le seuil*, the threshold, and sometimes as *le tracé*, the layout, the tracing, that which is traced – what is taking place in the trace is not the creation of the sign of a concealed presence, as it is in Heidegger, nor is it a sign of absence, loss or darkness. The trace is rather, again, a force, an inscription of power in writing itself: the trace permits the potential for meaning while never permitting meaning to come to rest; it is an active force in the written text, a metaphoric force, a force of cross-reference and lateral exchange, of linearity, of association with context, of order, and of disruption. It is the antidote for the great trap of what Nietzsche calls 'metaphysical comfort', permitting Nietzsche to declare that the artist who understands this power 'will not submit to the tyranny of actuality'. Derrida's formulation makes *le tracé* into the disruption of metaphysical tradition *and* its remedy; he calls it the *pharmakon*.

Three significant applications of the Derridean/Nietzschean trace are at work in Beckett. These are:

(1) Trace and the nature of action
(2) Trace and meaning in the text
(3) Trace and the power of distance, what I will here call the *étrangeté* of the text

1. Trace and the nature of action

Confronted by Murphy in his chair, Hamm in his wheelchair,

Winnie in her heap, and myriad other images in Beckett, the reader or viewer becomes aware of Beckett's provocative dialogue with action. Action is always a problem (see Aristotle's *Poetics*), being both profound and mundane, a function of metaphysics and blocking. The question as to whether Gogo's 'action' at the opening of *Godot* is the removal of a boot or a manifestation of the human dilemma of desire and unfulfillment remains in dispute. But the advent of the trace gives us another way to see action – particularly dramatic action, and particularly in Beckett: action for Beckett is a performance of the trace, which as the force of difference is not and can never be merely an imitation; therefore, Beckettian action is always a confession of the *un*substantiality of action. The trace is a performance of action in the theatrical sense of *Darstellung*, a representation and a making-present, Beckett's bringing-forward of *physical* action as an emblem of the *absent* grounding action seems to signify. This is not action in the Aristotelian sense, the 'action' of the drama as the *significant act* out of which physical and metaphysical interaction creates conflict and drama, but an acknowledgement – again, a performance – of the divorce of action from meaning. Scene: Gogo sits on the ground trying to remove his boot. After several attempts, he mutters *'rien à faire'*, 'nothing to be done'. This is itself a parable of the trace and the nature of action, since that which *is* 'to be done' is 'nothing'. The tension in the line itself, delivered as a throwaway to set up Didi's ensuing misinterpretation, is that of writing's action (the text of *Godot*, like the tightrope of Nietzsche's Zarathustra) stretched across the void of that initial *rien*, 'nothing.' Of course, Gogo *is* doing something, but the words and the purported (and aborted) action are worlds apart, the words more 'substantial' than Gogo's non-action. Enter Vladimir, unable to enact the simple movement of walking across the stage (he advances, Beckett says, with 'short, stiff strides, legs wide apart'). Vladimir responds to Gogo's words at another plane:

GOGO: *'Rien à faire'*?
DIDI: I'm beginning to come round to that opinion.

But neither Gogo nor Didi can 'win' here: the words are no less unsubstantial than the mundanity of Gogo's actions. And Didi's unwitting nonsequitur is not really a nonsequitur at all. On one level, this first engagement between them is not boots but existential stasis, the 'nothing to be done' signifying to Didi a *condition* in the world rather than Gogo's aching feet. On the other hand, it is Gogo who does not understand Didi's response, that Didi thinking of both existential (physical and metaphysical) stasis and essential stasis (bowel problems). The subject is missing in either direction, at either level. This makes the exchange funny, in the sense that Beckett is funny. Both Gogo and Didi present themselves as thinkers and doers in their austere, ascetic world, but conclude by engaging in a Nietzschean comedy, as Alexander Nehamas defines it, as the 'effort to reveal the inner contradictions and deceptions of asceticism, to denounce it, and yet not produce a view that itself unwittingly repeats the same contradictions and deceptions' (133). This comedy is sometimes funny, but always fraught with revelatory tension. Indeed, in this moment, at the opening of *Godot*, Didi goes on deafly and blindly to say that he has tried to alter his interpretation of being in the world, of *Dasein*, but has not found grounds for doing so. Beckett expects us to come along with *him*: Vladimir's *méprise*, taking Gogo's cliché about aborted action for an abstract declaration of *angst*, echoes throughout the play and the plays that follow.

This mistake, which is also a *méconnaissance*, a misunderstanding, is a function of difference, as a layering of significance, what Derrida calls 'the active, moving discord of different forces, and of differences of forces' ('*Différance*' 18) set up first, according to Derrida, by Nietzsche 'against the entire system of metaphysical grammar', and clearly at work in Beckett, for whom stage action is a residuum of the action of, and in, the text that 'produces' it. This is most clearly visible in Beckett's theatre and television pieces. In *Not I* the text stipulates four 'movements', the only actions in the play, which consist of the raising and lowering of the arms of the sexless, silent 'auditor', 'in a gesture of helpless compassion'. *Ghost Trio* shows this tracing of action even more clearly: its three sections are named 'pre-action', 'action', and 'reaction', but the only significant action is given to the television camera. *Footfalls* is a piece of choreography in which walking and speaking cannot occur simultaneously. And *Act Without Words* directly, so to speak, asks the question of the validity of action by instilling each action with heavy gestural symbolism, but here everything is *either* highly significant or utterly meaningless: the choices invalidate choice. Beckett's characters are alienated from any insight into how to go about understanding textuality *or* action; as Ross Chambers says, 'Beckett's characters do not struggle with language; Beckett's language struggles with characters' (166).

2. Trace and meaning in the text

The trace of action on the stage or in narrative sets up the conditions for meaning. This means that meaning is what Nietzsche calls the 'mobile army of metaphors' of which texts are made. The trace is the threshold of meaning, the membrane between text and interpretation, what Derrida (quoting Mallarmé) calls the 'hymen'. As such, *la trace* does not partake of meaning-as-being but of theatricality, the returning of theatre, as in Artaud, to Nietzsche's 'danger of becoming'. Meaning, then, is what Hesla calls 'the final idol which the poet and the critic in their human weakness are tempted to fall down and worship', 'the last literary absolute' (227). The dilemma of Beckett's drama is that his characters *want* this absolute and cannot have it. They try to find order, but find the arbitrariness of order. Since we have seen that for Beckett all action is in fact *disorder*, the play itself is quintessential disorder and disjuncture, in which characters do not have control over their bodies, their minds, their hats, or their words. Nor, indeed, their meaning. Theatre here, *cruel* theatre, is a ritual of questioning the ritual of meaning. Meaning here is not message; for Beckett, the meaning is the insoluble problem of delivering messages. Beckett's messengers invariably have no intelligence; they are the parodies of the 'off-stage voice' Beckett mocks. No matter how close Beckett's characters try to get to what Lance Butler has called 'the experience of being', they find that gesture and word, as uttered in the dramatic context, do not compose meaningful action but perform a questioning of meaning. My point is that this questioning, this absence, is relative to the convention of heartfelt human meaning posited in the voice with which Beckett speaks in 'Cascando' when he derides

> the churn of words in the heart again
> love love love thud of the old plunger
> pestling the unalterable
> whey of words.

The play of order and disorder, of the desire for human validity where it is not available, wrought by Beckett into the beautiful image of the 'heart's' 'pestling' of the 'whey of words', an intentionally mixed metaphor, since whey cannot be powdered and therefore not pestled, shows the power of the trace: the image in the metaphor cannot contain a meaning that is inevitably added on as supplemental baggage. The human condition is one in which one constantly attempts the impossible with words: tries to make them be what they will not be and do what they will not do, simultaneously constructing with them the images out of which they seem to circulate within a system of concerted meaning.

But meaning is precisely what Beckett's words perpetually leave out; the more theatrically heightened and idealised human experience becomes, the stronger and more obvious this estrangement becomes. In *Catastrophe*, when the protagonist finally lifts his face to the audience, at the end, the running tape of a 'distant storm of applause' falters and dies (300–301): again and again Beckett shows that desire for meaning in human consciousness, where it is not. Beckett, like Artaud, protests against what Derrida calls '*la lettre morte qui s'absent loin d'haleine et chair* [the dead letter which absents itself far from breath and flesh]' (*Writing and Difference* 187) but at the same time acknowledges that theatre, the perfect fleshly place for this revolt, is itself the imitation of writing, so that the so-called 'centre' is not experience but what Derrida calls '*le puits innommable sans fond dont le signe du centre était . . . le centre comme le signe d'un trou que le livre a essayé remplir* [the unnamable bottomless well whose sign the centre was . . . the centre as the sign of a whole that the book attempted to fill]' (Derrida, *Writing and Difference* 297). Thus Derrida states Beckett's programme from the *other side*, that of the voice of plenitude relative to which Martin Esslin develops his concept of Beckett's absurdity. In Beckett's plays, that plenitude is cancelled. On Krapp's last tape, for example, it is precisely the moment of meaning that is denied:

> What I saw then was this, that the belief I had been going on all my life, namely—(KRAPP *switches off impatiently, winds tape forward, switches on again*).   (60)

This occurs over and over, that threshold of meaning that remains looped within the text.

This self-referentiality is clear in Lucky's monologue and in Hamm's final soliloquy, as he retreats behind the virgin page itself, the unfolded white handkerchief that is mask, veil, and infinite latency. Hamm speaks to the mask, a kind of last voice of meaning in a place where the meaning of voice, its substantiality, is denied. Indeed, in Beckett, voice is denial and absence of meaning beyond the text, just as action is denial and absence of order.

3. Trace and the power of distance, the étrangeté of the text

Beckett derives his power precisely from the questioning of action and meaning's validity in the text, and the gap or *aporia* that opens through the etiolation of spirit and person. The threshold Beckett is always inviting the reader/viewer/listener to cross with his text is that at which, as Butler says, one has come to 'the end of the normal world, the end of surface realities' (163). This is a world of *étrangeté*. The implication here, however, that therefore Beckett presents an alternative reality, is misleading. Beckett's reality is like Borges' imaginary realities: the cosmos of Beckett's text is a combination of Einstein and Heraclitus: 'all is flux, [and] the only principle of consistency is that all possibilities are possible' (Dearlove 28). His is a world not of a dialectic with reality, but with the estrangement from reality *at all*. This kind of opening can only occur in a text dissociated from the presence of voice, not the world of what Ross Chambers calls 'Beckett's dimensionless interiority' (153) but of the distance and difference of the order of the written which, being metaphoric and not corporeal, can only be 'encoded' in that corporeal world as part of the teleological 'reinvigoration' of reading or watching.

Text for Beckett is the ultimate solipsism of print, the indifference of type, and the dramatic tension of the page, without reference to any reality outside the formulations that give experience order, and with the barest skeletal references to the dark, liquid, latent imagery of some experiential well posterior and subordinate to the written one. For Beckett, the idea of 'meaningful reality' is itself apocryphal, in that reality consists of the constant abrogation and subversion of meaning. Indeed, existence itself is called into question in Beckett's textualisations: no longer will existence conveniently or conventionally link itself with an extra-textual world of experience the essence of which is its imitation in language. The entire concept of 'external reality' is ironised by Beckett, and the additive of 'meaning' to that chimerical context makes it the more fantastic. Reality becomes, in the Beckettian text, the index of the merely possible, the hypothetical, the imagined – but the imagined that bears no necessary connection to conventional reality, perceived as a transcription of experience or of fact. Beckett is always at the edge of a definition of reality; Ross Chambers calls attention to that 'threshold' – as he too calls it, and names it 'that region of being where existence and essence, nonself and self, time and timelessness endlessly co-exist, in the strange, ambiguous, inescapable half-world of semi-exile' (168). But Chambers stops short of Beckett's brinksmanship. One could go further: the *threshold*, that brink, edge, or fold from which the text derives its power, like Derrida's and Mallarme's 'hymen', is writing itself, *le tracé*, grammatology's *étrangeté*. Beckett's writing is always an allegory of writing, a positing in text itself of that which cannot be written and which must be written about just because it is lost in or absent from writing.

The astonishing thing about this *u-topos* is that is is so joyful and (which is different) so humorous. Beckett is amused by the cusp on which human consciousness hovers, the precipice on which it totters. He has been educated by the Nietzschean joy of insecurity. Our response to Beckett, that we can never be sure whether what we are getting from him is comic or sad, whether it is potentially *full* of meaning or utterly devoid of it – or, more worrying, that what is sad *now* will be comic in an instant and what is devoid of meaning *now* will be significant, this response is produced by a Zarathustran jester who is ready to overleap us at any moment. Beckett plays on our convergent need to predict, to construct our individual and cultural identities out of a continuity of moments connected by a seemingly consistent consciousness, but then proceeds to operate outside this framework himself, to play with it as a cat does with a bug. If we are about to signify something, we never do, it seems, and the play of that possibility (the implications of its elation and its horror) form a comedic context that crosses generic lines just as it cancels predictability. This is the nature of Beckett's *étrangeté*. He reserves for himself, or rather for 'himself', the position of authority from which these questions of authority emanate, then obscures, mocks, and inverts the questions. Beckett's writing might say, as Estragon does, 'either I forget immediately or I never forget' (39). Beckett's writing creates the illusion that it *itself* speaks, from its own place. In *Company,* this 'place' of writing, formulated in an ephemeral first person, asks the appropriate Nietzschean question:

And whose voice is asking this? Who asks, Whose voice is asking this? And answers, His soever who devises it all. In the same dark as his creature or in another. For company. Who asks in the end, Who asks? And in the end answers as above? And adds long after to himself, Unless another still. Nowhere to be found. Nowhere to be sought. The unthinkable last of all. Unnamable. Last person. I. Quick leave him.   (24)

The oscillation between first and third person, calling the nature of the 'bio-graphical' exercise into question, is itself conflated with that other, capitalised Third Person, who is also subsumed into the writing hand. But that revered third person is not the god of Christian tradition, however Biblical its formulation might at first look, since in context that 'His soever who devises it all' clearly can refer to the bio-graphical hand itself, to the writer. To further complicate this text, the quoted passage is uncharacteristic. These first-person echoes, here of Nietzsche's *last man*, the etiolated perceiver of his species' failure to triumph over failure, reiterating the fundamental psychic question, 'who asks?', occur in *Company* as part of a text written overall in that *other* perfect Beckettian voice: second person. Always combatting aloneness, the narrator creates the false voice of the interlocutor, the listener, *as if there were* a second person. Mocking this most human of possibilities, however, Beckett holds out the normal and then withdraws it: in the text, no relationship to reality occurs in second person, since the listener is 'hidden' in the text, unidentified. The only conceivable 'company' is pre'existent in the articulation itself. The writing hand is responsible for, encompasses, and creates *all* writing/voices.

Encapsulated in his dramatic world of tensions is Beckett's 'ruthless criticism of experience' (Mayoux 78). Since in this world of over- and under-determined observation, in which the relativising of value never can be permitted to normalise itself, experience first posits itself as an 'it' and then cancels that existence, its only solution is to claim that the 'thingness' of experience is a function of the senses of it one accrues from the forces capable of shaping it. And since, as Deleuze points out in his long discussion of the nature of the will to power as *force*, those tensions are uncountable (4), even to try to establish a solid relationship between thing and force is to mock the notion of essence. Estragon's claim that 'we always find something, eh Didi, to give us the impression we exist' (44), is echoed at every level of Beckett's text. Experience must be seen as a series of vectors whose additive accumulation achieves a weight of what we refer to as meaning. The Deleuzian centrality of *force* derives from Derrida, for whom

> *le distinction entre force et sens est dérivé en relation à un archi-trace; c'est aux métaphysiques de la conscience et du présence, ou plutôt du présence dans le mot, dans la hallucination d'un langage déterminé sur la base du mot ou de la réprésentation verbale. Le métaphysique de la préconscience, Freud dirait . . .*
>
> [the distinction between force and meaning is derived in relation to an archi-trace; it belongs to the metaphysics of consciousness and of presence, or rather of presence in the word, in the hallucination of a language determined on the basis of the word or of verbal representation. The metaphysics of preconsciousness, Freud might say. . . .]   (*Writing and Difference*   213)

But the 'metaphysics of preconsciousness' relates to the world of experience in a very problematic way, as we see over and over in Beckett. The notion of the 'archi-trace', the apocryphal stasis of trace and the origin of a relationship between force and meaning, is seen in Derrida and in Beckett as an *original differentiation*, a kind of absence which is not necessarily a loss. The report at the conclusion of *Molloy* demonstrates the non-referentiality of experience in terms of its power to create a simulated experiential world:

> in the end I understood this language. I understood it, I understood it, all wrong perhaps. That is not what matters. It told me to write the report [that we have been reading as *Molloy*]. Does this mean I am freer now than I was? I do not know. I shall learn. Then I went back into the house and wrote, It is midnight. The rain is beating on the window. It was not midnight. It was not raining.   (176)

What matters is that the voice of the 'report' of the 'novel', which again here writes itself, has been 'told to write' and that 'it' proceeded to produce a series of untruths that pass for experience. Since events cannot be verified, we are left with Beckett's formulation that 'where we have both dark and light, we have also the inexplicable. The keyword in my plays is "perhaps"' (Hesla 230). The desire to believe in a transcendent reality or even a transcendent power, or even in the transcendence of writing itself, is always powerful in Beckett, but can be exercised only as a question. This is the distance of *étrangeté*.

Two of Beckett's works best domonstrate this *étrangeté* of writing. The first and most obvious is *Waiting for Godot*, written in French, according to Martin Esslin, *'parce qu'en français c'est plus facile de'écrire sans style'* (8). Beckett has corroborated this, declaring that in French he is 'anonymous', a 'tool-user', which allows the play to be more 'purely written'. The dramatic form, which denies generic delineation, consisting of repetition and pause, is nonetheless what Foucré calls 'the opposite of an anti-theatre, since there is no other reality than the gestures that make it up, the words said on the scene itself' (51). And if Beckett is writing here the opposite of anti-theatre, does that mean he is writing theatre – itself? Anti-anti-theatre? How far do these designations hold; or rather, how far out along the vectors of designation must one go to come to the *beginning* of meaning in *Waiting for Godot*?

Of the *dramatis personae* one confronts in *Waiting for Godot*, Lucky stands at the crossroads of the themes of absence and language-power. Lucky, the encapsulation of the possibility of all possibilities, is the embodiment of Heraclitean chance, the plenitude of change that lies behind all seemingly predictable order; he is, therefore, the ironic embodiment of *pure text*: his famous monologue is memorised and forgotten simultaneously, not because it is receding into the impossible, Romantic obscurity of the interior, but because it is 'emerging', in Joycean fashion (as in 'Oxen of the Sun', or throughout *Finnegans Wake*), a protean energy that belies Pozzo's assertion of Lucky's 'falling off'. Lucky is a dramatic emblem of the emergent text. In the French version of *Godot*, much more engaged in the play of *étrangeté* than its English translation in which Beckett slips back into the 'voice of the music-hall', Lucky's speech is presented on the page as a learned treatise with marginalia, further mocking the scope of human interiority: the text is self-sufficient, not even, in a sense, needing Lucky to deliver it (indeed he delivers only a *fragment*). The conclusion of his speech, which gives the impression of being overfull of meaning but through which he fights his way as if caught in the actor's nightmare of being on stage without a clear sense of purpose and, more importantly, *without lines*, is an index of desire, alienation –

étrangeté – the threshold, and because of Beckett's own *self-alienation* into French and then back into his own English I want to quote both:

> *la tête la tête la tête en Normandie malgré le tennis labeurs abandonnés inachevés plus grave les pierres bref je réprends hélàs hélàs abandonnés inachevés la tête la tête en Normandie malgré le tennis la tête hélàs les pierres Conard Conard . . .* (Mêlée. Lucky pousse encore quelques vociférations.) *Tennis! . . . Si calmes! . . . Conard! . . . Inachevés! . . .*

the skull the skull the skull in Connemara in spite of the tennis the labors abandoned left unfinished graver still abode of stones in a word I resume alas alas abandoned unfinished the skull the skull in Connemara in spite of the tennis the skull alas the stones Cunard (*mêlée, final vociferations*) tennis . . . the stones . . . so calm . . . Cunard . . . unfinished . . .

For Beckett the concluding word, in any languge, is always 'unfinished'; the listener sees Lucky as emerging through and engaging in a fragmented and never-ending recollection, trying to connect with a world (and a speech) he has known and lost, which was presented and is not absent except in this *tracé*. Phrases of a pregnant richness with which the speech is seasoned, seemingly remnants of a significant *other speech* which lies behind this one, phrases such as 'the labors abandoned left unfinished', 'abode of stones', and 'alas alas abandoned unfinished', are locked in an invisible but logical relationship with others of a quite different nature, phrases such as 'in spite of the tennis'. This relationship is at once, once again, comic and serious. It mocks the oracular nature of natural genius Lucky seems to possess when he speaks, and still permits the reader/listener to codify Lucky in that guise: he *is* scintillating in the sharpness of his phrases, and he *does* have a seeming gift for connections that lies beyond the normal. He is not like us and yet he seems to mirror us. Like us, his phrases soar and then thud, but unlike the 'us' we imagine ourselves to be, Lucky's speech is always at the precipice of dis-association (and dissociation). He finds (rediscovers?) words that suggest a deep but always hidden meaning, and follows them with words that are clearly gibberish – or does tennis somehow invite a significant interpretation here, if only we knew the rest of the speech? Thus does Beckett engage the Idealist tradition, from the Platonic dilemma of insight and knowledge to the Heideggerian one in 'On the Origin of the Work of Art', of truth's being 'untruth insofar as there belongs to it the reservoir of the not-yet-revealed, the un-uncovered in the sense of concealment' (180). Lucky allows us to glimpse these possibilities, and then he is forced back into the world of his masters. His subjugation is accomplished by the restoration of his 'lid', the bowler of convention and metaphysical presence. Hat restored, Lucky stops. In terms of conventional, 'realistic' logic, and in terms of a normative world of experience, Lucky's speech is indeed, as Pozzo suggests, a winding down, but it is also pure trace.

The paradigmatic text of Beckettian estrangement, however, is *The Unnamable*, the text of the grammatological moment. It is the musing of text itself – the world's most self-reflexive text. Constantly denying its own textuality in a mockery of the presence of voice, it dares to imitate (and therefore mock) the Nietzschean-Joycean-Derridean creator, the voice not *in* but *of* the text. As we have seen, this is the voice, as it were, of the centre where the question is displaced. In *The Unnamable* the *tracé* is revealed as the outpouring of the *écart*, the gap of what Tom Conley discusses in his essay 'A Trace of Style' as not merely an inversion of letters in an alphabet, a pun to amuse, but an interaction of language and chance, of meaning and freedom-from-meaning that leads to the anxiety, what Conley calls the 'verbal apprehension' (80) so prominent in Beckett's – and Derrida's – writing. Conley points out how this word-play is in fact the opposite of the facile exercise it seems at first to be: it demonstrates the slippage inherent in and endemic to any text, which must not be overlooked, but which cannot be relied on for meaning. *The Unnamable* is the text of the trace – the unnamable. The easy power of the voice 'in' the text is fluent, trustworthy, and absent. It establishes its authority as it denies its fleshly metaphoricity; it becomes more authoritative as it denies Beckett:

> To hell with silence, I'll say what I am, so as not to have been born for nothing, I'll fix their jargon for them, then any old thing, no matter what, whatever they want, with a will, till time is done. . . . First I'll say what I'm not, that's how they taught me to proceed, then what I am, it's already under way. I have only to resume at the point where I let myself be cowed. I am

neither, I needn't say, Murphy, nor Watt, nor Mercier, nor – no,
I can't even bring myself to name them, nor any of the others
whose very names I forget, who told me I was they, who I must
have tried to be, under duress, or through fear, or to avoid
acknowledging me, not the slightest connexion. I never desired,
never sought, never suffered, never partook in any of that,
never knew what it was to have, things, adversaries, mind,
senses.   (325–6)

Again that play of opposing phrases, some substantial and some
flippant, almost slapstick, indicate those poles of writing in which
voice resides. 'I'll say what I am,' says the voice, 'I'll fix their jargon
for them.' But then it turns to denial, to *étrangeté*: 'I'll say what I'm
not.' What the voice is *not* is substantial character – certainly not
those Beckett has created in his previous works, which are listed,
then personified ('others whose very names I forget, who told me
I was they, who I must have tried to be, under duress'), then
denied. We have seen that this voice, in its various guises, cannot
be 'trusted' in a conventional way – which is certainly not to say
that the voice is that of Beckett himself 'lying', but it is equally not
to say that any sense of conventional identity resides in such a
voice.

This radical declaration, an *auto-biography* in the sense that the
writing hand writes itself, must because of the nature of the distance
of writing/telling itself, conclude for Beckett *at* the threshold, which
he calls 'the door'. This door is the fold at which *tracé* must always
dialectically divide itself, as Nietzsche saw. It is a turning aside
from the directness of voice, a concealing and an opening at once,
the perfect metaphor and the mundane, the symbol and the tool.
For Beckett, as for the Nietzsche of *Zarathustra*, self-inscription is
worse than over-simplification, it is an invitation to the rigidity of
that death-in-life, self-iconisation, the eschatology of the archi-
trace. Biography removes the *bios*. For Beckett, self-telling is self-
denial, and so the text itself, denying itself, tells of its power. On
its last page, *The Unnamable* asks

what's a door doing here, it's the last words, the true last, or
it's the murmurs . . . a dream silence, full of murmurs, I don't
know, that's all words, never wake, all words, there's nothing
else, you must go on . . . as long as there are any, until they
find me, until they say me, strange pain, strange sin . . . per-

haps they have carried me to the threshold of my story, before the door that opens on my story . . . it will be I. (414)

In this simulation of a reality that extends into the physical world, the text of the unnamable gives an image (and a metaphor) to the power of *étrangeté*, and immediately cancels it again. The door is 'the last words, the true last', opening on to the vista of a phenomenal world that always constitutes itself of 'murmurs'. In that 'dream silence' which is not a silence but 'full of murmurs' the only imperative is to follow the murmurs, to constitute the text, which can never be ended and, by extension, never begun. When the door is perceived, the *tracé* of power, one must, indeed, 'go on . . . as long as there are any, until they find me, until they say me'. Because this distance is the power of the text and at the same time an acknowledgement of the impossibility of that power outside the metaphor, it is a 'strange pain', and because it brings the voice back to a world in which disconnection, chaos, and estrangement are causes not of strength but of guilt, it is indeed 'strange sin'. Beckett then transposes his position within the metaphor of the space before the door: 'they' have carried him to the threshold of 'my story', which has comprised these words – he has not carried the words – and yet when he is at the threshold of that narrative opening, Beckett qualifies this localisation: 'before the door that opens on my story' – the story is still beyond the door, the fold of the narrative, the unfolding of the writing. He then comes full circle to the displacement that must always enshroud the narrator: 'it will be I'. That future tense, and the use of the expletive (a false subject, 'it', that places the formulation in the passive voice), accumulated with the final pronoun that stands so rigidly for the nothing it always 'represents', all these combine in a final, ironic formulation of what seems solid prose, but the 'I', the *récit*, is avoided in that repeated 'until', 'until they say me', in the trace.

What is Beckett tracing? The obvious first assessment, that he is tracing absence, seems on reflection to be incorrect. The skeletal nature of his writing, writing without a skin, as though it had been flayed off, does not 'produce' absence. Beckett's is indeed a flayed writing, '*écriture écorchée*,' stripped to the bone and cruelly humorous, a continuous play on the conditions of a solid language leading to a solid world; language for Beckett points to the not-there, a '*langage écorché*', the vernacular expression for 'murdered language' from which the experiential life has been peeled away and removed. In Beckett, this tracing is a flaying of the corpus of metaphor, writing without comfort.

SUPPLEMENT

Friedrich Nietzsche ('On Truth and Lies in a Nonmoral Sense', §1):

In irgend einem abgelegenen Winkel des in zahllosen Sonnensystemen flimmernd ausgegössenen Weltalls gab es einmal ein Gestirn, auf dem kluge Thiere das Erkennen erfanden. Es war die höchmuthigste und verlögenste Minute der 'Weltgeschichte': aber doch nur eine Minute. Nach wenigen Athemzugen der Natur erstarrte das Gestirn, und die klugen Thiere müssten sterben. — So konnte Jemand eine Fabel erfinden und wurde doch nicht genugend illustrirt haben, wie klaglich, wie schattenhaft und fluchtig, wie zwecklos und beliebig sich der menschliche Intellekt innerhalb der Natur ausnimmt.

[Once upon a time, in some out of the way corner of that universe which is disposed into numberless twinkling solar systems, there was a star upon which clever beasts invented knowing. That was the most arrogant and mendacious minute of 'world history', but nevertheless, it was only a minute. After nature had drawn a few breaths, the star cooled and congealed, and the clever beasts had to die.—One might invent such a fable, and yet still he would not have adequately illustrated how miserable, how shadowy and transient, how aimless and arbitrary the human intellect looks within nature.]

First there is a mountain
One's first reaction to reading Beckett is that he is not only the most obvious choice of an author to whose works one can apply post-structuralist strategies but that he is almost too good, programmed, it seems, for a Derridean treatment. His themes of absence, loss, darkness, and silence (particularly when seen in the context of humor, the style of play so common to Beckett and deconstruction) require a deconstructive response.

Then there is no mountain
Reflection makes one suddenly doubt this assumption. Beckett is

tied to his text; it is a privileged place, as for Joyce, for example, and Pound. Beckett can be seen to be making vehement statements about identity, difference, presence, Being – the right themes but on the wrong side. Beckett is obsessed with PRESENT-ing the voice, and the text that, so to speak, produces it. This doubt comes when one listens to Beckett's nomenclature of failure.

Then there is
But Beckett's power derives not from text, not from voice, presence, identity, Being, but from questioning, from failure itself, from distance/distancing. Seen as a palimpsest of strategies of presence and absence, the threshold on which Derrida's *trace* occurs, Beckett's is the dangerous, precipitous writing of and for deconstruction.

Jacques Derrida (*Positions* 38):
> *Le jeu des différences suppose en effet des synthèses et des renvois qui interdisent qu'à aucun moment, en aucun sens, un élément simple soit présent en lui-même et ne renvoie qu'à lui-même. Que ce soit dans l'ordre du discours parlé ou du discours écrit, aucun élément ne peut fonctionner comme signe sans renvoyer à un autre élément qui lui-meme n'est pas simplement present. Cet enchaînement, ce tissu, est le* texte *qui ne se produit que dans la transformation d'un système, n'est nulle part ni jamais simplement présent ou absent. Il n'y a, de part en part, que des différences et des traces de traces.*

[The play of differences involves syntheses and referrals that forbid at any moment, in any sense, that a simple element be *present* in and of itself, referring only to itself. Whether in written or spoken discourse, no element can function as a sign without referring to another element which itself is not simply present. This interweaving results in each 'element' – phoneme or grapheme – being constituted on the basis of the trace within it of the other elements in the chain or system. This interweaving, this textile, is the *text* produced only in the transformation of another text. Nothing, neither among the elements nor within the system, is anywhere ever simply present or absent. There are only, everywhere, differences, and traces of traces.]

Samuel Beckett (Addenda to *Watt*):

> *qui du vieillard*
> *l'histoire contéra?*

dans une balance
absence pesera?
avec une règle
manque mésurera?
des maux du monde
la somme chiffréra?
dans des mots
néant enfermera?

[who may tell the tale
of the old man?
weigh absence in the scale?
mete want with a span?
the sum assess
of the world's woes?
nothingness in words enclose?]

Jacques Lacan (*Ecrits* 692):

L'homme ne peut viser a être entier . . . dès lors que le jeu de déplacement et de condensation ou il est voué dans l'exercise de ses fonctions, marque sa rélation de sujet au signifiant.

[Man cannot aim at being whole . . . while ever the play of displacement and condensation to which he is doomed in the exercise of his functions marks his relation as a subject to the signifier.]

Samuel Beckett (quoted by Schenker):

In my work there is consternation behind the form, not in the form.

Samuel Beckett (*Endgame*):

CLOV: What is there to keep me here?
HAMM: The Dialogue.

Samuel Beckett (*Molloy*):

No wanting to say, no knowing what one wants to say, no possibility that one can believe that one wants to say, and always say, that's what is important not to lose sight of in the heat of composition.

Democritus [in answer to Parmenidean certitude]:

We know nothing in reality, for truth lies in an abyss [*en bythoi*].

Samuel Beckett (*Molloy* 64):

To know nothing is nothing, not to want to know anything likewise, but to be beyond knowing anything, that is when peace enters in, to the soul of the incurious seeker.

Jacques Derrida ('*Différance*' 28) [on *trace*]:

Cet innommable n'est pas un être ineffable dont aucun nom ne pourrait s'approcher. . . . Cet innommable est le jeu qui fait qu'il y a des effets nominaux, des structures rélativement unitaires ou atomiques qu'on appelle noms, des chaînes de substitutions de noms, et dans lesquelles, par example, l'effet nominal 'différance' est lui-même entraîné*, emporté, réinscrit, comme une fausse entrée ou une fausse sortie est encore partie du jeu, fonction du système.*

[This unnamable is not an ineffable Being which no name could approach. . . . This unnamable is the play which makes possible nominal effects, the relatively unitary and atomic structures that are called names, the strings of substitutions of names, and in which, for example, the nominal effect '*différance*' is itself *infused*, carried along, reinscribed, as a false entrance or a false exit is still part of the game, a function of the system.]

Jacques Derrida ('*Différance*' 23):

La trace . . . s'éfface en se présentant, s'assourdit en resonnant.

[The trace . . . erases itself in presenting itself, muffles itself in resonating.]

Works Cited

Anders, Gunther, 'Being Without Time: On Beckett's Play', in *Samuel Beckett: A Collection of Critical Essays*, ed. Martin Esslin (Englewood, New Jersey: Prentice-Hall, 1965), pp. 325–41.

Artaud, Antonin, *Le théâtre et son double* (Paris: Gallimard, 1967).

Barnard, G. C., *Samuel Beckett: A New Approach* (New York: Dodd, Mead and Co., 1970).

Beckett, Samuel, *All That Fall* (London: Faber & Faber, 1970).
——, *Collected Shorter Plays of Samuel Beckett* (New York: Grove Press, 1984).
——, *Collected Poems in English and French* (New York: Grove Press, 1977).
——, *Company* (New York: Grove Press, 1980).
——, *En attendant Godot* (Paris: Les Editions de Minuit, 1952).
——, *Endgame* (New York: Grove Press, 1958).
——, *Fin de partie* (Paris: Les Editions de Minuit, 1957).
——, *Happy Days* (New York: Grove Press (Evergreen), 1961).
——, *The Lost Ones* (New York: Grove Press (Evergreen), 1972).
——, *Murphy* (New York: Grove Press, 1957).
——, *Nouvelles et textes pour rien* (Paris: Les Editions de Minuit, 1958).
——, *Play* (London: Faber & Faber, 1964).
——, *Three Novels by Samuel Beckett: Molloy, Malone Dies, The Unnamable* (New York: Evergreen Books, 1965).
——, *Waiting for Godot* (New York: Grove Press (Evergreen), 1954).
Butler, Lance St John, *Samuel Beckett and the Meaning of Being* (London: Macmillan, 1984).
Chambers, Ross, 'Beckett's Brinksmanship', in Esslin, *Samuel Beckett: A Collection of Critical Essays.*
Cohn, Ruby, *Samuel Beckett: The Comic Gamut* (New Brunswick, New Jersey: Rutgers University Press, 1962).
Conley, Tom, 'A Trace of Style', in *Displacement: Derrida and After*, ed. Mark Krupnick (Bloomington, Indiana: Indiana University Press, 1983).
Dearlove, Richard, *Accommodating the Chaos: Samuel Beckett's Non-relational Art* (Durham, North Carolina: Duke University Press, 1982).
Deleuze, Gilles, *Nietzsche and Philosophy*, trans. Hugh Tomlinson (London: The Athlone Press, 1983).
Derrida, Jacques, *'Différance'*, in *Speech and Phenomena*, trans. David B. Allison (Evanston, Illinois: Northwestern University Press, 1973).
——, *Dissemination*, trans. Barbara Johnson (Chicago: University of Chicago Press, 1981).
——, *Writing and Difference*, trans. Alan Bass (Chicago: University of Chicago Press, 1978).
Esslin, Martin, *The Theater of the Absurd* (New York: Doubleday, 1961).
—— (ed.), *Samuel Beckett: A Collection of Critical Essays* (Englewood Cliffs, New Jersey: Prentice-Hall, 1965).
Fleissner, Robert F., '"Godotology" Revisited: The Hidden Anagram for *Gott/Tod'*, *Germanic Notes* 13.3 (3 November, 1982): pp. 35–6.
Fletcher, John, *The Novels of Samuel Beckett* (New York: Barnes and Noble, 1970).
——, 'The Private Pain and the Whey of Words: A Survey of Beckett's Verse', in Esslin (ed.), *Samuel Beckett: A Collection of Critical Essays.*
Foucré, Michèle, *La geste et la parole dans le théâtre de Samuel Beckett* (Paris: A.-G. Nizet, 1970).
Goicoechea, David (ed.), *The Great Year of Zarathustra (1881–1981)* (Lanham, Maryland: University of America Press, 1983).
Heidegger, Martin, 'On the Origin of the Work of Art', in *Basic Works*, trans. and ed. David Farrell Krell (New York: Harper and Row, 1983), pp. 143–89.

Hesla, David, *The Shape of Chaos* (Minneapolis: University of Minnesota Press, 1968).

Hoffman, Frederick J., *Samuel Beckett: The Language of the Self* (New York: E. P. Dutton and Co., 1964).

Kenner, Hugh, 'The Cartesian Centaur', in Martin Esslin (ed.), *Samuel Beckett: A Collection of Critical Essays*.

——, *Samuel Beckett: A Critical Study* (Berkeley: University of California Press, 1973).

——, *The Stoic Comedians: Flaubert, Joyce, and Beckett* (Berkeley: University of California Press, 1974).

Lacan, Jacques, *Ecrits: A Selection*, trans. Alan Sheridan (New York: W. W. Norton, 1977).

Mayoux, Jean-Jacques, *Samuel Beckett* (Harlow, England: published for the British Council by the Longman Group, 1974).

——, 'Samuel Beckett and Universal Parody', in Martin Esslin (ed.), *Samuel Beckett: A Collection of Critical Essays*.

Mercier, Vivian, *Beckett/Beckett* (Oxford: Oxford University Press, 1979).

Nehamas, Alexander, *Nietzsche: Literature as Life* (Cambridge, Massachusetts: Harvard University Press, 1985).

Pronko, Leonard Cabell, *Avant-garde: The Experimental Theatre in France* (Berkeley: University of California Press, 1964).

Robbe-Grillet, Alain, 'Samuel Beckett, or "Presence" in the Theatre', Martin Esslin (ed.), in *Samuel Beckett: A Collection of Critical Essays*.

Ulmer, Gregory L., *Applied Grammatology* (Baltimore: The Johns Hopkins University Press, 1985).

Zurbrugg, Nicholas, 'Beyond Beckett: Reckless Writing and the Concept of the Avant-garde Within Post-Modern Literature', *Yearbook of Comparative and General Literature* 30 (1981): pp. 37–56.

Index